Canyon Dance

Canyon Dance

My Visit To the Deepest Canyon on Each of the Seven Continents

Jeff Budd

ISBN-13: 9781533122216
ISBN-10: 1533122210
Library of Congress Control Number: 2016908485
CreateSpace Independent Publishing Platform
North Charleston, South Carolina

Dedication

This manuscript is dedicated to: An Budd, my brother's wife, Leonard Jackson, and Ryan Kauffman. An for her constant support and friendship, everything from sending my twenty-nine re-supply boxes on the Pacific Crest Trail through hike, welcoming me in Hawaii, and being an awesome aunt to Amelia. Leonard for being such a great co-worker, he put our Ketchikan youth agency on the state map and was a true friend, funny, wise, and supportive. Ryan, a Sitka Bike & Hike co-worker and Sitka Monthly Grind co-producer for being a great friend who could and would get as far out as there is to get. Thanks to my brother Mike, who always has time to join me on parts of my adventures: the PCT, biking cross country, and paddling the Yukon.

Thanks to the following for reading, editing, and their support: Greg Mandel for the most excellent and appreciated finishing touches and suggestions. Mike Budd, Robin Emmens, Amelia Emmens-Budd, Cheryl Call, Don Muller, Jon Wunrow, Cara Flag, John Michner, all who read it, edited it, and/or gave encouragement. Laura Kaltenstein, the woman who has let me hang out with her for, the last 15 years and endured my starts and stops in this process. And to my granddaughter Hazel, the new canyon of my life.

Jeff Budd December 2016

A forward: Holy smokes. This attempt at going to the deepest canyons was hatched sometime in 1994, completed 2000 to 2001 and now the manuscript has finally been completed very late 2016. Some things have probably changed since I did this quest. I still have not heard of anybody getting to all seven – but I hope someone takes the time and effort to do it – it is a worthy challenge, I think.

A note: Any mistakes on the facts are mine.

One

Begin the Beguine
Canyons: An Introduction

"A man never goes so far as when he doesn't know where he is going."

--Oliver Cromwell

"If you don't know where you are going – any road will get you there."

--Lewis Carroll

It was early October, 2000, and I was in Namibia, Africa, about to hike the Fish River Canyon, that continent's deepest. It was the beginning of my journey, a pilgrimage, really, that would take me around the world to hike the deepest canyon on each of its seven continents. As you can imagine, I'd packed for everything – the hottest heat, the coldest ice, the wettest rain, and the brightest sun. When I left my home in Sitka, Alaska ,and landed in Seattle and later, Frankfurt, the huge pack was more than awkward, what with its size and weight. Dragging it around, I felt like Igor in *Young Frankenstein*. There I was with that pack on my back, limping along and trying to look a bit dignified, or at least, like I was a competent traveler.

Now, getting settled in my room at the Chameleon, a backpackers, (what a youth hostel is called there), I started to unpack. It was more than just heavy gear that came out of that huge bag. I also unpacked some of my travel fears, phobias, and anxieties, which were not heavy on my back, but plenty heavy on my mind. I remembered reading in *Passage to Juneau*, by Jonathon Raban, that such jitters were the norm. He would describe my anxiety as "nervous elation – half high hopes and half cold feet – that marks the start of a big adventure." My high hopes and cold feet involved surviving this canyon and, then again, so much more. Would I make it to the other canyons on the six other continents? Would I survive them? I was on a journey that would take me 51,000 air miles. Between now and March I'd be racking up still more mileage on the ground - hiking the many canyons and whatever they might throw at me. Then there was managing all of the different cities in between with their many strange currencies and language barriers. What brought me here to this place inside my soul and to Africa? It was canyons. This canyon journey was one that started many years ago.

Canyons touch me: mind, body, and spirit. The first time I saw the Grand Canyon was in the summer of 1974, and I fell in love. It was a late evening in July, and I was leading a youth group from the Dayton, Ohio, YMCA, where I was a youth worker. My working partner and I had talked our boss into letting us take a group of city kids on a backpacking trip to the Colorado Rockies and to the Grand Canyon. After driving all day from Ohio, we arrived very late at night and pulled up to one of the overlooks. I couldn't see a thing, but there was no doubt that something was out there, something really big. Its energy flowed up like smoke from a campfire, hugging the ground, washing over me, passing right through me, and heading toward the stars, giving me a slight hint of what was to be. As my eyes adjusted, I could make out the darker shape where the canyon was. In that darkness, I sensed a huge hush, a presence of place.

We awoke the next morning and went back to the rim. It was right then and there that I fell head over heels. Cupid shot his arrow, little love birds chirped round my head, stars were in my eyes. I was in love – with the Grand Canyon. It was not unlike my first love and the accompanying feelings for my high school girlfriend. I am not sure which of its aspects caught me up so.

Maybe it was the size, the shapes, and the constantly changing colors. Maybe it was the tranquility or the views that just kept going farther and farther to the horizon, as the eye, all the while, tried to take in the entire landscape. Maybe it was its unattainability, its aloofness, the catch-your-breath beauty. Whatever it was, I was hooked. It was over the top, incredible, like nothing I had ever before seen. No picture could do it justice. I was stunned, almost falling to my knees in wonderment and awe; my breath literally taken away by its sublimity.

Who among us can tell why we fall in love? If it is true that only fools fall in love, I became a fool for canyons. With more Grand Canyon experience under my belt, I came to better understand that the views from the rim truly were overwhelming. Hiking into a small side canyon or amphitheater, trying to grasp the epic film one frame at a time, made it almost comprehensible, a bit more on the human scale. The more I explored, the more in love I became. Not once have I left the Grand Canyon without making a pledge that I will be back. I suppose in today's parlance you could say that canyons are part of my spiritual touchstone.

Since that first encounter, I have visited the Grand Canyon fifteen times over a span of over forty years, while living in three different states: Ohio, Oregon, and Alaska. Twice I went with my daughter, Amelia, once when she was four, and again when she was eight. The first time we hiked to its Indian Gardens, about four and a half miles down, and walked out to Plateau Point for a good view of the Colorado River and a good chunk of canyon. We spent the night and then hiked back up. The second time we hiked again to Indian Gardens and camped. The next day it was down to Phantom Ranch where we overnighted. The following day we returned to Indian Gardens for our third night out, and then it was back to the rim.

Four times I've gone with youth groups. On a trip with an alternative high school from Eugene, Oregon, I learned a valuable lesson. I had been told it never snowed or rained in the Grand Canyon. That was a myth I enjoyed propagating until I learned the truth. On that trip we were ready for everything but snow or rain. Rain was, however, exactly what we got.

It was then that I found out it does, indeed, at least rain in the Grand Canyon!

I have been there twice with the guys; once to Hermit's Rest and down to the river, and then back up the Boucher Trail, what the guidebooks call "one of the more difficult Grand Canyon trails." It was there that I first heard and saw positive proof of a trail being so steep you could see "nose prints." The other time I went with my brother and a co-worker from that original YMCA trip. I've done five with then current girlfriends as well as two solo trips. These ranged from one night hikes to one solo trek that lasted for more than three weeks. As an aside, I went eight straight days on that trip without seeing or talking to anyone. On the ninth day, I ran into two hikers and commenced to talk their ears off. I talked and talked for what I'm sure seemed to them decades. I learned then and there that I was not a hermit.

All these hikes took me from the south rim to the north rim via the Kaibab Trail as well as the Bright Angel Trail. I went as far west as Bass Canyon, as far east as the Tanner Trail, and took the trails in between. I've been to the north rim and hiked east to the Clear Creek River. I hiked the Tonto Plateau for more than 100 miles on the south side. These hikes introduced me to different parts of the canyon and, also, to the different parts of my heart. My numerous times in the canyon allowed me a glimpse, a peek into my own psyche – the psyche of a canyon freak. The sunburn, light head, clear eyes, glimmer of passion, mirthful smile (or was it a smirk?), bounding joy that seeped from my veins, and the love of Mother Nature were all signs of it. These were signs shared by those of us who had been in the canyon, thinking, feeling, acting as if we were one with the canyon. Not to be a canyon snob – but this takes at minimum a week, and usually longer.

Not only did I make those many return visits to the Grand Canyon, I expanded my canyon experiences with trips to Hells Canyon (nestled between the Oregon and Idaho border, and, which some say, is the deepest canyon in North America – more on that later); the Grand Canyon of Yosemite, Canada's Frazier River Canyon in British Columbia, Arizona's

Canyon De Chelly, and Monument Valley, Bryce and Zion Canyons in Utah, and Waimea Canyon in Hawaii on Kauai. It seems that since my love-at-first-sight Grand Canyon experience, I have indeed become a canyon freak; a certified canyon junkie.

With time, my love for canyons continued to grow, and it was now taking me to the deepest canyon on each of the planet's seven continents. That world-wide marathon is what this story is all about – my personal canyon dance with each one of them. My partners awaited in Africa, Europe, Asia, Australia, Antarctica, South America, and, finally, North America, and in that order.

The seed for this quest to visit each continent's deepest canyon, if we discount Freud, was probably planted by Dick Bass when I read his *Seven Summits*, co-authored with Frank Wells who served as president of the Walt Disney Company until his death in 1994. Bass was the owner of Snowbird Ski Resort in Utah, and a well known self-promoter. The book is an account of their race to be the first people to reach each continent's highest summit and to do so within one year. Their goal was not only ambitious and daring, it was also very expensive, time consuming, and technical. And did I say costly and difficult? I will admit to a certain intrigue with firsts – the highest, the longest, and the like, but climbing that high requires extraordinary ability; it had never made its way onto my own list of goals.

By the way, Bass and Wells met their mark. They became the first to bag all seven summits on April 30, 1985, having climbed Denali, aka Mt. McKinley (North America), Aconcagua (South America), Mt. Elbrus (Europe), Mount Kilimanjaro (Africa), Vinson (Antarctica), Mt. Kosciusko (Australia), and Mt. Everest (Asia). It is worth noting that on that date, Bass established yet another record. He became the oldest person, at age 56, to have climbed Mt. Everest.

I had never hiked over 13,000 feet, but I had hiked canyons. It was on a long distance hike in 1994 that the deepest canyons seed planted by Bass germinated in my brain. Over a six-month period, I through-hiked the 2,600 mile Pacific Crest Trail (PCT) and it afforded me plenty of time to daydream, to muse, you name it. With all that musing, a spark was ignited. Somewhere on that journey, while trying to fill my mind with something other than the questions that preoccupied it – *Where is the next water? – How many different ways can my feet hurt? – Am I on the trail? – Do I have enough food? – What will I order? – And how much of it will I order when I get to a town?* – that the idea came to me. While enjoying the scenery, watching my steps, and counting calories (or the lack of them), I wondered what I would do next. From out of the blue, I said to myself, "OK, I'll visit the deepest canyon on each continent." I wondered if I had stumbled upon a first; one that I might, indeed, be able to do.

It was along about 1997 that I started to get somewhat serious about my musing and sought to find out just where these deepest canyons were. It wasn't an easy task. The canyons were remote and the technology for measuring their depth wasn't always available or hadn't been applied. Additionally, there wasn't always consensus among the "authorities." In a Guinness-type book of records, I discovered that the Copper Canyon in Mexico (not the Grand Canyon or Hells Canyon) was the deepest canyon in North America, and that Peru's Colca Canyon was South America's deepest. A valley named the Yarlung Tsangpo (also called Yarlung Zangbo) in Tibet kept turning up in the literature as Asia's deepest canyon. The other four deepest canyons remained elusive, and my search a bit haphazard. I wasn't totally serious yet, but as time allowed, and the notion would strike me, I'd dig into whatever sources I could find. As far as I knew, there was no single go-to source that would answer my question. I searched by continent, looked in encyclopedias, visited libraries, and Googled. At a book store, I'd peruse *Lonely Planet* or *Footprint* travel guides or other guidebooks on Australia, Europe, Antarctica, and Africa, hoping to learn of other deepest canyons. On one such quest, I came across Africa's Fish River Canyon which is located in Namibia.

I then began to keep a "possible canyon" list and would jot down the odd note that might be of help somewhere along the line. At the same time, I was single parenting my then high school-age daughter, Amelia. In 1995, we had moved from Ketchikan, Alaska, where we'd lived for ten years, to Sitka, where I took a new job. My daughter, my job, and other regular parts of life kept me busy. The canyon hunt remained more than a passing fancy, but it wasn't all-consuming. I pretty much kept the search to myself, partly because I didn't want anyone to steal my idea, which was possibly a tad hubristic, for those few who knew about it really didn't seem to care. A few of the outdoor types who did were intrigued, but I didn't pursue any details about it with them. In my mind, this journey was going to be a solitary effort if it was ever to be at all.

It took another year before I learned about Antarctica's Dry Valleys. I did so while reading an Antarctica Foundation book and studying a huge topography map of that southernmost continent. As to Australia, I'd been reading about a King Gorge or King's Canyon as a possibility. While searching the internet, my friend, Jon Wunrow, and I discovered a European canyon that seemed to fit the bill. Our efforts had uncovered the Tara Canyon in Yugoslavia. I had met Jon via the telephone when I interviewed for my job in Sitka. He chaired the board of the Sitka Teen Resource Center, the agency to which I had applied. On my resume I'd noted my PCT hike. Jon, his wife, and their dog had done the hike six years earlier. We hit it off pretty well and he hired me. Now, it was Jon, who I reluctantly suffered to be one of the muses for this journey.

It was 1999 and four years had gone by since I had taken the Sitka job. During that time the Teen Center had merged with a local adult alcohol treatment program, and I became the director. Our programs expanded, we added a new building, the size of our budget and staff grew, and so did my responsibilities. Getting to the canyons could easily get pushed aside. I didn't want that to happen. With these accomplishments behind me, my sense was that it was about time for me to leave my job. I stayed on, though, until May of 2000.

In the midst of those workplace responsibilities, I started to become truly serious about the canyon venture. In 1998 I took a big step. I drew a grid on a large sheet of paper. Serious planning was in order. Across the top I wrote: best season to visit - money exchange rate - shots needed - airlines for getting there - visa needed - special permits needed - water issues - special equipment needed - primary method of transportation to get to the canyon once in the country - maps needed – and more. Down the side, I listed the seven continents and their canyons, at least the ones with deepest designations that I considered to be a done deal. I tacked this 3' by 5' planning chart to my bedroom wall and began slowly but surely to fill in the blanks.

I like to think of myself as an organized person and the planning grid was evidence. Besides that, compiling to do lists makes me happy, but not as happy as crossing off my entries. For me, a good part of any trip is the fun of planning it, and that involves making those charts and lists with lots of to-dos. Indeed, there is that previously mentioned sense of satisfaction in crossing items off the to-do list. But, of course, there is also the reality that every time one scratches an item off, one adds two more.

Long ago I read a blurb from a business magazine suggesting one ought to plan the next day's tasks before going to bed. For years I awoke most mornings to small bits of paper strewn about the floor. They held mostly illegible notes of middle-of-the-night thoughts about what I needed to do the next day. I wasn't always a list person. After all, I moved to Oregon in 1975, and not due to any plan. I ran out of gas money in Eugene and stayed for ten years. But, while working at a runaway home there, I attended a training session during which the presenter asked the crowd of fifty or so how we organized things. No one had an answer. Vern Madison, the trainer, quickly showed us his fool-proof method: decide on the goal, brainstorm all the things that need to be done, prioritize them, and divide them up if there is more than one of you, make a time line, and set up some type of evaluation, and begin. That method has stood me in good stead and it was what I used to try and figure out this canyon conundrum.

In mid 1999 I began searching for a travel company to help get me here and there. While looking through a big city newspaper's travel section, I found several agencies that specialized in booking round-the-world travel arrangements. That there were masterminds who worked at getting folks around the world was good news. I started calling and e-mailing several of these agencies with my intentions. I also mentioned my plans to Becky Johnson, a friend who was the owner of Kruzof Travel, a local travel agency in Sitka. Becky said she'd help, that she could underbid the others, but she needed a time line that included ordered destinations. I needed to get more specific.

Originally, my plan was to go around the world in a clockwise fashion, west to east. It was to be modeled on the Kora, a type of pilgrimage and meditation in the Tibetan Buddhist tradition. It would thus follow the religious direction that pilgrims take when circumambulating a shrine or sacred place. This trip certainly had an essence of pilgrimage to it and canyons were my shrines; hence, my directional choice. My Kora, though, would not include the usual108 ambulations that one made around the sacred object on many such excursions.

Even though I had quit my job at the center in May, my huge, round-the-world Kora couldn't begin until September 30 of 2000. The reason – I had started a bike and hike tourist business in the summer of 1999. With my business season running from May 14 to September 20, I figured I would need ten days to close up shop. As it turned out, the end of September became a pivotal date. Due to the extreme heat, that's when the Namibian government closes their section of Fish River Canyon, and it would remain closed long past the date I would be returning home to Alaska. Summer heat begins there in October and daytime temperatures can get dangerously high, well over 100 degrees Fahrenheit. I would need to get to the Fish River Canyon as soon as possible. It would have to be my first stop.

Also, as it turned out, there was only one outfit, Quark Expeditions, that went to Antarctica's Dry Valleys. They listed two departures a year: one in December and one in January. As with Namibia, North America's winter was Antarctica's summer. To get to this canyon, I'd leave Tasmania on a Russian icebreaker, sail to Antarctica, and 24 days later, return to New Zealand. There went the idea of the Kora. With that knowledge, a reverse Kora would have to do. I presented my newfound plans to Becky and the others.

Then there was the budget. Yes, what about my budget? Its consideration had taken a back seat to the foremost questions of where to go and in what order. These were the priorities that would determine my expenses, but how much time I'd spend at each site entered into my costs. My original and foolish hope was that the entire journey would cost about $10,000 (in the year 2000), a big laugh in hindsight. I'd read and heard from the same friends who'd told me about snakes as well as smaller, creepy-crawly things that climb in your ears while you sleep, and bats that suck toe blood, that for $2,500 I could go around the world. TWA allowed a passenger one year to fly in the direction originally flown - always flying either east or west. That would leave about $1,000 per continent, a good deal, or so I thought.

Wrong! The cheapest seat for the three-week "cruise" on the Russian ice-breaker was $10,000, and that was sharing a cabin-room with two others! So, I envisioned working my way to Antarctica, sleeping in the engine room, swabbing decks, peeling potatoes. I tried. I called, wrote letters, e-mailed, and faxed Quark, the outfitter that ran this extravaganza. I was begging them for help. Their response was, "Thank you for your message and your continued interest in Quark Expeditions. Unfortunately, we are unable to accept your barter services. Our vessels are chartered from Russian ship owners. They are fully staffed with crew who maintain the operation of the vessel including the kitchen and cabin services. Quark does hire staff specific to each expedition but these are individuals who are highly experienced in icebreaker operations as well as polar expedition cruising or are lecturers/naturalists/scientists." I asked myself, "What now?" Was I prepared to spend $10,000 in an **attempt** to get to the Dry Valleys of Antarctica? Attempt was, indeed, the operative word. You see, Quark offered no guarantees. Setting sail was one thing, but arriving in Antarctica was weather dependent.

There was another "option." Rent a helicopter out of Argentina for $150,000 to $300,000, and run my own operation! No, there seemed to be only one way, but $10,000 for a ship that was dependent on the right weather and ice conditions to get me even close to the Dry Valleys seemed absolutely absurd. And where was I supposed to get that kind of money, even if making it to my destination was guaranteed?

Understandably, I had second thoughts about doing that canyon. Who would fault me for only getting to six canyons when the expense was so great? The aforementioned Jon Wunrow is who. He faulted me for even thinking of leaving Antarctica out of this trip, and, I must say, it seemed perfectly okay for him to needle me about my stinginess. Jon's bona fides included not only the aforementioned PCT, but other kudos as well. He was a mountain climber, a well-respected regional figure in the youth work world, chair of the board of the agency, and, essentially, during much of the time of this debate, my boss. He had also just returned from Tibet with his son. As the self-proclaimed conscience of my journey, Jon said something along the line of, "Come on, you big weenie. If you're gonna do the seven canyons, you gotta do them all. What's an extra $10,000?"

I suppose a bit of self-disclosure on my financial situation is in order here. I had been saving for the trip for six years or so. I'd put back a little here and there. I'd opened a special bank account just for the seven canyons and it grew. Slowly. It was supplemented by the annual "Permanent Fund" dividend that each Alaskan man, woman, and child receives every October. It was about $1,000 a year then, and had gotten as high as $2,000. It helped fill the coffers, but I still didn't have the $20,000 I thought I'd need.

I did, however, own a house in Eugene, to which it was unlikely that I would ever return. I had been holding on to it with the idea that my daughter might attend the University of Oregon, but sacrifices had to be made. I put the house on the market; it sold, and I made a few bucks. Uncle Sam, got a huge chunk of it. So with the meager income from my summer business and the sale of the house, I had the finances to take the $10,000 trip to Antarctica. Good thing, because before I put the house on the market, I'd sent a $2,500 non-refundable check deposit to Quark.

The round-the-world folks quoted me a cost of $5,600 for the trip. Becky offered me the same for $5,000. My airlines would include Alaska Air, United, Lufthansa, South African Air, Olympic, Singapore Air, Air China, Ansett, Air New Zealand, Lan Chile, and Tans Peru. That left $5,000 of the original $10,000 I had figured for the whole trip before I learned about Antarctica and its money realities. That meant about $700 per continent for all of the other expenses I might encounter. I sensed it would be a challenge to stay within that figure, but a no-frills journey was better than no trip at all. It would be a stretch, a long stretch as it turned out.

The cost for Antarctica continued to nag at me throughout the entire trip. It was crazy. The internal argument would flow back and forth between. Are you out of your mind? You can't afford to do this trip. – What about your responsibilities, duties, obligations?" – and – "This is a once-in-a-lifetime opportunity, a quest, a pilgrimage, a noble journey to visit the deepest canyon on each continent."

The entire trip would be a real challenge and I still hadn't come across anything in my reading to tell me if it had already been done. I had the money; I would go. Thus with my budget and time-line in place, I started getting my shots.

Then there was the 11th hour planning change. As noted earlier, my research had pointed to Tara Canyon in Yugoslavia as Europe's deepest canyon. Enter Richard Fisher, premiere canyoneer, guide, photographer, and the first person to get to the deepest part of the Yarlung Tsangpo in China. He was also one of the first Americans to figure out how to work with the Chinese to get permission to enter there. His book *Earth's Mystical Grand Canyons* and his photographs had inspired me. Richard was "the" canyon expert in my mind, and I had written to him about my canyon quest, laying out my plans. He was incredibly kind to me, taking me under his wing in a manner of speaking. He wrote back asking why I was going to Yugoslavia when Europe's deepest canyon was the Vikos Canyon in Greece. I got right on the phone to Becky and changed my reservation from Yugoslavia to Greece.

This situation may call to question the thoroughness of my research. However, as I've noted, there is some conflicting information on which canyons are the deepest, just as there is some dispute on whether Fisher was the first to encounter Yarlung Tsangpo's deepest reaches. Early explorers had staked that claim years ago. However, back then they didn't have the technology with which to verify the depths to which they'd gone. Fisher's "rediscovery" and scientific reports are accepted by authorities in the canyoneering world. He was acknowledged in the *1996 Guinness Book of Records* as the first to document Yarlung Tsangpo's depth of 16,650 feet, and to have led the expedition.

Conflict regarding the depth of various canyons does exist. Although the Fish River Canyon is firmly designated as Africa's deepest, I did find those who would vote for Ethiopia's Rift Valley. The latter is a rift, a fault, a fissure that runs from the Syria/Lebanon area of southwest Asia to Mozambique in southeastern Africa. It represents a separation of earth's African and Arabian plates that has been going on for millions of years. It will eventually result in the splitting of the African plate into two new ones, turning the Rift Valley of East Africa into an ocean.

Let me be up front from the get-go. All of this research to verify the planet's deepest canyons was conducted by a man who flunked out of college twice (although I did eventually graduate and go on to earn a master's degree, but that is neither here nor there). My information was based on searching the internet, travel guides, and libraries. I pored over the likes of Richard Fisher's *Earth's Mystical Grand Canyons*, *The Guinness Book of Records*, and *Traveler's Challenge: The Sophisticated Globetrotter's Record Book*. I likewise made calls to tourist bureaus of various countries. Though I did much homework, I hesitate to claim 100% accuracy, but I would go about 99%. Then there are the differences between canyons, valleys, gorges, chasms, crevasses, and gulches. Some of these terms are often used informally and sometimes interchangeably, adding to the confusion. The differences between them and the depths of their related designations would make a fine graduate research paper for someone. A standardization of terms and definitions might help to clear up some of the confusion about just which of the abysses are the deepest.

After almost six years of saving money, reading, and reviewing all of the literature I could find, Googling all of the continents I could Google, planning what to take and what not to take, and gathering the equipment I would need, my departure date was drawing nigh. It was time to pack. Some friends who had just returned from their own around-the-world tour took only carry-on bags. If it didn't fit in them, well, they didn't need it. Not me. I was on a special trip with many different requirements. I would need all of my paraphernalia and more.

The first time I tried to get all of the things I thought I'd need into my North Face black gear bag – a 9,000 cubic inch, non-rolling, special expedition, extra tough, reinforced, extra-thick plastic/rubber pack – I couldn't get half of my gear inside the darn thing. After three more attempts to winnow it down, it fit. Inside that pack went everything I thought I'd need from Africa to Antarctica.

Ever alert to my anxieties, I knew I was toting more than that gear. I was susceptible and impressionable. When it came to people with lies, exaggerations, true-but-horrific-experiences, tall tales, and woeful things than can and do befall travelers, I was all ears. As I prepared to leave, friends regaled me with tales of robbers, missed flights, con artists, deadly spiders and snakes, airplane accidents, exotic microscopic critters that can climb up your urine stream to enter your body, and all manner of other disasters and near misses.

My friend Jon had some interesting, not to mention descriptive, examples of ailments and their aftermath. These included Montezuma and "the revenge," tropical sprue, and HACE (high altitude cerebral edema). I was more worried about low altitude! His mantra was the old adage, "peel it, boil it, cook it, shell it, or forget it." These and all manner of other untoward medical misfortunes like typhoid, malaria, elephantiasis, and diphtheria were just waiting for a naïf like me.

The 30th of September finally arrived and I left Sitka as planned with all of the deepest canyons designated, except Australia's. I figured that would get decided when I arrived in the Land Down Under as my long distance research had confirmed nothing. With my feet on Australian soil, I'd get straightened out as to which canyon in Oz would be my target.

For now I was in Germany where I'd spend two days in Frankfurt catching up with my jet lag. I also welcomed the break from dragging around all of that equipment. I e-mailed family and friends: "Just a hello from Germanz, sorrz for the goofz spelling the z is where I am used to the y being and vice versa. Can't saz I am not OK, still a bit over whelmed, but excited and nervous and looking forward to heading off to Africa tomorrow. I actuallz found my waz to a czber café onlz had to ask once for directions and that was with a map in hand, so I am building confidence for mz map reading skills that maz be necessarz as I trek on the thru these canzons. Peace, Jeff."

Two days later I'd be headed for Windhoek, the capital of Namibia. The first of my canyon dances was within reach. I wouldn't be traversing the entire length of any of the canyons, this one included. My goal for all of them was to just get to the bottom, and not even to the deepest part – just as close as I could. My friend Cara had opined that if one "bags peaks," then one must "pocket canyons." That, indeed, was my plan: to pocket several of the world's canyons. Now, it was off to the Fish River Canyon where this chapter began.

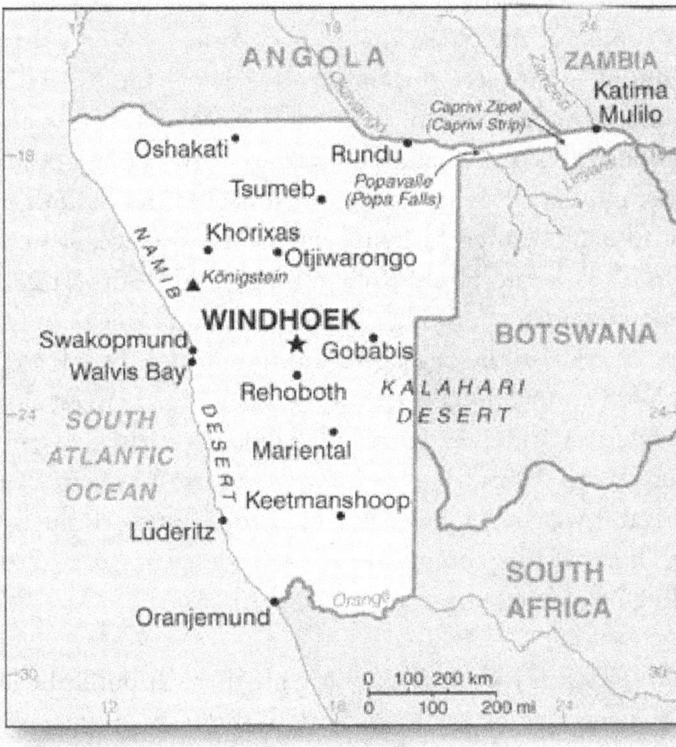

Africa

The Fish River Canyon

**"I want to ride to the ridge 'til the west commences,
Gaze at the moon 'til I lose my senses. I can't stand
hobbles and I can't stand fences, don't fence me in."**

--Cole Porter

Fish River Canyon in Namibia was my first destination. I was heading for a canyon reported to be the hottest and most remote in the whole wide world. At least that is what the Namibian government boasted. It was also Africa's deepest. Located in the Namib Desert, the planet's most ancient, it likewise laid claim to some of the oldest dirt in the world. The Fish River Canyon developed during what were predominantly pluvial times – rainy climatic epochs – hundreds of millions of years ago. Two major factors played a role in its formation and depth. In addition to the erosive action of the Fish River over the ages, movement of the earth's crust caused the bottom of the river valley to collapse. Now, after the many eons of its existence, it waited for me.

To get to it I flew into Hosea Kutako International Airport 28 miles west of Windhoek, Namibia's sprawling capital. It would be one of only two times that my gear beat me to the baggage claim. From there I took a taxicab into Windhoek. With around 300,000 people, it is Namibia's largest city, as well as its cultural and financial center. Purple Jacaranda trees, native to Latin America and introduced into Africa, dotted the wide streets of the cityscape. Shortly after my arrival, I watched a presidential convoy blasting through town; cars in front with horns blaring, accompanied by jeeps bearing armed soldiers. No one, including me, hesitated getting out of their way.

My time in Windhoek was limited, but while there, I found the locals to be friendly, the streets free of traffic gridlock and the town quiet and relaxed. There were small craft markets set up here and there in the shade, and the parks always seemed to have drumming going on under the cooler canopy of their trees. While wandering around the city, I couldn't help but notice that it seemed somewhat familiar, sort of Germanic. It reminded me of parts of Frankfurt that I had just wandered through on my stop over there. I discovered that was because Germans, in the 1880s, had colonized what is now called Namibia, annexing it, and naming it German South-West Africa. It remained under German occupation until the end of the First World War.

After the war, South Africa moved in and occupied the German territory. In 1920, according to a League of Nations mandate, South Africa began its rule over what it would call South-West Africa, imposing its system of apartheid in 1948. Namibians began the first resistance to South African domination in 1959, and in 1966 the South-West Africa People's Organization (SWAPO) launched the Namibian War of Independence. Freedom was eventually won. In 1978, the UN Security Council called for free and fair elections that were finally held in 1989. March 21, 1990 marked the Republic of Namibia's Independence Day. As an aside, Ziggy Marley, Bob's son, wrote *Namibia* the song that promoted their independence.

By area, Namibia is ranked the 34th largest country in the world, and is about the size of Germany and France combined. It is located in the southern part of the continent, just north of South Africa. To its north lie Angola and Zambia, to the east is Botswana, and to the west the waters of the Atlantic Ocean. A country of almost two million people, it is home to more than ten different ethnic groups and varying lifestyles that range from traditional hunter-gatherers and herdsmen to urban dwellers. Many of its people are still subsistence farmers, but that is changing. These days, the economy includes agriculture, mining, and tourism. Mining is, and for many years has been, a mainstay of the economy. Various metals, diamonds, gold, silver, copper, and uranium are among the targets for excavation. When I was there, the average income for a Namibian was about $2,000 U.S. a year, not that much, but apparently pretty good compared to other African countries. The country struggles with poverty and unemployment, the AIDS virus, and land distribution problems unresolved since pre-colonial days. Under German occupation it had become a trading station. Later, an economy of agriculture was established that included vineyards, fruit, and vegetable exports.

Namibia is now becoming a popular tourist destination due to its excellent wildlife; its Namib-Naukluft National Park is the largest game reserve in Africa. Namibia is one of the few countries in the world to have incorporated conservation into its constitution. Article 95 of that document reads: "The State shall actively promote and maintain the welfare of the people by adopting international policies aimed at the following: maintenance of ecosystems, essential ecological processes and biological diversity of Namibia, and utilization of living natural resources on a sustainable basis for the benefit of all Namibians, both present and future." What is written on paper sounds good and promising. One only hopes that it will translate into enduring reality for Namibia, its wildlife, and its people. The fact remains that mining is extremely important to Namibia's economy, and mining can be extremely hazardous to the land, its people, and wildlife.

Wildlife conservation is actually managed today by the people of Namibia through the Community Based Natural Resource Management (CBNRM) project established in 1993. This program links the health of Namibia's wildlife to the prosperity of the local people. It is the people who've been given the authority to oversee wildlife conservation through the establishment of communal conservancies. Poaching is not now socially acceptable and populations of various creatures are on the rise. These include cheetahs (the world's highest population of which is now in Namibia), black rhinos, lions, desert elephants, and more. Cultural sustainability is valued, too, with traditional villages and crafts benefiting from tourism.

In addition to its wildlife, Namibia has magnificent deserts as well as the world's highest sand dunes, and, of course, my destination: the Fish River Canyon. Fish River Canyon is part of a nature conservation park, the southern end of which hold the Ai-Ais Hot Springs. Pronounced eye-ice, Ai-Ais is an oasis whose name means "burning water" in the Nama language. Thermal waters from deep within the earth are said to be therapeutic for those suffering from muscular and joint aches and pains, and wonderfully soothing for just about everyone. It's no wonder that these ancient waters are now a part of a resort spa. Good news for those who've just hiked the canyon that it's in the vicinity!

With all of these facts about Namibia and my anticipated explorations of the Fish River Canyon going through my mind, I continued to stroll the streets of Windhoek. Its skyline had a few very modern buildings. One that caught my eye was the Supreme Court Building, a mixture of modern and hokeyness, but in a grand way, with huge columns and a stately manner. It appeared slightly off kilter, too, due to the older styles surrounding it. That it seemed to have been thrown up recently created an unbalanced effect of nice and old coupled with a bit of the garish new. Another building, the Sanlam Center, was built to look like stairs climbing up to the sky. It sat on Independence Avenue, the main drag, which held many examples of old colonial architecture.

My lodging, the Chameleon Backpackers was a 40-minute walk from downtown Windhoek. The Chameleon is a sprawling compound that sits behind a high brick wall with concertina wire and glass on the top to keep out local thieves, predators, or both. Against the back wall was a small pool, shaded by trees. Here two tame resident meerkats hung out along with a well-scarred pit bull-like dog. The main two story building held a small e-mailing space and the owners' rooms. I was ensconced in one of the smaller cabins which held a bed, small desk, colorful African wall hangings, and barely enough space to spread out my gear. I unpacked, and as I did, those aforementioned fears came tumbling out. They included this canyon's infamous debilitating and dehydrating heat; my numb feet failing me (from my hike on the Pacific Crest Trail); my route-finding or, more precisely, not route finding acumen catching up with me; being in an unfamiliar place; and being alone and lonely. How was I going to deal with all of these mentally weighty fears? I didn't know, but I figured that my planning and past hiking experiences would help me in the long run. Whatever good omens were out there would get me through.

As an Alaskan who has been a guide for kayaking, biking, and hiking and for more than ten years the owner/operator of a small eco-tourist businesses in Ketchikan and Sitka, I'd been guilty of filling visitors' heads with wilderness stories: *"Oh yeah, they shot three bears in town last week."* – *"Yeah, a brown bear is the same as a grizzly but bigger and meaner."* – *"No, we don't have black bears, the brown bears eat them."* – *"Why, I once saw an eagle fly off with a small dog."* I knew the drill. Try to wind up the guests. Give them something to be scared of, to dwell on, as we hiked through a part of the world's largest temperate rainforest, the Tongass, which is also known for having the greatest concentration of brown bears on the planet. These stories often made me nervous, in the best tall tales there is always an element of truth, in this case a very large and furry element.

After unpacking and inventorying my mountains of gear, I was reassured that I'd packed something for any and every event. What I still wasn't sure of was whether I was prepared to deal with my mental fears that were every bit as heavy as that gear. Well, I'd just have to deal with all of that later. It was now time to repair to the shade of the umbrella by the bar. It was a small, dark, hole-in-the-wall place adorned with a few local artifacts: old deer and zebra jawbones; small elaborate carvings of elephants, zebras, and fanciful creatures; along with what looked to be a typical mask carved from ebony, the dense, dark wood I was pretty sure didn't grow in Namibia. Decorating the dim hallway was a table holding postcards and small flags. The latter were emblems representing the many different homelands of current employees and past visitors. In front, was a giant umbrella shading a picnic table at which sat two weather-beaten men. I said "hello," and was in luck, as they "gooddaymate"-ed me. Ah! They were English speakers; we could communicate!

The Aussies had been "in country" for a month. They were tanned, had permanent sweat stains on their ball caps, shorts and shirts with dust from last month that wouldn't wash out, and shirts, pants, and hats faded by heat, sweat, and grime. Just how I hoped I'd look in a few weeks. Their casual attitude, friendliness, and sun-scorched arms, legs, and faces were how I imagined a true traveler should look. They seemed authentic to my eye; I was a bit jealous. We traded pleasantries. Where you from? How long you been here? Where you going? The usual. They were two friends from Perth on holiday for a few months, and were traveling throughout Africa. They'd been in South Africa and were on a northward crawl. Namibia was their second stop, and here they'd been sucked into a vortex of cheap lodging and free pizza delivery, complete with plenty of new people passing through the backpackers with whom they could chat. "Inertia," they said, "can be hard to overcome when you got the "'Pondi Fever.'"

"Pondo, what's that?" I'd spent so much time getting shots and hearing the various stories about different diseases; here was one that was totally new. I was curious and a bit concerned.

"No, no, mate, Pon-dee fever."

Those two did look like they had something; too much sun or too much fun. I wasn't quite sure.

"Oh, Pondee. How do you get that?" My bullshit alert wasn't sounding any alarms yet, and, if there was a new disease, I for sure didn't want to get it on the first leg of my trip.

"Oh, it's serious, if a bloke gets it, you gotta lie in your hammock for a long time." They were both slumping, as if they were in a hammock. Their poses made the chairs they were poured into seem as flexible as a hammock made of wet spaghetti, or, maybe it was their bodies wracked with "the fever" that was causing such loose jointedness.

"And then what?" I could see they had something. I'm nervous now, and told them again, "I'd never heard of this one and I didn't get the shot."

"I seen a guy with it just last week, all red-and-stuff like that; horrible it was to look at." I think they sensed that my anxiety level was on the rise; a strange faint smile was on their lips, and, for some reason, I saw a bit of a twinkle in what had been bloodshot eyes.

"Holy smokes, how'd it happen?"

"Oh you can catch it or it can catch you, it's right bad, it is."

"Oh. Great! What can the clinics do about it?" I am now leaning forward looking back and forth between the two of them.

"Well it's bad stuff; you gotta lay around a lot to recover."

I'm getting more concerned. "Whoa, is it that bad?" I could see that they had been laying about for quite a while, what with the pile of beer bottles strewn about the table.

"Bad, its serious stuff, mate. Affects almost everybody who comes down here."

"Shit, I never even heard of that. The health folks in the States aren't hip to that one. Are there pills or shots to cure it or prevent it?"

The answer was, "No." Then immediately I heard, "Yeah. It's a new strain. Bad stuff, mate."

Hmm, one says no and one says yeah. Which is it, are they totally suffering? "I thought Australia had all the really bad stuff."

"Oh yeah, we do, but so does Africa," they acknowledged.

"So what happens if you get it?" I'd taken out my little notebook and was ready to take notes on this condition.

For some reason this put even more of a smile on their faces as they both looked at each other at the same time. Some message had passed between them. "Well, you get a few beers, lay back, and watch the river flow by. You then 'Pondo (er)' the meaning of it all." Hook, line, and sinker – I'd fallen for it. They got me. I was had, and at the same time relieved, like I'd dodged at least one medical problem. With that, I was more than happy to buy each a beer. Upon my return home I came across a word that added some credence to their Pondi Fever tale. The Swedes have a word, Resfeber, which means "the restless race of the traveler's heart before the journey begins, when anxiety and anticipation are tangled together; a "travel fever" that can manifest as an illness.

After learning the truth about Pondo Fever, I left the two Aussies to contemplate their illness and its medication. I went back to my room where I did some pondering of my own. Why subject myself to the costs, time away from family, the heat and the cold, my fears, and not the least, Ponder Fever? Those among you who are either professional or armchair psychologists may be able to trace my obsession with canyons back beyond that first visit to the Grand Canyon. Maybe it goes back to my childhood toilet training, maybe even further back than that. Maybe it is truly Freudian.

Some refer to canyons as Mother Nature's womb. Such references go way back. I'd seen one old scroll painting of Asia's deepest canyon in the cradle of Tibetan civilization. It depicted a local Tibetan goddess with the river symbolizing her spine and with a mountain peak as her breast. It doesn't take much imagination to figure out the rest. Some other canyon legends are tied to creation stories. There is a legend told among some Native American tribes that explains how the Grand Canyon was formed. Two Gods were battling for control of the earth. One decided to flood the world. When the flood waters subsided, mountains were revealed, along with the huge chasm we know as the Grand Canyon. Fish River Canyon has its own creation legend. San Bushmen believe that a large serpent, Koutein Kooru, was being pursued by hunters. In his frantic flight to get away, he twisted and turned through the land, forming the torturous contours of the giant canyon that awaited my visit.

Other stories tell of civilizations that sprang from canyons. There are Australian aboriginal tales that have people coming from a hole in the earth. Some present day notions aren't far off. When I told one of my friends about my wish to visit the deepest canyons, she e-mailed that "…searching for deep canyons is a metaphor for re-birthing, getting in touch with your feminine side, or maybe it's just as close as one can get to the center of the earth."

Maybe there were some truths in these analyses. I knew that the idea of going into something, a canyon "for example" had significance. I'd heard the Grand Canyon called Mother Nature's Jellyroll and on and on. None of this is original and as noted in the long histories of people, canyons are seen as part of a woman and nature. Nevertheless, looking for the deeper truth within my psyche, I don't really think I was trying to get back to my birth experience.

After pondering the many canyon legends and some of the hunches about the reasons for my trip, it was back to the reality of the present. My plan was to hang out for a few days here at the Chameleon, which was billed as the "Friendliest Hostel in Southern Africa" by my *Footprint* guidebook. As far as I was concerned, it was indeed a most friendly place even if the two Aussies had had a good laugh at my expense. Later, after I'd returned home to Sitka, Richard Fisher wrote asking me to recommend a place where he could stay while he photographed the Fish River Canyon. His experience, it turned out, wasn't mine. He found it quite lacking in friendship and professionalism.

Upon leaving the Chameleon, it was my plan to take a train south to Keetmanshoop for an overnight stop at the Chapel Inn B & B owned by Louie and Re'etTourie. I'd then be transported to my new digs at another of their establishments: the Fish River Lodge. From there I'd be able to hike the canyon, even though the Namibian government closed the hiking trail between October and April. During these long summer months the temperatures can get dangerously high. I was in luck. Louie and Re'et owned the upper forty miles of Fish River Canyon. After learning of my hiking experience, they were happy to let me traipse around their section of canyon despite the searing conditions. It was the resourceful owners of the Chameleon Backpackers that I had to thank for this opportunity. They had secured for me all of these arrangements. It seems they were pros at helping misfits like me, and I was most grateful.

I came to find out that the Touries had moved to Namibia from South Africa, where they had grown tired of the big city life and the strife. They now made the Chapel B & B their home; it was where they were raising their family. After having experienced a bit, a very small bit, of the tourist trade in Keetmanshoop, they reasoned that adding a world famous attraction to their repertoire couldn't hurt. The private area of canyon became available to them when an old time farmer died. His wife was willing to sell them the farm and the land. Who wouldn't want to buy into such a venture? They took the risk and transformed the farmhouse into the Fish River Lodge.

Meanwhile, back at the Chameleon, I'd met a German couple who would be driving to the rim of the Fish River Canyon. Heading out with them would save me on transportation costs as they'd be going through Keetsmanshoop where I was to rendezvous at the Chapel B & B before heading off to the lodge in the Fish River Valley. I rode with them the 400 miles south from Windhoek to Keetsmanshoop in a small black car that was great for absorbing the heat!

Along our way we crossed the Tropic of Capricorn, one of those five foremost lines of latitude that encircle the earth. This one separates the tropics to the north from the southern temperate zone and pretty much bisects Namibia. It was the first time for all of us to experience what we'd only seen before as a line drawn on a map. I knew from my reading and from a few of my friends in the sailing world that crossing the equator is marked by a rite of passage. Once you've sailed across it, you morph from a "Pollywog" to a "Shellback." Our threesome didn't undergo any transformations. Neither did we have to entertain the typical crossing-the-line dignitaries one encounters at the equator such as King Neptune, Queen Amphitrite, the Royal Baby, the Royal Barbers, or the Royal Constables. Our passage across Capricorn on terra firma was uneventful.

We drove on, in companionship with a two lane paved highway, through rolling, dusty, hot terrain, cooked brown by the heat. Along the way, every now and then, as if to give us a break from the monotone colors, we flashed past some houses painted in various shades of pastel. Our stops were at outposts, gas stations with general stores where we'd buy gas and bottled water, stretch, and then move on. The landscape could only be called dun-colored and barren, but there were cattle and ostrich ranches. The only people we saw were at those quick gas stops; it must have been too hot in the unforgiving sun for most people. We arrived in Keetmanshoop where they dropped me off at the Chapel B & B. My German charioteers then headed to the rim of the Fish River Canyon to camp out.

Keetmanshoop, one of Namibia's oldest towns, dates back to the end of the 18th century. The small, southern town was settled by Germans who'd used it mostly for sheep ranching. When those settlers arrived, it was a mission and trading station. The name derives from a wealthy German patron of the time, Johan Keetman, and means "Keetsman's hope." It is now a transit point for goods heading to South Africa, although they must not have been trucking anything when we were on the highway as we had the road to ourselves. It is also a jumping-off point for the Fish River Canyon and the famous Quiver Tree Forest.

The quiver tree is an odd duck sort of plant. It has a stout, straight, but gnarly trunk, and then literally bristles out to form a cluster of pointed branches or "quivers." It isn't a tree at all really, but part of the aloe family. It's loaded with features that allow it to survive the desert conditions, those characteristic, succulent, aloe leaves being only one of them. Its proper name is Aloe dichotoma, but its common name comes from the fact that San Bushmen, some of the earliest inhabitants of Namibia, along with the Nama people, have used its hollowed out branches as quivers for their arrows. The Quiver Tree Forest holds around 250 of these plants, with the biggest ones having been rooted there for two to three centuries. Later, I'd see a great specimen at the Fish River Lodge. Even with the canyon walls nearby, the tree, somehow, seemed to always get my attention.

It should be noted that quiver trees are now important in the study of climate change, being victims of it themselves. Though these plants have grown in the arid lands of Namibia and South Africa, adapted to desert conditions as they are, today's increasing temperatures and expansion of desert are proving too much, even for them. They'll need to head south, become polar bound, or spread to a higher and cooler altitude if they are to survive. Their survival – where they stand or through their spread, turtle-slow as it must be for plants such as them – is being watched as a benchmark of the impact of global warming on the delicate desert ecosystem. They have been listed as one of the indicators to measure the migration of plants and animals in today's changing world.

When it comes to heat, (maybe not global warming), I usually acclimatize fairly quickly. As a little kid in Redlands, California (technically in the desert until it was irrigated for the orange groves), I grew up with summer temperatures that got into the hundreds, those "dry heat" temperatures for which southern California is noted. Southern Ohio, where I also lived for a time, had 95 degree days complete with 90 percent humidity. It was also the case that I'd not only lived in hot temperatures, I'd hiked in them. In some sections of the PCT, I trekked with temperatures that got way into the hundreds. I had survived it all, but I was now in Africa. During the hottest part of the year, the force of the heat in the Fish River Canyon is reported to be akin to that coming out of the oven when you bend down to remove a cake. It has that dry, take-your-breath-away, blast furnace force, as if it could broil you right then and there, and Fish River Lodge – where I'd be staying – sat in the hottest part of the canyon.

The heat was definitely a concern. There was no doubt about it, but I was pretty sure I could handle it if I went slow and carried enough water. The Touries agreed, and, thankfully, were okay with me stomping around in their desert, frying my brains, though they preferred I do it with company. That was okay with me.

As fate would have it, others arrived at the Chapel B & B at the same time I did. They were Michael, a 27-year-old Peace Corps volunteer, and Astrid, a woman from Holland. The three of us were all headed out the next day for the Fish River Lodge. After a nice shower we looked for a café, but it was after 6pm and they were all closed, so the local gas station stood in for an eatery. Without too many worries, I returned to the B & B, and slept the sleep of the innocent under the humming ceiling fan.

The next morning we were all up early. We piled our gear as well as cartons of food - supplies for the Fish River Lodge – into the truck and headed off. Re'et was a talker: fun, interesting, and confident. We learned during the drive that she was 40 with two kids and an "oops" on the way. As we drove, she shared stories of the heat and asked us what our various plans were. We had all come to hike. Rolling along the dirt road, we spent most of the time looking out the truck window at the endless desert landscape, lost in our own thoughts; maybe just a bit concerned about that heat and our hiking. When asked how many people did the hike, she said, "No one at this time of year and not that many during the 'season,'" but they had plans to increase their advertising and hoped they'd be able to lure more adventure-hiker-type visitors.

The ride took us through more bush country, although we did pass a dam with an oasis. It made for an interesting juxtaposition of desert, oasis, and back to desert within thirty seconds. At the halfway point, two hours down the road, we were met by Christy, the lodge foreman who was in his early

20s. We emptied out the gear and supplies from Re'ets truck and restacked everything in Christy's car. Re'et then headed back to Keetmanshoop, and we headed off towards the Fish River Lodge, bouncing on the dirt track for a few more hours of heat, dust, burnt out scenery, sheer nothingness, and absolutely zero traffic.

Fish River Lodge was a welcome site. We got out of the truck and, after picking ourselves up from having been knocked down by the heat, helped to unload the supplies. The main building had a flat roof with a rounded, domed center that reminded me of a very miniature U.S. Capitol Building. It had no purpose that anyone could figure out after the inevitable question arose as to why a dome was there. Perhaps the answer was, "Why not?" A long, covered veranda sported a touch of grass at its border. The lodge sat among a grove of quiver trees, a few young ones abutting the porch were home to several birds that came and went. The original "farm" had been more of a ranch with sheep and ostriches as its main "crops." It must have been home to a hard scrabble livelihood.

The main building had several guest rooms plus space for the caretaker. Astrid would stay there. Michael and I would stay in "the stable," a large bunkhouse converted from the barn. It had three sections. One, to the side, held six three-tiered bunk beds; the middle realm was the cooking area, and the last third held the shower and bathrooms. We had it all to ourselves. The walls were of stone, the roof corrugated tin, and the floor a cement and stone combination. It was significantly cooler there than in the sun, and it had a dusty smell owing to its desert location.

There were several outbuildings, one of which housed the staff. Others included a groaning windmill that slowly turned in the intense heat to the sound of its own moaning. A hugely extravagant, room-sized birdcage was home to several weather-beaten, parrot-type birds. Several vehicles in various states of disrepair were a part of the usual clutter one finds on any farm.

The location of Fish River Lodge was truly amazing, for it sat perched directly on the western rim of the canyon. It was one giant, spectacular view of 650 million years of geological history. There, before your eyes, was an abyss that stretched out for 100 miles, measuring about 20 miles across, and, in some places, 1,800 feet deep. There was only it and the desert rim on which we sat. As someone said, "It was like being on the edge of eternity." A land-use plan is now in place to ensure that this natural wonder and its fragile ecosystems are minimally impacted by tourism. Fish River Lodge is a partner in the public-private Greater Fish River Canyon complex that seeks to co-manage conservation efforts while providing employment for the Namibian people.

With the immensity of the canyon ever present, due to our perpetual sweeping views of it, Michael and I set about storing our gear. We then walked up the dusty hill to the main building, the center of the then new tourist operation, and looked at the map to decide our route. It had been our intention to hike alone. It was only to quell Re'et's concerns for our safety that we'd agreed to hike together. He, however, wanted to spend four nights in the canyon; I wanted to spend two. Since Re'et was back in Keetmanshoop, we decided to revert to our original plans to hike separately. We'd both be dropped off at the starting block early the next morning to begin our adventure before the heat took over.

That night we all had dinner on the patio with its view of the stable/bunkhouse, the dry desert scene, and our very own quiver tree with birds still flitting about catching the evening bugs. When I told Christy's wife, Francy, our cook, that I was a pseudo-vegetarian, her eyes got wide, her hair started to curl, and her nostrils flared. Her reaction reminded me of my own incredulity when asking people, "Who's the King of Rock and Roll?" – and getting answers like "Sting" or "Cyndi Lauper." Her reaction was understandable. I had correctly intuited that my diet was new to her. Christy and Francy had grown up on farms and had always eaten meat. At the time of my visit, the idea of vegetarianism hadn't yet reached the far away corner of the world they called home. Later, after dinner, with the stars out, Christy asked me why I was a veggie. I told him "I was poor and dating a veggie woman when I first began the practice," to which he responded, he hadn't met any woman so good that she'd put him off his steak. Re'et had warned us that Francy was very new to the hostess business. As a pseudo-veggie, I eat fish when I can and turkey on Thanksgiving. I decided to eat a piece of chicken if it would keep the cook's eyes in her head and save the innkeeper from apoplexy.

The candlelight dinner was delicious and the bright, nearly full moon lent it a peaceful ambiance. We talked, as visitors will, asking about lodge logistics. We had witnessed their food delivery system, and while it was called a ranch or farm, they really didn't raise anything except a few chickens that roamed about the place. There was some hunting of game, but it was a subsistence life. The hoped-for-crops were visitors like us. Christy talked about having been raised on a farm in Namibia where they had some cattle, goats, and sheep, most of which were exported to South Africa. Now the Fish River region was being touted as a possible grape growing area and the farm was thinking of growing grapes. Not being a farmer, I had no idea of its feasibility, the land looked pretty barren to me.

Astrid, Michael, and I shared our stories. Michael was winding up his Peace Corps project; some type of small business adventure. He allowed that, like most Peace Corps volunteers, he probably benefited as much if not more than the wonderful people he came to know. Astrid was on holiday and looking for heat and some photo opportunities before she had to return home. It was a most pleasant evening of camaraderie with locals and travelers blending, asking, and listening. Maybe the magic of the continent was present there too. The warm breeze, cooling as the evening went along, was accompanied by a sky full of big bright stars. It wasn't much like what I'd become used to, a typical Southeast Alaska evening being 40 degrees F, cloudy, and raining. I felt it was a good omen for the eve of my first canyon dance.

The next morning Michael and I were up early. It was just us, for Astrid had decided not to hike. After a quick breakfast, we climbed onto the "buffalo" for the 1½ hour ride to the starting point for our canyon hike. The buffalo wasn't a large, hump-backed wild ox. It was a motorized contraption; a truck and carryall. A giant jeep monster vehicle it was, with huge five-foot tires, and a granny gear that allowed it to go up the side of a building. Its engine was enormous and the driver was perched next to it. There was no cab; all was open to nature. There were no hoods or bonnets or trunks or doors or windows or anything - just engine, tires, steel and wheels. The passengers rode behind on four benches that were bolted down to the steel floor. They might have thought of bolting us down too.

I have ridden on dirt bikes (admittedly small ones), in four-wheel drive jeeps, in Armored Personnel Carriers (APC) while in the Army, and in all manner of all-terrain vehicles, but this was the bounciest – slam-you-around, shake-our-breakfast, use all the blender settings to stir-and-whir-and-dice-and-mince you – ride of my life. I don't think it would be fair to call what we were on a road or even a track. It was, hopefully in the general direction of where we were going; a bee-line; a sort of compass point. Good thing there wasn't a roof or we'd have butted our heads right through it. Good thing, too, that my hands were free as I literally hung on for dear life. The awesome driver took us up, down, sideways; over hill, and under dale, and, somehow, managed to stay stuck to his seat. Oh, but us passengers!

Finally, we arrived literally in the middle of nowhere. No signs, no X number of miles to the campground, no "Welcome to the Fish River Canyon" - just bleakness, dirt, dust, and washed out hot rocks. Christy stood up from his seat, looked around, looked again, sat down, and instructed the driver to go a bit more "that way." We jounced around some more before arriving at another nondescript spot. He stood up again, looked around, and pointed towards what appeared to be an old path that led toward the canyon. We said our "thanks" and "so longs." It was hot, 37 degrees Celsius; that's close to 100 degrees Fahrenheit. My worries, already unpacked way back in Windhoek, were the searing heat, my numb feet, and route-finding. It was time to face the music! If you give a dance you gotta pay the band. The time for the first canyon dance was upon me. Michael and I headed into the Fish River Canyon -- its thousand million year old-self.

Over those thousand million years, Mother Nature has had her way with the canyon throwing heat, pressure, wind, water, and earth movement its way to create what I was now walking through. For geologic techies out there, it all began those many eons ago. First there were layers of shale and sandstone that, with heat and pressure, morphed into dense rock. With time, fissures and magma allowed a horizontal stratum of dolomite, or basalt, to form. It's visible in the inner canyon. Then major tectonic plate movement caused the rock to warp and buckle. The Fish River found a place through which to course. With wind, water, erosion, and infinity added, voila! The Fish River Canyon came into existence! The lower river area, (not where I was hiking), has a granite complex and some precious gems, diamonds among them.

The 33 mile section I would hike, while no more or less difficult than the government section, was said to be more spectacular. It was harder to get to, making it less traveled, and, thus, unspoiled. It was also the deeper section of canyon. As it turned out, I was not disappointed. The only trash I saw while hiking was one piece of an old nail clipper. I must admit, though, I wasn't on a trail, per se, that much. That is if there really was one. Christy claimed there was, but I never found anything I'd call a trail. He'd supplied me with mimeographed maps that were old, worn, aerial photos of the canyon. The so-called trail existed, so far as I could see, only in pencil dashes marked on the maps. I managed to find a way of my own. The canyon walls kept me hemmed into a limited area, and water runs downhill, so off I went.

No permits were required in the private section where we hiked, and there was no lottery system assigning us a hiking time. We showed up, were driven to the trailhead (we hoped we were at the right place), and then were on our own with several options – there were camp sites numbering one through four. Michael would hike the whole distance, about 50 miles or so. I didn't feel compelled to hike for four nights even though I had come a long way; I still had a long way to go to get to six other continents. Thus, I opted for a shorter route. We walked down the dry, rocky drainage together, following painted white dots on the rocks. My plan was to find Camp One, or if making good time, Camp Three. Camp Two was halfway along the northern route. I wasn't going there. The next day I'd hike to Camp Four where I'd spend the night. On the third day, I'd hike back to the lodge. At the bottom of our starting point, Michael turned right and I headed left on an unmarked section of the trail. His route made a sweeping loop to the north. I headed basically south.

I was happy to hike alone, entering into the unknown-to-me Fish River Canyon with my bag of fears. Just before we left, Christy had added a few more when he said, "If you see leopard tracks, don't follow them. They don't like to be followed and will turn around and attack you. If there are baboons above you, don't walk close to the canyon walls 'cause they like to throw rocks at the hikers." And my personal favorite: "Yes, there are snakes: most are poisonous, but will usually move when they feel the vibrations of your footsteps. Except the puff adder, which looks like the color of the rocks and will actually chase you." And then the Colombo aside, "Oh yeah, and make sure you cover your toes at night so the rabid bats don't bite them." I later learned that there was also a very poisonous plant called the Melkbos, similar to our milkweed, but what I didn't know didn't hurt me that time.

Classic canyon features were before me: crumbling walls, a meandering river with green bushes next to it, rocks, and more rocks, all baked by the blazing heat. The canyon's first section, about two miles long, included the dry Lowen River, an intermittent stream that's a tributary of the Fish River. Rocks covered the dry river bed that was now rimmed with brown, dried-up plants. My other companions were sand, sky, heat, and solitude. I hiked on, trying to figure out where I was. The mimeographed map had no contour lines like a serious topo map, but it did show the meanders and some of the major drainages. Michael, like me, had also looked for official maps or a hiking guide, but to no avail. There just weren't any for this part of the canyon, underscoring its remoteness and those claims of it being a more pristine area of canyon. With my compass, I at least knew in which direction I was headed. It allowed me some sense of relief in dealing with my route-finding worries.

On my way to where I thought Camp One would be, I came upon flat, smooth ground. It was a well-used space under the spreading limbs of a tree. I walked up the drainage and crossed to the other side looking for the painted number that would indicate it was the "official" camp site. It would allow me to feel like I knew where I was, or at least my location on the map. But no luck; there was no campsite or footpath. I searched some more. Ordinarily I would have been a bit anxious, but, oh well, it was early. So I decided to press on to Camp Three. It was only a few more miles, and then I would know where I was for sure. I trooped on. It was hot, but I availed myself of the occasional shade from trees or rock overhangs. To keep myself hydrated, I'd brought along three liters of water, and I'd already downed a liter before leaving. We'd been told that there ought to be some water in the river, but so far its bed had been dry, adding a bit to my early worries. The Fish River, the longest in the interior of Namibia, is no longer the mighty river that helped form this canyon. It now only runs in the late summer during the rainy season. The rest of the year it is nothing more than a series of narrow pools.

I was going through my normal hiking ritual of checking the map and compass, taking breaks, looking for puff adders and leopard tracks, eyeballing the cliff walls for rock-throwing baboons, and generally feeling okay about the pack on my back. Soon, I arrived at the site where Camp Three should have been, but nothing looked like a camp to me. Rumor had it that a large number three was painted in white on a rock, but I never saw it. Again, I consulted the map, walked up the drainage, then down the drainage, in circles, and then climbed the hill for a better look-see. I took a short break, and then looked some more. I could see Michael eventually coming upon my footprints-to-nowhere, and thinking me in the final stages of heat stroke. In several spots near the dry riverbed, I sank below my boot tops in sand. It wasn't really quicksand; it was more like slow sand. Well, shit-o-dear, I still couldn't find that camp.

I decided to wander downstream a bit more. Gradually, water appeared in the riverbed which, at first glance, looked strange. Seeing water, period, was a bit odd. However, this was odder still because the water looked to be flowing upstream, and I was sure I was going downstream. I realized then that a nice breeze was playing tricks on me. It was blowing the water upstream. And so I ambled on. I heard a clatter of rocks falling and looked up, expecting a horde of baboons to be gathering for a stone throwing party, but it was a zebra scampering up the side of the cliff. It looked a bit on edge. So, I reassured it by saying, "Take it easy." Upon gaining surer footing, it was out of sight. Earlier in the day I had passed what looked like a mummified zebra. The skin was intact, but there wasn't a lot of zebra left under it. Due to the extreme conditions, spotting large game in the canyon isn't all that common; but I had witnessed a mountain zebra in the wild. These creatures, though they like the rugged terrain of canyon ravines, are, themselves, a rare sight, or so I'd been told.

In retrospect, I ought not to have been surprised about not finding the campsites since I'd never really found the trail. If I'd had a bucket of paint with me, I would have left a big "3" on a rock just to make myself feel better about my path-finding skills. I'd been walking game trails, just bushwhacking down the stream trying to head in the right direction, at least according to the compass. I'd polished off my three liters of water, so I stopped to refill at the riverbed pool, and eat some lunch. There was a nice sitting rock under the "umbrella" of a shaded overhang. I plopped down, dug out the crunchy peanut butter, crackers, and cashews, dropped a Halazone purification pill into the water, and surveyed the canyon wall across the river. I was looking for wildlife, of which there was none. Brochures claimed there were antelope and gazelle type critters: kudus, klipspringer, springbok, and steenbok. I was also to be on the lookout for leopard, zebra, and baboons as well as a slew of smaller critters: mice and rats, including some called Dassiers/Dassie-rats. The bird list included pelicans, black eagles, fish eagles, kingfishers, wild ostrich, herons, and waterfowl. I saw none of those, but heading right for me was a dime-sized, VW-shaped, black bug that left a track on the ground that looked like treads from a four-wheel drive vehicle. I followed its progress for about a half hour, and then decided that this might not be the best spot for night camping. Leaving the large black bug behind, I packed up and headed further downriver, seeking better accommodations.

The temperature had risen to furnace hot, but not so hot that I couldn't walk. As noted, I've experienced both hot-humid and hot-hot. Hot-hot has always seemed to have had less impact on my hiking enjoyment. I was definitely now "enjoying" hot-hot. According to more brochure info, summer temperatures here could get to 48 degrees Celsius, or about 118 Fahrenheit, aka hotter than hell. Slathered in sun screen, with a wide brimmed hat providing my only shade, and a pair of light nylon wind pants for leg protection, I was feeling pretty good, so I kept on walking.

A game trail soon appeared. I followed it for the next four or five miles, sometimes thinking it was a good idea as it made walking easier, and sometimes thinking it was a bad idea because animals used it. Big, wild animals. Seeing a herd of springbok, not leopards, in the distance took my mind off the dangers inherent in my own personal debate. Two ducks flapped by, their wing beats loud enough for me to hear them before I saw them. Right after that a blue heron and a fish eagle went flying upriver. I'm not sure who was hectoring whom, but they were giving each other what for. My appearance called it off for the time being as they flew off in separate directions.

As the afternoon wore on, I established a routine. I walked for half an hour, and then rested for half an hour in the shade. It was near 5 p.m. and I figured that I ought to be darn close to where Camp Four was supposed to be, or where I thought it ought to be. The original plan of getting to Camp Three had been abandoned as I wandered down the animal track. I was, as it turned out, just above Camp Four, which was across the river near its big bend. I was pooped. There was a nice overhang for shade complete with an outstanding view to the other side of the river.

Across from my campsite was a classic little notch in the canyon wall. A lone palm tree grew out of it. I surveyed the wall for animals and then began dinner. My dinner drill was familiar from past backpacking trips: two packs of ramen noodles mixed with a soup stock; oily-melted yellow greasy cheese; a packet of butter, and a few crackers. It wasn't gourmet, but I cleaned my plate. The box I'd mailed ahead with backpacker food never made it to Namibia, at least not while I was there, but it did arrive about two months after I'd left. In spite of that, I ate okay and drank plenty of water. My only complaint was the taste of the Halazone in the water. Some strawberry Kool-Aid to mask that taste would have been nice. It occurred to me that I should market a Halazone/Kool-Aid cocktail. I'd call it "Koolazone."

I debated making a fire, but decided against. I was just too tired. So, I put up the tent and did my evening ablutions: brushed my teeth as I took a gander around camp to make sure everything was put away, made sure the tent was correctly staked out, eyeballed a pee trail for those nocturnal callings (so as to not step on the guy-lines or any major rocks), bid adieu to the stars, took a big breath of the cooling night air, climbed on top of my sleeping bag and wondered how long Colin Fletcher's "test of the spirit" would last. Fletcher is the author of *The Complete Walker*, one of the original how-to backpacking books, as well as *The Man Who Walked Through Time* (about his solo walk the length of the Grand Canyon). He also wrote *The Thousand Mile Summer* (about his walk up the California and Nevada border).

That test of the spirit, as I understood it, usually happened during those first few evenings when noises of the night, and your anxieties, coupled with whatever other boogie monsters you have in your head, loomed "out there." The test was to get through those first few days or nights. I usually had it worked out by the second day. That night, worries of animals stumbling over me where I was camped on their trail, or of monsters creeping up on me, didn't have a chance to get inside my head. Before it hit the rolled-up clothes I was using for a pillow, I was sound asleep.

At first light, I still wasn't exactly sure where I was. The sky was a baby blue and it was cool then in the early morning. Good walking weather. I followed the game trail and saw a few more springbok, noticed a couple more ducks, and heard some baboons in the distance. I could tell by the sound of all the rocks being thrown around. Walking was pleasant on the firm ground, and as I made my way around the river bend, I spotted what had to be Camp Four, with several small huts and lots of green. At this point the river went underground, and I boulder-hopped across to its east side, and the 4x4 track that led back to the Fish River Lodge. Finally, I knew where I was.

I turned and walked back down to the dry riverbed to look for a rock. I had decided to take a rock from each of the canyons as a token. One day they'd be a special remembrance of my dance with each of them. I knew the rock couldn't be too big, but I wanted something representative. I settled on a small, white, triangular-shaped stone that had a bit of glitter to it. The glitter was to remind me of my first canyon, and the white of its dry searing heat.

Something about this canyon had been eating at me since I first entered it, but I wasn't sure exactly what it was. Hiking had given me time to ponder, or was it just the Australian's "pondo fever" I suffered? I'd had some uneasy feelings, some qualms, but the reasons eluded me. Something just wasn't quite right. I liked the Fish River Canyon, but it was missing something. Finally, it occurred to me that I'd been comparing it to the Grand Canyon in Arizona. The Fish River Canyon while certainly a fine canyon – a spectacular canyon – it just didn't possess the enormity or grandeur that I was expecting or wanting or needing. Such thoughts made me a little nervous. While not wanting to admit it, I do have hiking related superstitions. To think a place less than perfect, especially where snakes, baboons, and leopards lurked, might alert the gods who oversee outdoor/hiking pursuits that a critic, a detractor, a petty backbiter was in their midst. You see, the gods live somewhere out there where they can watch only me; they wait to catch me in the ultimate hiking taboo: an insult. I tried not to think negatively, but this canyon was small compared to my first love. As I hiked along thinking about that, I realized my foolishness. I was the one suffering from such an outlook. I was cheating myself of the importance of enjoying the moment, of respecting where I was now. I was on a long-awaited journey that would bring me to dance with the deepest of canyons, to bear witness to the singularity of each of them, not to comparison canyon shop. I relaxed then and enjoyed my hike and the surrounding area with a greater peace of mind, trusting I hadn't unleashed any bad juju with my negative thoughts.

At this point I was now near a road that wound up and down through the desert landscape. In the distance I heard an approaching motor. It was that of a four-wheel drive vehicle carrying two couples. They were from Holland and had been driving all around Africa on an extended holiday. We exchanged the usual traveler's pleasantries. I, then, hiked on. If I'd known they were heading for the farm, I'd have accepted a ride, if one had been offered (which it wasn't). About four hours later I crested a hill and there it was: Fish River Lodge with its white-domed main building, the stable, the windmill, and the single green splotch of grass. It's cliché, I know, but every now and then one comes around a bend or over a hill, and there it is, what could be called home.

With that view, I had crossed the finish line. My first canyon dance was over; I had just hiked Africa's deepest. Given my previous experience, I'd been confident that I could do it. I'd thought myself more than able to hike this canyon, despite the warnings of its extreme heat. Heck, if I couldn't hike thirty-some miles through it, even with snakes and tigers and searing heat, then I probably wasn't the experienced hiker I liked to think myself. And, being mostly level and without too much sand, it hadn't been that strenuous for me. Nevertheless, I did impress myself. My feet felt fine. It wasn't until I was back at the lodge with them propped up and taking an air bath, that I noticed a large water blister on my left foot. I popped it, cleaned it, wrapped it up, and reminded myself that I would need to check out my numb feet more often. Not doing that could be dangerous in the future. In reviewing the hike, I gave my route-finding an okay, of sorts. I'd prevailed despite the challenge of the faded mimeographed maps, the lack of any discernible trail, and my inability to find the numbered campgrounds. While rarely did I know for certain where I was, I knew I was going downriver and, basically, where I had been, sort of. I had done the hike in fewer days than I'd originally intended, but the heat and route-finding had kept me honest. I'd gained confidence in the Fish River Canyon. Would it help with the other canyons yet to come? I didn't know, but it couldn't hurt.

That evening I reintroduced myself to the two Dutch couples I'd briefly seen earlier that morning as I'd walked away from Camp Four, when I had no idea that they were staying at the lodge. Over dinner that night, they told me they were traveling around Africa in that four-wheel-drive rig and having a blast. We began bantering and ended up talking about the "green flash." One of them was an industrial optical engineer and he explained how, yes, there is a green flash. The instant the sun sets, given the right atmospheric conditions, the brilliant green flash can, indeed, occur. Mariners around the equator report seeing it, and I have friends who have seen it. I never miss a sunset without looking for it on land or sea. To experience the green flash is one of my continuing goals and dreams.

The good optical specialist explained how it's really an illusion; the mind is playing a trick on us, which seemed a contradiction of what he had just said. However, as he elaborated, it became clear that the green flash is real. It just isn't green. In fact, the green flash is bright red, but we see it as green. He also said that once, on a bright, full moonlit night, while it was raining, he saw a rainbow complete with its bands of colors. This revelation came after I'd told him I'd been moon-burned one full moon night in the Grand Canyon. I remembered it clearly. I was sitting on a rock, reading a map in preparation for the next day's hike, and stayed in the moonlight too long. The next morning I awoke with a moon-burn on my neck, arms, shoulders, and nose, which made for an uncomfortable day of hiking. The good optical specialist had read dozens of accounts of the green flash and heard several folks tell of night rainbows.

He'd even seen one himself, but he allowed as I was the only person he'd ever met who had suffered a moon burn.

After two more days of relaxing at the lodge – reading, chatting up the other guests, and, basically, indulging in a bout of pondo fever – I was chauffeured by Christy back to Keetsmanshoop. There, at the Chapel B&B, Re'et patiently and generously let me nap until it was time to catch the bus back to Windhoek. She even insisted on driving me to the bus station which was only two blocks away. I arrived, promptly, at the designated departure hour of midnight for the bus that, finally, arrived at 5 a.m. Lulling around the gas station/bus stop, I watched five drunks break dance in the parking lot, did a few crossword puzzles, and chatted with a young teacher who was waiting for the same bus. Later, when I noticed her curled up on the cement asleep, I took out my ensolite pad and lay down too. It was just then that the bus arrived.

I don't know about buses in other places, but this was a pretty snazzy bus. It had two decks, not like the British type of double-decker bus, but more like a train double-decker. Each floor had spiffy, uniformed attendants who brought coffee around, and there was a TV with a movie playing. I dozed, thought more about my hike, and looked out the window at the arid scenery on the long ride back to Windhoek.

Back in Windhoek, I caught up on my sleep and e-mailing. I felt a sense of relief being able to so easily check in with the home front. Messages from my daughter, Amelia, would make me laugh out loud. She had dropped her college biology class, but assured me she was doing "a hell of a job" on her other three classes. She was taking Spanish, a writing class, and a drawing class. There was some discussion that she might join me in Mexico and be my interpreter.

Back at the Chameleon I did my laundry and started packing the ton of gear in preparation for my departure. I wouldn't be leaving for several more days, so I looked for something else to do to make good use of my time. I'd heard about Swakopmund from other travelers. It was a beach town four hours west. It looked sunny in the pictures, although the guidebook called it a foggy beach town. It was foggy; magically foggy; life-giving foggy. The fog is produced by the cold Benguela Current that moves north along the western coast of southern Africa. Swakopmund has so little rainfall that its flora and fauna depend on the fog as their moisture source.

A Side Trip to Swakopmund

"There wasn't hardly a morning that I didn't awaken with a feeling of disorientation, surprised and joyful at finding myself involved in a highly improbable scenario"

--M. Thompson

There were several ways to Swakopmund. I could hitchhike, take a train or plane, or go by bus. Hitchhiking was out of the question for me, although "back in the day" I liked to think of myself as one of the patron saints of hitchhikers. My fears about hitchhiking here were that I'd be unable to communicate with random drivers. English is the official language of Namibia and has been since independence from South Africa. It allowed for greater international communication and promised to pull together different cultural groups that spoke varied languages. Afrikaans (spoken in South Africa and Namibia) and German are both stigmatized as vestiges of Namibia's colonial history, but I was under the impression that German wasn't uncommon in Swakopmund. I'd probably get an English speaker, but I didn't want to take any chances. Besides, it was too hot to stand in the heat waiting for someone to stop. Hitchhiking would take way too long. It had taken staff at the backpackers three days to hitchhike the normal four-hour run to the Atlantic coast. The train trip took too much time as well, and flying cost too much money. That left the bus. Two types were available:the small, VW type vans that went all over the place with passengers piled higher and deeper, or the big old regular bus.

I opted for the VW-type van. A Winnipeg couple, Shane and Janet, were also heading to the coast to meet up with an overland trip, so we shared a ride from the backpackers to Rhino Park, an area north of downtown Windhoek. The bus people tell you, "Yes, we're going to the coast," and "Yes, we're leaving right away." But right away is as soon as the vehicle is filled up, which can be right away or hours later. We were ready to go at 7 a.m., but it was 10 a.m.

before we got on the road. With the exception of the three of us, the passengers were all locals. The driver liked reggae and the blues, so the tunes were good. The scenery was familiar with its dusty hills and a few plants scattered here and there. On that ride, I was reminded of just how hard a seat can be if you can't move, and I couldn't. We were crammed in, jammed up, and jelly tight. Nevertheless, the breeze kept it cool, and I chatted off and on with Janet who told me that Shane had been hit by a car three years ago while riding his bike. After several years of skin grafts and legal battles, they had finally collected the insurance money. According to Shane, it was not a recommended way to fund an 11-month around-the-world trip.

We arrived in Swakopmund four hours later, having traveled through the "oh so arid" Namib Desert, and were driven through a township where our fellow passengers were dropped off at their destinations. Many towns in Namibia -- from the smallest to the largest -- have townships. They are remnants of apartheid and their former South African rule. The Germans too had segregated native Namibians long before South Africa took over. Townships are similar to our slums, ghettos, the "wrong side of the tracks," only worse. They made me nervous. They stand as symbols of colonialism, violence, and racism, people who have been marginalized in their own land. Buildings were made of cinder block. Some stood side by side, others stood alone. Some were mere lean-tos, but all were surrounded by dirt and piles of rubble, shrouded in the fog, and with a palatable feeling of hopelessness. Many of those who lived there were waiting and hoping to get a job that would allow them to move to better conditions. But, there, camaraderie and culture were alive. Tourist buses now pass through the townships. Passengers can disembark to talk with the residents. I'm not so sure how I feel about that.

In stark contrast to the township on its outskirts, Swakopmund is a resort town for the more upscale Namibians on weekends and holidays, especially during December and January. During these hottest summer months, hotels are full and reservations are required for meals as many come to escape the heat of central Namibia. The locals can't even find parking spots then, due to the great influx of people to the cooler coastal town. Because it was September when I was there, it was mostly empty.

The entire coast of Namibia is magnificent. From Angola to its north to South Africa to the south, it is hot desert meeting the frigid waters of the south Atlantic. That collision of sorts is what creates the fog. Along with the Benguela Current, which moves the cold waters north from the Southern Ocean surrounding Antarctica, conditions make for an amazing diversity of marine life, perhaps the most abundant array in the world. The Namibian Coast Conservation and Management (NCCOMA) project was established to protect that resource. They may have a big job ahead of them. Threats to the coast are many and include off-shore mining of minerals, oil and gas exploration, over-fishing, tourism, and climate change.

Though sailors of old are long gone, the threats they faced along Namibia's coast are still visible. Skeletons of wrecked ships from the 19th and 20th centuries are scattered here and there. The same conditions that spawn the teeming marine life also create turbulent surface waters and waves that are continuous and heavy on the beaches. Together with the blinding fog, they've tested many a sailor. The Portuguese thought these seas "the gates of hell," and the Bushmen referred to the area (including further into the interior) as "the land god made in anger." It's not just the skeletons of past explorations that have come to rest here; it's those of whales and seals too; bleached leftovers of the 19th century whaling industry. For these reasons, Namibia's seaboard, from Angola to the Swakop River, has been nicknamed the "Skeleton Coast," although some use that name in reference to the entire seaboard. The designated area is now a national park. No skeletons of anything did I see while there. I remained in town.

Swakopmund, which sits on that coast, is surrounded on three sides by the Namib Desert as is anything that sits on Namibian's coast. The Namib Desert, is vast and extends from Angola, down the entire Namibian coast, and into South Africa. Namibia takes its name from this coastal desert. In the native Nama language, it means "vast place" just like the desert that occupies so much of its geography. The western border of Swakopmund is, of course, the Atlantic Ocean. It is here that the Swakop River, which flows through western Namibia, meets those icy cold ocean waters. "Mouth of the Swakop" was founded by Germans in 1892, and for many years it served as German

South-West Africa's main harbor. German influences, which include the colonial architecture, abound in Swakopmund. It is filled with these historic buildings.

I was dropped off in front of one of them, the Villa Wiese, another backpacker's, and was met by the hostess who welcomed me in. We chatted over a cup of coffee and I learned the building, built in 1905, had originally been a private home. In the 1980s it was converted to a church. The current owners had bought it two years before my stay and turned it into a backpacker. It was actually a compound with a walled-in main house and four or five other buildings that were used as cabins. They could house up to forty visitors.

Its present occupants consisted of a couple from Holland who I'd met when flying into Windhoek, three round-the-world surfers toting three surfboards each, and moi. Two of the surfers were brothers from New Jersey, and the third was an Irishman who they'd picked up along the way. Their goal was to go to as many beaches as possible on their world surfing tour. They'd already been to Tonga, Honduras, Australia, and several other countries, and had six months yet to go on their surfing marathon. For now, they were surfing the Skeleton Coast. We talked and played with the three resident children who were eight, ten, and twelve years old. I chatted with their dad who had spent eighteen years as an explosives worker in the mines. I had a darn good time with the company, but soon it was just the surfers and me. One of them made the mistake of asking me, what was the longest hike I'd ever done. I paused, but not too long, before answering, "Oh, 2600 miles." They guessed I was referring to the Appalachian Trail, which goes through a tip of New Jersey. No, it was the west coast equivalent, the Pacific Crest Trail (PCT).

With that we were off and running. I was impressed with their acumen. They immediately "grokked" the ideal of the "meditation of the trail", which was akin to the "perfect wave syndrome." Jack Kerouac in *Dharma Bums*, wrote, "Try the meditation of the trail, just walk along looking at the trail at your feet and don't look about and just fall into a trance as the ground zips by. Trails are like that: you're floating along in a Shakespearean Arden paradise and expect to see nymphs and fluteboys, then suddenly you're struggling in a hot broiling sun of hell in dust and nettles and poison oak… just like life."

The term "perfect wave syndrome" probably originated with surfers, but is now used by others too. It can occur for me when I'm hiking, biking, or kayaking, while everything feels to be in harmony. It might include the weather, the path, the speed, and the ocean; everything melds into one. I have also gotten into the groove at work and been lost in time; totally wrapped up in what I was doing, making for a great feeling. It is such a rush that I am always ready for Mother Nature, preferably, or my work, to make that great feeling happen again. Roald Amundsen, in his book *The South Pole*, described it thus, as he skied to the southern end of the earth: "I had long ago fallen into a reverie – far removed from the scene in which I was moving; what I thought about I do not remember now, but I was so preoccupied that I had entirely forgotten my surroundings."

Wilbur Wright of the Wright brothers, after one of his first flights with a motored aircraft, was asked how he would put the experience in words. He said, "When you know, after the first few minutes, that the whole mechanism is working perfectly, the sensation is so keenly delightful as to be almost beyond description." And further stated, "More than anything else the sensation is one of perfect peace, mingled with excitement that strains every nerve to the utmost, if you can conceive of such a combination."

Fifteen years out from my trip I have read more research is being done on this idea – now called *flow*. A Professor from the University of Chicago, Mihaly Csikszentmihaly, began studying the idea of flow in the 1960s and has written extensively about it. A blurb I read from a review about his book said, "Psychologist Mihaly Csikszentmihalyi's famous investigations of 'optimal experience' have revealed that what makes an experience genuinely satisfying is a state of consciousness called *flow*. During flow, people typically experience deep enjoyment, creativity, and a total involvement with life. In this new edition of his groundbreaking classic work, Csikszentmihalyi demonstrates the ways this positive state can be controlled, not just left to chance. *Flow: The Psychology of Optimal Experience* teaches how, by ordering the information that enters our consciousness, we can discover true happiness and greatly improve the quality of our lives." A bit pointy-headed for me, but he acknowledges this idea of flow, the perfect wave syndrome, and the mediation of the trail can happen while playing piano, closing a business deal, playing with a baby, again described as the "optimal experience" with a good dose of joy and I suspect adrenalin for many. Maybe so, whatever it is - it sure feels good and has many adventure thrill seekers after it as if it were the holy grail, while a new parent can also have the same feelings. Maybe that is why there are so many of us.

I was up early the next morning, borrowing a shot glass from the kitchen and filling it with dish detergent to take a shower. I said my "so longs" and headed into town to buy a book, get my bus ticket, and window shop. Just as I was reaching for the bookshop door I heard, "Hey, you going to Windhoek?" It was yesterday's driver.

"Yes," I replied. "But let me buy a book. Are you leaving right away?"

His reply was, "Yeah."

Two hours later, after another excellent tour of the township, where he tried to drum up more business, we were headed back to Windhoek, only half-full for the return trip.

On the way I debated with myself whether the four hours of riding each way was worth the 15 minutes I'd spent at the Atlantic Ocean. Probably not. Did the conversation I had with the three surfers make the trip worth the time? 100 percent!

Back in Windhoek I did my e-mailing: E-mail to Mike, Robin (Amelia's mom) and Michele (friend) 16 Oct 00. "I am on my last day here in Namibia, just back from the coast, to Swakupmond (sp), saw the Atlantic Ocean, met three surfers who are going around the world surfing all the way, each has three boards, fun talking with them. I depart Africa the 17, fly from Namibia to Jburg to Frankfurt to Athens to Ionnia (sp) where I am spozed to arrive the 19 I think. When I get there I will try and catch up and let you know where I am. Just wanted you to know I am doing OK and having a decent time, getting a bit of sun, and looking and hearing and clearing a few cobwebs. Hope all is well with you. Peace, Jeff."

I showered, ordered my last pizza (delivered by guys in tuxedos!), and chatted with the other guests. When I related some of my early worries and some things that had happened along my way, I was informed by one of the guests that, "Namibia is the beginner's Africa."

Two

Greece
Vikos Canyon Dance

"The world is a book and those who do not travel read only one page."

St Augustine

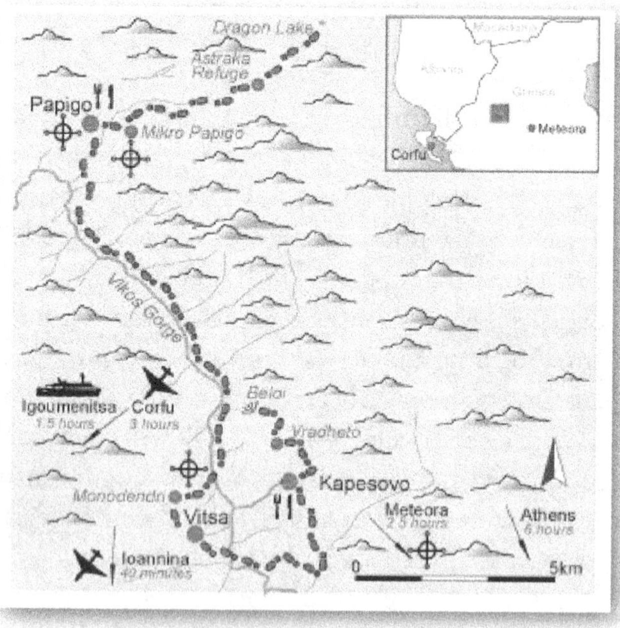

My impression of Greece from reading about it and friends' accounts was of sunny beaches, good cafes, islands, blue sky and balmy temperatures, with plenty of cultural opportunities. A place one went for a holiday. Greece, they said and wrote, was a place of warmth, luxury, and relaxation. But that wasn't to be my time in Greece. No five star hotels for me, or summer festivals, nor any digging into the history. I was not there to patronize the arts. No, I was there for a canyon dance, my second, and I didn't know what to expect. But I did know what not to expect: sunny islands.

I flew into Athens from Frankfurt, early in the morning ,and spent a week there one hot afternoon waiting for my evening flight to Ioannina. To kill some time, I took a cab, an adventure in itself, to the other airport to see if I could get extra legroom on my return flight. Why I had to go to the other airport, I didn't know. Why there was another airport, I also don't know. I just followed directions. Someone at the first airport said the other airport is where the airline's main ticket office was. One airport is in the west part of the city, but most international flights come into the eastern airport, which allows people like me to help the cab drivers' children through college. So I dutifully got a cab for what turned out to be a Mr. Toad's Wild Ride with Mr. Toad, himself, driving. We careened around corners on two wheels, shook our fists at those "lousy women drivers," and honked our horn at every pedestrian. We arrived in what I gathered was record time. I shakily exited the cab, paid the driver his drachma, a currency I never figured out, but the money was pretty and coins ancient-looking. Then I stumbled, thankfully, into the airport. There I was given the chance to wait in line for an hour to be asked why I was at this airport when I was flying out of the other one, and told to go back there and work out my seat arrangements. So I went back outside and got another cab back to the original airport, this time with a driver who wasn't in a hurry and actually told me a bit about Athens. I knew from my own ancient history that Athens is a classical Greek city, famous for the Acropolis, the Seven Hills, and lots of museums, galleries, and other assortments of ancient artifacts. There were great bazaars to visit, excellent food, and the Olympics were supposed to be coming that way soon too. The driver told me about how Athens was just a burg in about 500 B.C., but due to trade in olive oil and silver it got quite important and grew to be "The Place" for its time. He was most proud that democracy, or a type of democracy, came out of this time, that Greek history still had its touch on the civilizations of today. But I didn't come to Greece for the history; I came to visit a canyon, and that is what I did.

At about nine p.m. I arrived in Ioannina via airplane, a town of about 100,000, the closest airport to the Vikos Canyon. The guidebook pages I had with me (I had torn most out, deeming the book too heavy to cart around), listed two hotels. I selected the Grand Palladion Hotel, which had room for me that evening, but could not promise anything past then. I took a cab, registered, dragged my gear upstairs, and fell asleep at once. My plan was to spend a few days in Ioannina, get to the Vikos Canyon, hike it, and return.

Ioannina immediately intrigued me. There were narrow streets and all kinds of shops, with the majority being shoe stores. Have you ever been to a town where two out of every three stores sold shoes with standing room only and lines out the doors? Yes, there were cafes, book shops (thankfully with a small section of books in English), stores just selling lamps, small motors, a butcher shop with the skins of dead animals hanging about, a fish shop, little grocery stores, but more than anything else, there were shoe stores. Men's shoes, women's shoes, kids' shoes, tennis shoes, boots, all kinds of shoes. I started noticing that people always seemed to be looking at my feet, making me more self-conscious of my size fifteens. It was a city with a serious foot fetish. Also, apparently there were no malls, because the downtown was vital and alive, until 1:30 p.m., when it seemed to turn into a ghost town. I was the only one about, the shops being closed. It was just me and the shadows cast by my feet, strolling about. But then from 5:30 p.m. until long after dark, streets were again jammed with buses, cars, taxis, motor scooters, and people, people all over the place, and they all seemed to be smoking and talking on cell phones and shopping and looking at my feet.

But I didn't discover any of this until the next day; as soon as I put my head on the pillow that night, I was asleep. But the next day brought one of those happy accidents of good timing, albeit good timing that started sixteen years ago. I had never been a joiner, nor was my father. But sixteen years ago I joined Rotary. Rotary is an international service organization, with clubs in more than 160 countries with 1,200,000 members, 400,000 of us in the U.S. of A. It was founded in 1905 in Chicago. Touted as the first service organization begun in the U.S., it likes to think of itself as the "Cadillac" of community service clubs. It is much like the Lions, Elks, Moose, Kiwanis, Shriner's, Eagles, the civic/service clubs that almost all cities, big and small, have. I think the general stereotype of a Rotarian, or other animal club member, is that of a good old boy working the business network. Now, at least in the United States, it includes good old girls. Rotary is also spearheading an effort to eradicate polio. It has spent more than $407 million for vaccinations around the world, and except for those countries at war, it has accomplished that incredible goal. World Peace is part of their efforts, too.

I was convinced to join Rotary in 1986 while living in Ketchikan, one year before women were allowed to join in the United States, but my co-workers, including women, encouraged me to join for the good of the agency. I knew nothing about Rotary except, like clubs around the world, it was made up of business people and community leaders: the suit, tie, and wingtip crowd, although in most Alaska cities it would be more like the XTRATUF, wool vest, and Carhart crowd. I joined for the business connections, to meet the movers and shakers. I slowly got hooked on the incredible larger picture that a worldwide organization can inspire, the influence for good that it can have, as well as the meaningful roles the clubs have on their local communities. Our Sitka club has a strong interest in youth exchange to foreign countries and has been in the forefront of bringing Chinese youth to America. The Rotary motto is "Service Above Self." Probably the three aspects I've enjoyed most are the fellowship, the service, and the connections. My daughter was a Rotary International exchange student her junior year in high school. She spent the year living in Japan, going to a Japanese high school and living with three different Japanese families.

I attend Rotary meetings most every Tuesday, help with a variety of projects, and have been a club officer. One must note there are differences between clubs, as there are no women in the Japanese Rotary Clubs, and most of the members there are all business owners of factories, wealthy people and managers. Amelia and I once visited the Rotary Club of Washington, D.C., which is, as one might expect, a premier club. The members at our table were vice presidents of airlines and ambassadors to different countries wearing $1,000 suits. We were welcomed with open arms, like long lost family, despite our well-worn travel clothes and my appearance, which might be described as shaggy.

What does Rotary have to do with Greece or canyons? The next morning I was sitting in the lobby of Hotel Palladion, eight a.m. or so, waiting somewhat impatiently for eleven o'clock when they would tell me whether or not they had a room I could stay in for a few more nights. It was as if they were thinking about it. I felt as if I was auditioning for a room. Was I good enough? I tried to look humble, to hide my chafing and anxiety but still look positive and upbeat. I sure didn't want to drag my half-ton of gear through the streets trying to find another hotel. I was hoping I looked small and polite, and kind of nice, when I noticed the manager talking to a man with a Rotary pin in his lapel. I got up and introduced myself as a Rotarian. Smiles and handshakes, and an exchange of club flags followed. I had Sitka Rotary flags in my duffle; I told you I was prepared. I then had an invite for a drink at eight-thirty p.m., and a room was suddenly available without further waiting on my part. And that's what Rotary has to do with canyons and Greece!

The Rotary meeting in the bar of the hotel included an Englishman, who was there in Greece exploring the possibility of the Ioannina Rotary Club doing some relief work in Albania. Panos, a civil engineer from the local Greece club, said, "It is better to have a rich heart than a rich pocket." The discussion turned to why I was there. Why indeed? I was there to visit the Vikos Canyon, the deepest canyon in Europe. They were surprised, but I assured them the Guinness Book of Records said it was so. It was also the deepest canyon in the world according to some sources, giving it a feeling of uniqueness. Within the space of a few weeks, I would have been to the two deepest canyons in the world on two different continents no less. Quite an accomplishment.

The Vikos Canyon also had a mission attached. Richard Fisher, the canyoneer par excellence and photographer, had sent me a package and a letter: "Dear Jeff, I would like to help you more on the Vikos as the people were very good to me there. Could you please take this book to Kostos in

"'Little Popinggo (sic)'" hotel (B & B)? He is a great guy and was a big help to me." Richard included a basic map along with his book, *Grand Canyons of the World*, for me to deliver to Kostos in Mikro (little) Papingo. Seemed like a worthy challenge. It wasn't until later that a couple of thoughts occurred to me: why in the world, two years after the fact, would Kostos still be in Little Papingo? I also learned that the name Kostos in Greek is like John in the U.S. Sitka has a small café called the Mad Greek, owned by a guy named ... Kostos. However, these thoughts didn't occur to me at the time and from the moment I was asked to deliver the book, it was part of the plan, never mind how. I had no idea where Little Papingo was located in relation to the Vikos Canyon, but I was on a mission within a mission.

The Vikos Canyon is about 250 miles northwest of Athens, very close to the Albanian border. Ioannina is near the Pindhos Mountains and is situated on Pamvotidha Lake. It is the largest city in Epirus and the capital of the region. The town is pretty modern but does have a few antiquities, such as mosques, and it is the jump-off point for the more remote Oracle of Zeus. The Oracle of Zeus is said to be very old, dating to around 1900 B.C. It was a site where locals used to worship Zeus. Today Ioannina is known for its silverware, brassware, woodcarvings, and by me for its numerous shoe stores.

I spent three days getting ready, which mostly meant finding the bus station, which turned out to be only a few blocks away from the hotel. It would seem that walking three blocks from one's hotel to the bus station would not be much of a challenge, and the walk itself wasn't, but locating the bus station was difficult and took the better part of a day, due to my inability to understand Greek. When asking for the bus station I was usually met with a blank stare. The signs also were not in English; after all I wasn't in an English speaking country, which was delightful. Ioannina was such a sweet town and it wasn't a tourist town in any way that I could see. After finally stumbling on the bus station, the next challenge was to purchase a ticket, not a straightforward operation either, again due to my lack of language. I did not have the language phrase book that I would later add to my kit. After several hours of pantomime, gestures, and mutual head-scratching, a semi-English speaker finally came around, and helped me get my ticket. I then spent a few more hours trying to backtrack through the winding, confusing, narrow, but attractive streets to the hotel. I did take notes and drew a map, which helped on the next day's practice run, but my skills still needed a bit of fine-tuning. Not to excuse myself, but the bus station was located in a courtyard-type space, so it wasn't that I could walk down the street and see a half dozen idling buses or smell their diesel fumes from blocks away. Also, there was only room for two buses in the space, so in some regards my direction-finding skills were not totally put to shame. Eventually I found my way there and back with some ease.

When I finally got back to the hotel, I did something easy; I began packing my backpack. The canyon trail -- from reviewing the guidebook map -- didn't look too long. It appeared that one took the bus, a six a.m. departure to Monodhenhri, a small village on the edge of the canyon. The bus ride would take about an hour, followed by a hike of six to eight hours, which ought to take me to either Big or Little Papingo villages. From there I could bus back to Ioannina. I decided to tempt fate and not only leave my tent at the hotel but also my stove as well.

On the appointed day, I shouldered my backpack and walked through the dark to the bus station. There was a young couple also with backpacks. I asked if they were headed to the Vikos, and they were. David and Meta were an Israeli couple. She had one week before she started veterinarian school, and he was an agricultural school graduate. The three of us boarded the bus with one older local gentleman, and drove off into the dark foggy morning heading north. As we gained altitude, I noticed the stars were out. I had rain gear but it was, as yet, untested. We went around hairpin turn after hairpin turn. Around one corner was a most startling site. It looked like candles on a birthday cake in a darkened room, but was just a village we were passing through. Since it was not on my map, I dubbed it Birthday Villa.

Vikos Canyon is located in the Zagori area, which is mostly limestone tablelands, forests, and mountains, near Mount Gamila. The area is known for its traditional villages and stone churches, homes, and public buildings. It is not farming land due to a lack of arable land leaving few jobs in the area. The Zagorohoria is what the forty-six villages of Zagori are called and are mostly all stone buildings, with walls surrounding them in a medieval fashion. The streets are cobbled. They look ancient but were generally built in the last few hundred years. In 1975 a national park was established to protect the Vikos Canyon area from over-development and dams. It is here that the 3000-foot deep Vikos gorge takes off, separating Mount Stouros on the west and the peaks of Tsouka Rossa and Goura on the east. The area has become very popular in the July and August months, and rooms at those times are at a premium. Weekend and holidays are also busy times. I was lucky and had very few folks for company.

At just about daybreak we arrived at the village of Monodhendhri, the south end of the gorge, where the three of us got off the bus. I asked if they would mind if I tagged along. Some of the fears the guidebook said I ought to take along included bears, mean farmer dogs, and "desperate, possibly armed" Albanians who crossed the border nearby, and robbed (and worse) lone hikers. Other suggestions included to bring a big stick to keep the snakes and wild farm animals at bay. I was also warned that there had been flash floods in this area. The cab driver at the airport had also suggested I have company. David and Meta were happy to have me tag along, lucky for me. They organized their gear (they had everything with them), and I had the luxury of just taking the basics of what I needed.

We found the trailhead after we hiked the wrong direction on the rim for twenty minutes, which brought us to an uninhabited monastery literally hanging over the edge of the gorge. We then trudged back another twenty minutes, and were told by a local woman to go back in the direction from which we had just come. We ignored this advice and around the corner from her abode we found the trailhead, hard by the church of Ayios Athanasios. It was steep and paved with stone steps making it pretty easy to follow but very slippery with wet leaves from the morning dew. Almost literally, I counted a switchback every fifteen steps. After an hour we hit the dry riverbed of the Vikos Canyon.

At this point the need for a good map became vividly clear. I had four pages torn from the guidebook, a small general map of the entire area, not just the Vikos, and a hand drawn map from Richard Fisher. David and Meta, who had no map, were stopping for breakfast. I didn't want to be a nuisance, so started heading south, down canyon.

"Hey Jeff, do you want some tea?" called David.

Oh well, with an invitation like that, sure, I returned and joined them. They were trying to lighten their load so they offered me bread, tomato, cucumber, and cream cheese, plus tea served in three small glasses! Upon comment, they informed me they always bring a third glass. It is customary in case of a guest, be it at home or while backpacking. I liked the custom as well as the sweet tea.

It was at this point I figured it was time for me to head off down the trail. But sweet serendipity, trail magic, or just good dumb luck interrupted us. I assumed we'd head south, but as I looked at the map, in Greek, it seemed not so. We discussed it. David thought down river was correct also. Well, even if I had left my tent and stove behind, I had not left my compass. We oriented the map to north and sure as shoot we'd have headed in the wrong direction. Meta just rolled her eyes at us boys as she had already said, "No we go this way." At least to our credit, we'd checked the map before heading off in the wrong direction. Later, I got shuddery thinking if I'd been alone, how long it would have taken before I realized my mistake. The information I had, if I had been paying attention, told me to go north. We finished breakfast, glanced once more at the map and saddled up.

The next few miles were a walk on the river bed, over bowling ball, basketball, volleyball, soccer ball, ping pong ball, baseball, and golf ball-sized rocks, mostly rolled smooth by the high water times. There were also VW and bigger-sized boulders to rock hop around and from, and small pools of stagnant water to get around. It was a nice walk, not too hot. The scenery was pleasant, and for some reason my fears were not unraveling all over me, even about the route-finding. About this time I started to wonder why I expected to find Kostos. Even so, I rehearsed my lines as well as his:

"Are you Kostos?"

"Ne." (Yes in Greek).

"Do you know Richard Fisher?"

"Ne."

"Wait, I've got a surprise for you!"

Then I would observe his reaction. This ought to be good, but would he be there? This became the gnawing question. Forget no map, forget it looked like rain, and forget the outlaws from Albania. Would I find Kostos?

The next section of the canyon was probably as good a hiking trail as I have been on, level, good hard-packed dirt, no question about where the trail went, not hot, not cold, a pleasant walk paralleling the mostly dry Vikos River bed, with steep limestone walls very gradually opening up as we headed north. I passed the shrine of Ayia Triadha. I was ahead of David and Meta, so found a pleasant sitting spot. It seemed idyllic, except for the cow poop everywhere. Heedless of it, I took out my sleeping pad and sat down for lunch. A green canopy surrounded me and lunch was rolls, peanut butter, and smoked cheese I had bought in the small grocery store near the hotel, washed down with bottled water. David and Meta caught up and we chatted and then I hiked on.

The trail remained level and true to the guidebook information I had, ever so slightly the canyon opened up. I remembered my task of getting a rock from each canyon. As the trail skirted the riverbed, I dropped down and began a search for my Greek rock. I decided on a semi-square kind of pale yellow one, smooth from the river washing it. It seemed to be as good a representative of the canyon as any of the other million rocks, so I pocketed it.

With rock number two in my pocket, I kept hiking. Ahead the trail was "well developed" and, after a bit, led to the village of Vikos. I knew somewhere to the right was a more 'obscure' trail that led first to Big Papingo and then Little Papingo, my goal. Again, I was reminded of the needle-in-the-haystack quality of the search I was on for Kostos. I was also getting a bit tired, and the weight of the book, about two pounds, started to seem a foolish idea. Where was the logic: bring the book, leave the tent? It was starting to drizzle. I am not a biblical scholar, but somehow I remember John the Baptist saying, "My book is my shelter." I suppose if worst came to worst I could have used Richard Fisher's book for a shelter, of sorts.

I found the trail junction, near the Voidhomatis Springs, about five hours from where I started the hike. I covered my pack with the rain cover, which I noted had holes in it, although it was only twenty years old. I sat under a tree for my rain protection and waited for David and Meta to show up. After a half an hour I knew I had to go because if I waited much longer, the old muscles would stiffen up. It was still at least two hours to the end of this trail for me, to Little Papingo. I hefted my pack. The rain was holding off, but dark would not. I found my way across the riverbed and started to climb up and out of the Vikos Canyon. The trail up, while dryer and less slippery than going down, was steep, so steep you could again see places where past hikers' chins scraped the trail. Those switchbacks appeared again every five yards, but they beat the trails built before switchbacks were invented. If you are an M.C. Escher fan, you may recall his picture that has a staircase that looks like it is going up. If you trace the actual stairs, they make a square. I wasn't on a merry-go-round, but there was a sense of the Escher eccentricity to the climb.

Fifteen minutes up the trail I looked back and saw David and Meta; they'd missed the cut off. I yelled and pointed and they headed in the right direction. I kept my upward slog going, up, huff, puff, sweat, pant, groan, stop, look, listen, and repeat. Earlier in the day I'd been completely fooled by what I thought were church bells. One fifteen p.m. may or may not have been a funny time for church bells to be chiming, but in a new country how was I to know? They were tinkling very melodically up the canyon. I knew Vikos, the village, had an 18th century chapel; the bells sounded good to me. It wasn't until later, when I heard the individual bells that it came to me. These were cows, goats, or sheep with bells. Well the one-fifteen chorus was well rehearsed. On the climb up I finally saw the herd of goats I had thought was church bells. I was fooled again, or, maybe it was that the Greeks think so much of their goats that they may have actually sent them to music school.

As I climbed, the view opened up so that I could see up and down river. If one could see the Vikos from the air it would be like looking at a long serpentine river course twisting its way through steep cliffs that run down at an angle to the river. In the fall the colors would be vivid reds, oranges, and purples, with green foliage, too (I know this from the postcards I saw). It had a dreamy look to it, fairytale land; it just needed a castle off in the distance and maybe a dragon roaming the countryside.

With each step, if I wasn't watching my footing, bemoaning the fact that I'd brought only one-and-a-half quarts of water, or catching my breath, the Kostos question was going round and round. What were the odds of him being there? Isn't it a bit preposterous for a book written and photographed by a Tucson, Arizona author, to be sent to me in Alaska, then carried halfway around the world to be delivered? Alaska to Germany to Africa to Greece. Put it in my backpack, and head off to some dime-sized village in the middle of nowhere and then there would be Kostos? Seemed a bit whimsical, if not downright goofy. Oh, well. I was almost to the top of the canyon where I would find out soon enough.

I had finished my water and had to admit I was still maybe thirty to forty-five minutes away. I was playing the game of, if I had my tent, where would I put it up? I was looking for the first flat spot to come to, where at that point I would have put it up, eaten a dry meal and gone to sleep, and worried about Kostos the next day. I was tired.

I had left Sitka twenty days ago and had been in reasonable condition. I had spent forty minutes on the stair stepper every other day, climbed a local mountain up and down for about two hours at a whack, comparable to about a third of what I had just done (without a backpack), been hiking and biking all summer, but that wasn't enough. All the time of no hiking between canyons was taking its toll. I was soft! My back hurt and my knees did too. But, all in all, it was still light outside, and with no tent, I would keep on keeping on.

Soon enough the sign in Greek announced Big Papingo, with about fifty buildings, to the left and Little Papingo to the right my destination. Big Papingo is also the place for the more upscale hoity-toity Greeks and their weekend dalliances. In peak season it is impossible to get a room. The tableau was kind of medieval in appearance, all stone buildings, and they seemed to blend into the background, like the buildings were comfortable where they were. It was as if they were made to feel at home in the mountains and I suppose they were. It turns out the gray rock buildings were made from the gray limestone rock on which the very site of the town was situated, thereby making it look and feel natural. But that was not where I was heading, so I kept my head down and put one foot in front of the other, Mr. Left, Right, Left.

Mikro (little) Papingo hove into sight, located under a gray limestone outcropping known as the *Pirgi Towers*. I followed the path, now littered with donkey doo, and came to a high stone wall and a stone path. All the signs were still in Greek. I heard voices and followed the sound of two men talking. I showed them the name of a hotel I had written down and one of them indicated I ought to follow him. He showed me to the entrance to what I was hoping was the hotel that Kostos owned or had owned, Xenon O Dhias. Two years seemed like a long time to expect a person to be around, but who knew? I entered an enchanting fairy-tale courtyard. Everything was in stone, the ground, the walls, the buildings; a low stone fence surrounded even the few trees. The trellis with grape vines and the wooden tables on the stone patio were the only non-stone things I saw. Even the pitched roofs on the three buildings in the courtyard were stones, piled on top of each other, like stone shingles.

Entering the café/bar, I asked the man behind the counter, "Are you Kostos?" I had incorrectly read that Kostos spoke English, but that was the Kostos in Big Papingo. And yes this was Kostos in front of me, but not "the" Kostos. This Kostos told me my Kostos was "busy but he'll be back." I checked into my room, up a set of ancient wooden stairs, and entered a large room, with white stucco walls, a bathroom, en suite, as the Europeans like to say, and flopped on the bed to catch my breath.

The next step was a shower. The man had boasted that they always had hot water, and so they did. The bathroom had a sink big enough to bathe a medium-sized child in, a square toilet seat, and the shower area had a two-inch raised area surrounding it with a hose for the shower apparatus. The shower in Little Papingo might not have been the best shower I ever had but it sure felt good. Refreshed and in clean clothes, at least to those who had not yet seen me, I went back down stairs to the café. I sat and began writing up my notes, like actual writers do, according to the books I have read. The phone rang, and was answered. The first Kostos -- not the Kostos I was looking for, but the one I first met who had a little English -- said, " That's Kostos." I thought he meant on the other end of the phone line, and thinking he spoke English, wanted to talk with me. I headed for the phone but before I got there, Kostos Number One hung up. Well, I went and sat back down.

"No – that's Kostos, right there," Said Kostos Number One. He pointed to another man standing nearby. I had rehearsed this scene for a while and had it memorized, so I jumped right into the scene. "Are you Kostos?"

He nodded.

"Do you know Richard Fisher?"

He nodded again, and his eyes lit up. He reached up and pulled down the first Richard Fisher book, sans the Vikos Canyon in it.

I said, "Don't go away. Wait right here." Mostly this was all in pantomime. I headed for the door and turned to make sure he hadn't moved. He hadn't. I rushed upstairs to grab the book, and hastened back down. With as much pomp, circumstance, and ceremony as I could muster along with a bit of dignity, a slight bow, I handed the picture book to Kostos. I told him, "Richard Fisher gave this to me to bring to you."

The other Kostos translated. As an aspiring travel writer, I knew I had to closely watch for reactions and record them. When Kostos finally understood that I came from Alaska and had hiked the gorge and brought him the book, his face was a combination of bemusement, incredulity, and wonder, all flashing by as if his face was a pinball machine and I was tilting it to get my ball to score as many points as possible. I can only guess what was going through his mind, but he was smiling, looking at the notes Richard had included in the book and turning right to the Vikos section. I stood and watched him and his friends look through the book, then sat down to write up my observations. I was brought a beer, on the house, and later the real Kostos gave me a map of the area, in Greek, but still a very nice gesture.

As the evening wore on, more folks, who must have been husbands and wives of the hotel workers, took turns individually looking through the book. It was my impression that they were pleased and excited. I would like to think that the book's arrival became one of the stories of the hotel, Kostos reminiscing, "Remember when that old tall smelly hippie guy from Alaska walked in here and gave me this book? I about shit. Can you imagine coming so far just to give me a book? Why didn't they just mail it?" I hope with time the story gets even further embellished: "Remember that cold, rainy, dark and stormy night, not fit for man nor beast and out of the dark came this wet, scraggly, old bearded guy, clothes torn by bears and wolves, almost dead on his feet? He knocked on the door and then fell when it was opened. We were all amazed. He dragged himself into the inn, pulled his torn and worn body to the fireplace, and after thawing, when he finally quit shivering, he feebly asked, 'Is Kostos here?' He then fumbled in his old worn out pack and pulled out this book wrapped in plastic and gave it to me. He'd been sent all the way from Alaska to bring me this book. Craziest thing I've ever seen. Those Americans must be nuts, maybe they don't have a mail system."

It was a worthy, maybe even a meritorious thing to do. It was a fine mission, a nice gesture on Richard Fisher's part. Apparently Kostos had hosted him. It was a trusting thing for Richard to do, to send the book with me to carry to Kostos. Maybe that is an example of trail magic. And then it hit me. I had just hiked the Vikos Canyon, done the dance, and pocketed the canyon. A small wave of warm awareness washed over me. By golly, I'd done it, pocketed canyon number two. Five to go. These were probably the easy ones, but by gosh I had done them. I knew I had more miles to fly and miles to walk, more money and housing to figure out, as well as language difficulties to overcome, large crowded cities, dizzying heights, poisonous mosquitoes, deadly snakes, rooms to find, and countless times to pack and unpack my various fears and phobias, but I had just hiked the deepest canyon in Europe, in eight hours no less, through beautiful scenery, great temperatures and my feet did okay. My spirits were happy. I had encountered no bears or bandits and I had even found Kostos. I finished up my note taking. My order for food, lost in the excitement (or my lack of Greek), did not appear, so I took myself up to the room, made two peanut butter sandwiches, and fell right to sleep.

I spent three days and nights in Little Papingo, reading books, sitting in the sun, taking walks, looking at the buildings, and waiting for an English speaker to happen by for some conversation. David and Meta did, and we chatted more. They asked about hiking in the Canyonlands in Utah and Arizona, well I had a story for them.

I was in the Canyonlands area of Arizona. I was with my army buddy Tim; he of the angelic looks in contrast to my more down-home swarthy appearance. As a quick aside, to give you an idea of how things were with us: Once, when in the army, Tim took shoe polish and painted a slogan on the side of a white shed near where we formed up every morning for reveille. When our sergeant saw the graffiti, he figured it had to be one of us. Don't ask me why. So they called the two of us into the office and said, "Budd, you did it." I looked at them with innocent incredulity. I didn't even know why we were there, but once they told me what I had done, I looked at Tim's hands and saw the black shoe polish. In the best manner of CYA (covering your ass) I said, "Look at Tim's hands and look at mine." They did, but I was still guilty. So our friendship was based on these kinds of events. The first time we met we almost got into fisticuffs, but that is another story.

The plan was to hike for four days or so in the Canyonlands. It was mid-September and the weather report said things were just fine. We geared up, told the next of kin where we were heading, and then, as is Tim's wont, we went somewhere else. Oh well, the car was at the trailhead. I figured so no big deal. We loaded up and headed down canyon, through the narrow slot canyons following the meandering, sensuous limestone riverbeds. We twisted and turned and kept heading for the river we knew was somewhere downstream. It was as fine a day for hiking as I could remember, great big puffy clouds, blue sky, and enough breezes to keep us cool in those narrow canyons. The day ended in perfect form as we saw the sky color over as the sun set. We had a nice little fire of old river driftwood. When the stars came out we headed for the sack.

The next morning there was a good foot of snow on the ground and tent; imagine our surprise. But, we had plenty of food and fuel and figured it was a freak storm and would melt off. We would just sit it out and relax. Why not? So all through the day as more snow fell, we sat and watched and sat it out. Unbeknownst to us, the snow was slowly piling up and preventing any possibility of walking out. The snow just kept getting deeper. It turned out this was the anniversary of the great 100-year snowstorm, the greatest amount of snow to fall in the area since records were kept. We didn't know, and figured it would pass and melt off. Maybe we'd have some wet boots, but the car wasn't more than a day's hike out, uphill though, as I reminded Tim.

Tim was raised in the jungles of Ethiopia, where his father was a missionary to lepers. They lived three donkey days from Addis Abba, and Tim was, if nothing else, proficient at improvising in difficult situations. By the third day we figured we were in for a long wait for the snow to melt and started to ration our fuel and food. The snow kept falling and we were just able to keep it shoveled away from the tent by using our cook pot. That kept us busy, that and melting snow to stay hydrated. We no longer had any firewood --- it being used up long ago, and what little might possibly be left was buried under four or more feet of snow. Who knew how deep it was on the rim, and we gave up any thoughts of hiking out. It was way too deep.

Somewhere along the fifth day, I started to bless out Tim for changing the plan. No one would know where to look for us. His counter was the car would be buried anyhow. My retort was at least they would know where to start, but of course this would get us nowhere. We knew not to panic and to take stock of our situation. This wasn't the first time Tim had gotten me in over my head, as it were. We had enough food, at quarter-rations, to last two more days, and fuel was about gone. We were almost dry, although our gear was getting closer and closer to being totally soaked, from the moisture of our breathing as well as the heavy labor of trying to stay dug out, plus cooking in the tent. So things were not looking that good from my point of view. I don't know what Tim was thinking because I wasn't talking to him at that point. We thought of trying to make improvised snowshoes from our packs, but didn't have enough material to make frames. That all had been burned up in the first evening's fire.

By the seventh day, the food was gone, we were wet, and I was seriously worried about hypothermia setting in on both of us. As a matter of fact, the next thing Tim did was confirm my worries. He was sitting at the door of the tent just staring out, looking in the distance, when he said, "I got it, we are going to be okay."

"Yeah right," I thought, but followed his gaze to what looked like a mini steam vent of sorts. Tim grabbed the cook pot and said, "Follow me." We waded through the snow, about waist deep, to this anomaly where Tim started to dig like a madman. Before I knew it, he had uncovered a whole den of hibernating rattlesnakes. Disgusting, raw snake didn't sound appetizing to me-- I wasn't that hungry -- but that wasn't the plan, as I was to discover. Tim uncovered four of the bigger and longer snakes, and after carefully straightening them out, placed them in the snow, again being careful not to bend them, except for the head, which he slightly curved up. He then instructed me to hold them by the head until they refroze in that position. It was not something that I was up for, but … they did seem to be asleep. He informed me that snakes are true hibernators and there was nothing to worry about -- he being a jungle boy of sorts -- so I did as bid. In the meantime he selected four rather skinny snakes of two different lengths and again, carefully straightened them out and laid them in the snow, but didn't bother with a slight bend at the end. This was all making me nervous. I didn't see how we were going to eat frozen snake. Was it a way to prepare snake sushi? Some time passed. Tim sat mute, watching the snakes, checking them every now and then, and ignoring my questions. Finally he said, "Get some of the straps from the packs and bring them to me." Again, I did as I was told. Why argue with a madman?

What happened next still sounds strange and unbelievable to me to this day. He took the straps and fashioned bindings as for cross-country skis. We loaded up our packs, strapped the snakes to our boots, used the smaller ones, tail up, head down, for poles and we began to ski out of there! Every now and then the snakes would start to warm up due to the friction, but we would be warned by a slight rattle. We'd stop, they'd refreeze and off we would go again. Actually, it was good they started to thaw every now and then because I wasn't in great cross-country ski shape. We made it back to the car just at dusk. We put the snake skis outside and repaired to the relative warmth of the car, where we had some extra food stashed, and a radio to let folks know we were okay. The next morning we skied out to the road and hitched to a friend's home. We left the snakes buried in a snow bank. As I wound up the tale I glanced at the Israelis and saw two pairs of rolling eyes. I swore it was true.

A few other visitors said hello, but my response in English quickly ended any discussion (or they had been warned by Meta and David), still I was flattered to be taken as a local. Nevertheless, I was well fed; coffee (Nes te is the word they used) is universal. For breakfast I had six to eight slices of toast, big slabs of butter, jam, and juice. Dinner was a delicious spinach pita and French fries. One couple bought me a drink of the local wine, not ouzo, but similar. I could see how that would warm someone up; a bit closer to moonshine was what I was thinking.

So I idled for three days and nights, then awoke in the dark and walked the mile to Big Papingo to catch the seven a.m. bus back to Ioannina. I knew not where or how I was to recognize the bus stop in the dark, but I did find where I thought it was. I wondered how the bus driver would turn around in such a small space. He didn't; he backed down the hill for about a mile to a spot where he could. It was a pleasant ride back to town, picking up locals all over the place. The highlight was the small tree, like a miniature bonsai, growing out of the driver's ashtray. The countryside in the daylight was rolling and verdant. At the outskirts of town, there were no malls, not even the normal clutter of McDonald's, tire shops, and Dunkin Donuts, and the like. They could have been disguised by their words in Greek, but the obvious American logos were nowhere to be seen.

I spent several more days in Ioannina, packing up, answering e-mails, writing in my journal, confirming that every other store sold shoes, and taking a day trip with a fellow Rotarian I had met upon arrival. We drove even closer to the Albanian border, and I saw more of the Vikos River and the local area. Then one morning I packed my bags, got a cab, returned to the airport, flew to Athens for another long wait and eventually headed back to Frankfurt and the next dance of the journey.

Three

Tibet, the Asian Canyon Dance

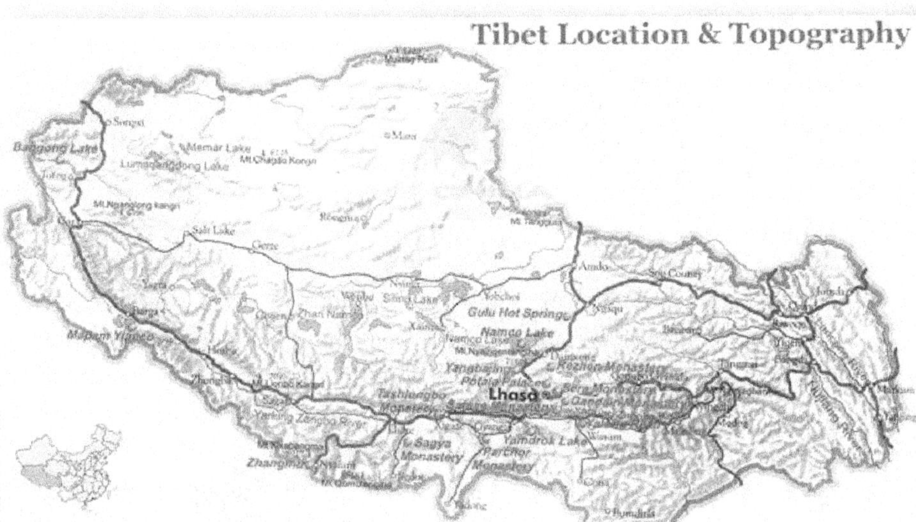

"There is an ambush everywhere from the army of accidents:
therefore the rider of life runs with loosened reins."

Hafiz

Even before I left home, the "To Go or Not To Go to Tibet" question was distressing me. Some folks were saying going to Tibet just encourages the Chinese in that they get hard currency and that being a visitor gives credence to the Chinese government's occupation there. To the best of my knowledge, there has not been a boycott of the country. Most of my reading and research on the matter indicated that the Dalai Lama and Tibetans welcome visitors. By having westerners visit, they feel the outside world gets a picture of the conditions of Tibet, and the hopes and dreams of Tibetans. The Dalai Lama "encourages people to travel to Tibet and bear witness to the occupation and colonization of Tibet." So with that as an understanding I knew I would go.

I think I am like most people; I have superstitions, one of which is that I am not supposed to tell you I have superstitions. I believe in omens too, particularly the good ones. I don't look for bad ones, even try to ignore them. My first good omen was a dream I had while in Frankfurt, waiting to fly on to Tibet. We were flying over China, when all of the sudden a herd of mid-sized black and white Great Danes came galloping through the airplane, down the aisle, and began running amok amongst us passengers. The captain came on the intercom and said, "Well … this looks to be an interesting flight. You all don't have to buckle your seat belts." Pondering this as a foretoken left me scratching my head.

My three-plus weeks in Asia had a three-part harmony if you will. The first, being in Lhasa and environs. Part two, the journey to reach the deepest canyon in the world, the Yarlung Tsangpo. Part three is the second attempt.

Part 1. Lhasa and Environs

I had been curious about Tibet, the fabled Roof of the World, the Mecca of East Asia, and the home of the living Buddha, for as long as I could remember. Tibet had always held a mysterious appeal for me, and many writers felt the same. Why? I am not sure when I first became aware of Tibet, but the image must go back to the ideal of Shangri-la. I first saw the movie *Lost Horizon*, from the book by James Hilton, in the early 70s around the time I first fell in love with canyons; maybe there was some synergy happening? Since then

I have read numerous books of the travel adventure genre about Tibet and Nepal, climbing stories, tales of searching for enlightenment, Zen stories, living with nomad stories, and travel for the sake of travel stories.

One quote I came across takes a good swipe at why many Westerners are so intrigued: "Tibet has become the symbol of all that present day humanity is longing for, either because it has been lost or not yet realized, or because it is in danger of disappearing from human sight: The stability of a tradition that has its roots not only in a historical or cultural past but within the inner most being of man, in whose depth the past is enshrined as an ever present source of inspiration." So said Lama Govinda in his book *The Way of the White Cloud*, a narrative of a pilgrimage that Lama Govinda took in the 1930s before the Chinese invaded Tibet in the 1960s.

In my own curious way I like to think I have some connection to Zen Buddhism, besides the last name of Budd. It figures into my own brand of spiritualism, nothing especially profound, not entirely superficial either. I have enjoyed the Koans (What is the sound of one hand clapping? What did the monk see when he looked into an empty mirror?) and other cryptic mysteries of Zen: when you get to the top of the mountain, keep climbing; or Zen is like looking for the spectacles on the end of your nose; or the eye with which I see god is the same eye with which god sees me. I find, in my limited knowledge, that overall, Buddhism offers a broader idea of life and spirituality than western religions do. I have also been aware of the ousting of the Dalai Lama and the Chinese bastardization of Tibet, as well as the atrocities the Chinese government continues to perpetrate on the Tibetan people.

I was delighted to learn that the deepest canyon in Asia (some call it the "Everest of Rivers"), as well as in the world, was the Yarlung Tsangpo in Tibet. Tsangpo means large river. The valley has two 7,000-meter mountains on either side. The Yarlung Tsangpo River starts as the world's highest river; its source is near Mount Kilas, a very holy site to Tibetans. The Tsangpo flows across Tibet before entering the deepest gorge and runs into India's Arunachal Pradesh where it then becomes the Brahmaputra. In the book *The Last River*, by Todd Balf, it is noted that the deepest part is about three miles deep and was "determined by shooting a straight line from the tops of Mounts Gyala Perei to Namche Barwa and marking where the line transects the river" somewhere past the village of Gyala. The two mountain peaks, Namche Barwa, at 25,458 feet, and Gyala Pelri at 23,461 feet, represent breasts, and the Yarlung Tsangpo River, the spine. Not only is it the deepest canyon, but also it is said to be the birthplace of the Tibetan culture.

Richard Fisher is usually given the distinction of being the first Westerner to visit the canyon in 1992. Since then he has returned at least eleven times. The Guinness Book of Records credits him with establishing the Yarlung Tsangpo as the deepest canyon in the world in 1996. My guess was that this would be the most spiritual of my quests, as well as the most physically demanding canyon, due to the depth and the altitude.

The flight to Lhasa was amazing; it shocked my sensibilities, nothing short of it! I had flown from Frankfurt to Beijing, with the original plan being to spend a few days in Beijing and then fly to Chengdu for a few more days before flying off to Lhasa. Upon arrival in Beijing, I was not too tired, even though I'd been flying for twenty-four hours. I didn't want to spend any more time than was necessary in a huge city, so I opted to fly on to Chengdu. The airlines said, "No problem." However, I buzzed going through the metal detector and the ensuing search found the one-and-a-half inch Swiss Army, key ring style, knife I had carried since leaving Sitka. It was deemed an "illegal item," and I would need to check it in with my luggage, which had already been checked through. It seemed to me the guard just wanted the knife. But, the oversize luggage people took me to the bowels of the airport to find my checked bag. I put the knife in it for the peace of mind of the Chinese officials. Then I paid 50 Yuan, about $8.00 U.S., for the airport tax and headed for Chengdu. In hindsight I might have seen this as an omen, trivial perhaps, but oh so Chinese.

Landing, I was lucky to see through the silty smog the soft curved puzzle pieces of landscape that made the outskirts of the large Chinese city. It wasn't the square farm acreage of the U.S., but a more random, serene and flowing pattern. We landed with a bump and all the smog and haze settled in. I found my luggage and took a cab through the murky twilight, the neon signs just visible, as were the bike riders, pedestrians, and vehicles of various types we seemed to just miss. The driver's night vision was sure better than mine, thank goodness. I'd heard that the dogs of Chengdu bark at the sun because it is so rarely seen.

We arrived at the Traffic Hotel, a tall building across from a river in a busy part of town. I got a room and was introduced to the notion of attendants on each floor, who taxed me for the room, as well as the room key. Who says the Chinese do not understand capitalism? I was not allowed to keep my sixth floor room key, so each time I wanted to go back into my room I was re-taxed for the key by the alert floor attendants. The hotel, I was assured, was a typical three star Chinese hotel, which meant it had running water. My room had two single beds, a worn and stained carpet, TV, and red shiny lacquered tables at the sides of the beds. While there were holes in the sheets, at least they smelled and looked clean.

My primary task in Chengdu was to find "George of the Jungle," the tour operator. His business card touted him as Chairman of the Tianfu Travel Service and his motto was "Travelers of the World Unite." George was one of the tour outfitters that could get travelers into Tibet. Individuals were not allowed permits, but groups were. So George rounded up minimums of six people, then for a fee would get them tours of Lhasa. The tour package included a flight to Lhasa, two nights at the Snow Land Hotel and a tour of four monasteries, including the Potala. The Chinese visa I had been granted while in the states was good for one month.

We, the Traffic Hotel group, were to meet in the lobby at five a.m. A guide showed up, counted heads, and we were off to the airport in a blur. We paid our 50 Yuan airport fees, again, dragged our luggage to the counter and were on the plane, a great big China Air Bus, before I was fully awake. I had a window seat with plenty of legroom. I dozed at first, but some powerful force woke me to look out the window.

We were cruising at 30,000' but the peaks looked to be just below the plane, and they were because they were 20,000 feet high. For the next hour I didn't take my face from the window. I got a kink in my neck from looking so long, but not even my need to use the bathroom budged me from the view. I watched the scene below unfold. I am going out on a limb here, but will call this the best scenery I had ever seen from an airplane, bar none.

I have been on Alaska Airline flights to Sitka, Juneau, Anchorage, Fairbanks, Bethel, Nome, Barrow, and down the Kenai Peninsula to Homer, on bright sunlit days, the beauty so awesome the pilots would announce a deviation from their flight route to do 360-degree tours around their favorite peaks, or the endless ocean dotted with thousands of islands, mountains and sky, over the Juneau ice fields, outrageous beauty, Mother Nature at her finest. I had plenty of comparisons to make for this flight, but Tibet thrilled me!

As we left Chengdu the sun was rising and I made out faint mountains and valleys. As the sun continued its ascent, I became more awestruck. The landscape included ridges, side canyons, wide and narrow valleys, and jagged mountain ranges to the horizon, all bare, nude and brown, every wrinkle, wart and stretch mark, all the cuts and bruises of the land displayed. We were heading west as the sun rose higher and the scenery below came more into focus. The farther west we traveled the more jagged the mountains became, as if they were rough hewn by a giant buzz saw abandoned to its own gone madness. Snow became part of the landscape. The peaks seemed to be pushing harder and harder to reach the sky, more glaciers, steeper and sharper, harsher, straining to bust from the earth's gravitational pull. This was one of those flights where the price of admission was worth it; the scenery was one of a kind.

The scenic visions continued to increase in ruggedness, raw stone, and cold windswept beauty. Knife-edged serrated ridges, and needle sharp peaks, valleys that were bare and severe with the white cold, pyramid-shaped, saw-toothed inclines, synclines and anticlines, razor ridges as far as the eye could see. A geological slam dance, mosh pit, muddy and funky Woodstock, a Jimi Hendrix guitar riff, Janis Joplin at her "Piece of My Heart" most brittle soulfulness, a rumble of mountains, street trash talking, bring it on to the max. I was breathless, gob smacked, and left to try and describe the scenery in some gonzo stream of consciousness that pales beside the actual scenery outside the window.

Eventually we peeled off south and the scenery began to settle down. The snow receded, I exhaled, and we entered the Lhasa Valley with the Kyichu River. The music on the airplane, some grandiose Chinese orchestra playing a bodacious classical piece, matched the scenery, and with a smooth landing I was in Tibet!

The bus ride from the airport saw me still giddy. We grabbed our stuff and headed toward Lhasa, the "Forbidden City." I was still agape at the dusty scenery and high mountains. Closer inspection confirmed my sky-view; it was brown earth down here. In Lhasa we only clipped one bike rider who got up and waved us on. I rubber necked through town and we entered the Snow Land Hotel courtyard, laid out in typical Tibetan fashion. It has been around for a while and, as the guidebook noted, "changed very little since the 1980s," (they certainly hadn't cleaned the toilets). Their brochure noted the hotel is entirely run by honest Tibetans who will be happy to receive you as guests and send you off as friends. The bottom floor on the street side held shops. On one side of the entry were a laundry, hair washing salon, and reception space. In front of these shops were street stalls selling fabric, teakettles, fruits and nuts, and watering cans among other things. The other side of the entry held the Snow Land Café and more vendors selling a variety of wares.

Inside the courtyard the space to the left housed a small internet and grocery shop, and more laundry. Upstairs were the guest rooms and offices for the travel agency, and the third floor had more rooms, some individual and some dormitory style. Opposite the main entry and across the courtyard were the upscale rooms. A dorm room ran for twenty-five Yuan, about $3.50 U.S. with a bathroom and shower down the hall, heat was not provided. I opted for the more upscale room, the one for the swells, with an en suite bathroom with hot water and flushing toilet, and a sign on the wall that read: "Please put toilet paper in the plastic container. Thanks all." The bathroom floor was tiled with a floral design and the door had a frosted panel like in the old detective movies. My living area contained two beds, a console between them, curtained windows that looked at the building next door, and a TV I couldn't make work, along with two small chairs and a round table that held two thermos bottles filled with hot water. Best of all, on the ceiling was a huge circular Tibetan design, the Wheel of Dharma, representing the path to salvation; I could use it. The walls were green, also sporting Tibetan design, this one the Knot of Eternity, the never ending passage of time, harmony, love and the unity of all things. This room went for 150 Yuan, about $16 U.S. a night. I think I made the right decision room-wise; most people abandoned the Snow Land as soon as they could. The communal bathrooms stank, the showers were moldy, and most of the staff acted like they worked for Exxon before (and after) the Valdez oil spill. They didn't care and they didn't have to. Snow Land controlled 90 percent of the tourist business, so it was a player in that sense, but it was not the only room in town.

My fellow travelers and I had a dinner of bottled water, Tibetan cheese pancakes, and a bowl of egg noodles, all of it very tasty. Later, as I lay in bed on my first night in Tibet, I was still overwhelmed: holy mountains surrounding me, monks walking the streets chanting and begging. There were pilgrims, nomads, cops, and seekers. The street outside was busy with vendors pushing ancient two-wheeled carts, cyclo drivers, monks, kids, business people, three wheeled bikes piled high with people, furniture, fruit, propane canisters, beds, more bikes, small animals, and me. All of them were either yelling or singing or chanting or spinning their prayer wheels. Old people, young people, people wearing clean clothes, raggedy, dusty, torn and worn out clothes. People in traditional dress and people in what would pass for western dress, dark suit of pants and jacket. There was a multitude of small sidewalk shops and sidewalk vendors. Smells, sounds, noise, and movement. It was like nothing I had experienced in all my years. I was still buzzing when finally my lights went dim.

The next day was our tour of the monasteries. At nine thirty a.m. our Snow Land Hotel group met with our Tibetan guide Nygile, a young man and student who was hoping to become a translator and travel agent. We were ushered onto a bus and driven the few minutes to the Potala Palace.

The Potala was built in the seventh century and has two surviving parts. In 1645 the fifth Dalai Lama extended the palace to its present size. It is thirteen stories high and was the Dalai Lama's main living space. Our tour started at the top and worked its way down. We saw the Hall of Gradual Paths. I learned from our guide the meaning behind the prayer flags. He said white meant clouds, blue, the sky, green, the water, and red, the protection in the sky. Later a different guide said the red was for fire, and yellow, for the earth. We saw a four-ton golden "Light Stupa," burdened with another ton of precious gems. Stupas are where the remains of the Dalai Lama are kept. I heard Dalai Lama means Ocean of Knowledge. On we toured, through huge rooms with golden mandalas, burning incense, burning yak butter, and monks huddled in dark corners chanting. We learned the six-word chant for "please take me to paradise," oh-ma-knee-bien-ma-hum. The Potala has been the home of each Dalai Lama since the fifth, who was credited with the original construction of the palace. The building was almost self-contained as the seat of Tibetan government. There were chapels, living quarters, schools, and tombs. The Chinese did shell it in 1959 but somehow the building survived. The Potala was reopened to the public in 1980 and had something like 4 million U.S. worth of renovations completed by 1995 by the Chinese government, who recognized it as a way to make a profit.

That night I dined on Tibetan noodle soup, and vegetable momos. The small deep-fried, dough-covered veggie concoctions became a staple of my diet. They were about half the size of spring rolls and could be filled with goat, cheese, potatoes, or yak. While eating I pondered the Potala. The guidebook had described it as "eerily empty", but I knew it was the most unusual, interesting, out of the ordinary, unique building I had ever seen. From a distance it had a feeling of aloofness, but also a presence that spoke to its serenity and wisdom, both ancient and present. Up close it was overwhelming, like being on the rim of the Grand Canyon. I tried to think of any building that surpassed the Potala, but none came to mind. I found my favorite building of all time.

After the Potala, we were transported to the Sera Monastery, about two miles from the city. Founded in 1419, in its day this monastery housed more than 5,000 monks. It has an assembly hall, three colleges, and thirty houses inhabited by the Yellow Hat sect. The guidebook says, "Don't judge a monk by his hat." It was the Chinese who differentiated the monks by their hats. I met a man from San Francisco who was spending a month in Lhasa. His goal: to get his prayer books blessed by the monks and collect as many "big hats" as he could. Some were skin-covered, some were made with cloth and had cardboard backing, some were used by monks, some were for the nomads, and some, well, no one really knew. This fellow searched the Barkhor for them, and each time he appeared he looked different, always blue fingernails, dread locks, and long soul patch beard, but his millinery splendor would be changed.

The Sera Monastery was outside the city, pushed up against the 14,000 foot - foothills. While we walked through the monastery, a monk blessed us with long life. We had to touch our foreheads to a certain spot, then look up to see a blue-headed horse on top of the Buddha. The highlight of the tour was the debating monks of all ages. When I say debate, I don't mean western debate, in which two people nicely dressed stand behind a lectern asking each other questions with a time limit and a moderator. I mean about 200 monks in their red robes gathered in an outdoor courtyard. One monk stood with two seated, the standing monk clapping his hands loudly while sliding one of the clapping hands to point at one of the seated monks. "Attention please! I want to ask you a question!" he said. The seated monk had to respond and defend his point of view. They grilled each other with great vigor, and of course, could have been talking about anything. The noise, enthusiasm, and dust level were high and tireless. I saw no authority figure. The monks had their own desire to participate. They talked; they yelled, pointed, laughed, kicked up dust and played with their prayer beads. The only serene being was a black and white dog, asleep among the debaters. After a while it woke, scratched, and went back to sleep amidst the pandemonium. The monks were all dressed alike, but in their strenuous debating, small differences were noticeable, a snake tattoo on one monk's wrist, a beeper on another's belt, and no one had the same style of shoe. To think that American students could or would show this type of focus was hard to imagine. The debates lasted four hours, without letup.

Our last stop of the day was to the Dalai Lama's summer palace, built in 1956 by the current Dalai Lama, who left in 1959 and went into exile. This space had a more human scale; it wasn't bigger than life like the Potala. It contained the first modern bathroom in Tibet, and looked to be a comfortable dwelling, though a rather large space.

I had met a few other travelers, a woman from Ohio who was studying Chinese in Beijing and on vacation in Tibet, an Australian woman who taught

Japanese, and a man from England. We agreed to go on a two-night excursion to see the Samye Monastery, the first monastery in Tibet, and Yamdrok-tso, a most sacred Tibetan lake. While this was being organized, we, the Traffic Hotel group, got our fourth tour. This one was right around the corner from the Snow Land Hotel. The Jokhang Temple, in the middle of the old Lhasa section, was founded in 647 AD during the time of the Tubo King Strontsan Gampo. The Jokhang, four stories and facing west, is a working temple, and is said to be the most revered religious structure in Tibet. It is the destination of many pilgrims from all over Tibet. Through good fortune it was not destroyed during the earlier Chinese occupation; however, many of the sacred icons were stolen by the Chinese, who showing a profound lack of respect, turned the Jokhang into a hotel. The main courtyard of the temple was used by the Chinese as the cafeteria, and the inner sanctum became a pig sty and butchering area. This is also the site of Lhasa's largest modern massacre, which took place on March 5, 1989. Chinese police stormed the temple, where Monks were protesting Chinese interference in the year's most important Buddhist ceremonies. More than forty monks were killed and hundreds more imprisoned.

As we approached the temple, we were enveloped in smoke from incense being burned in a stupa in front of the Jokhang. Here, pilgrims were gathered, some from thousands of miles away, many prostrating themselves. Some wore thick leather aprons and had wooden knee and hand pads to help in their process of standing with hands raised over their heads, then brought down in front of their faces, while they knelt and sliding forward – arms extended - into the prone position, touching their foreheads to the ground, then back up to a kneeling position, then standing up, arms stretched over their heads, then repeated, over and over and over again. This wasn't happening just around the temple. Many pilgrims young and old had traveled hundreds, or even, thousands, of miles to get to this most scared of temples. Some opted to do this ritual without the protection of the leather and wood or any heavy clothing. How many Westerners would leave their home and walk even across a small city to go to church, mosque, or synagogue, on hands and knees? Then think of spending day after day until the days turn into weeks, until they turn into months, and then months on end. The rule of thumb is 1,000 miles of travel in this manner will take four years. It doesn't happen in our country and maybe we are the poorer for it.

We entered the Jokhang through a dimly lit space, the only light coming from yak butter candles. In the center of the main area were long rows where the monks sat during meditation or training. Around the inside of the building pilgrims moved slowly, taking one step at a time, waiting a few minutes, and then taking another, until they'd circumnavigated the inside three times, then outside three times, and then the Barkhor three times more; nine circumambulations in all. People were belly to backbone, snaking in and out of the small rooms, some spinning ancient prayer wheels, some with yak butter candles in small chalices, all of which was conveniently for sale in the Barkhor. They shuffled along in the semi-darkness amid ancient vibes emanating from the walls, floors, and ceilings.

In the center of the temple a dozen monks played large drums, creating a single droning sound; bong bong bong, no conga rhythms here. Bells, chanting, and drumming were the groove of the sounds that shook and pulsated in my senses. My eyes adjusted to the dimness; luminescent yak butter candles and outside sunbeams made their way into the temple.

As I spent time in Lhasa I became more comfortable. I am admittedly a small town boy, so at first the city was overwhelming. As I became more at ease, I began to notice more and more. The sidewalks were not smooth pavement, but rather large stones set in cement, leaving a very uneven path of crater-sized potholes and occasional piles of poop and puddles of pee. And then there was all the traffic. With no real flow or rhythm to the traffic, the most exciting, most dangerous time of the day, usually between 8 a.m. and early evening, was trying to cross at a busy intersection. Some corners had traffic lights – but that was mainly a suggestion. I adopted the strategy of mentally grabbing hold of a local who looked the savviest and shadowing them as they evaded and dodged the oncoming hazards: bikes, cars, cyclos, buses, taxis, and other pedestrians. Good sport!

The Barkhor is the square in front of the temple. All around it were twisting alleys, small shops, street vendors, you name it. It was part of the clockwise circular route, the *kora* that the pilgrims, nomads, and travelers religiously walk. I walked it several times a day while I was in town, not so much for any religious reason as for the tableau that unfolded with each step.

I also tried my hand at the local pasttime of bargaining in the Barkhor. The rule is - there are no rules. Whatever you wished to purchase as you strolled past the vendors, you asked. "How much?" This was not a game for the meek, and I turned out to be meeker than I imagined. At home we have a thrift store, the White Elephant, where I was regularly chased out by the more serious combat thrift-shoppers. Common knowledge in the Barkhor held that the prices were extra high for westerners. If the price were ten Yuan for a local it would be 100 for us. Thus, if one wanted an item, the first ploy was to knock the price down about 90 percent. Some of us could do that and get away with it, but I did not possess the warrior spirit that shines so strong in some true bargainers. The Tibetans saw right through my act. I would see some piece of plastic turquoise that looked pretty good to me, draw myself up to my considerable full height, peer down over my glasses and pretend great indignity and outrage at such an exorbitant cost. I would go through my act and then spend sometimes an hour caught in the amazingly firm grip these old ladies had. I could not pry their fingers loose from my arm, and would submit to all kinds of verbal abuse while we haggled with pointing fingers over pennies. Even though I was a poor player it was fun to participate and observe.

My view from the Snow Land entrance was a pretty good composite of the area. Immediately to the right of the portal was a sidewalk stand selling porcelain cups, teapots, and plates. To the left were flags and pennants. Across the street were stalls selling cigarettes, fruits, and shoes. Sitting directly across from me were four monks, seated on the curb, feet in the gutter, chanting "Om mani padme hum ("the jewel is in the lotus"), and begging. Most of the westerners were of the mind that to give money to beggars, holy or not, was not the correct thing to do; however, many Tibetans gave willingly. Eventually, I gave to the very old and crippled, and then moved on to adopting the monks in front of the Pentoc Hotel. Pentoc is short for Pentecostal, and was established by affiliates of the Pentecostal missionaries. I also slipped a few fractions of Yuan into beggars' hands or cups as I circled the Barkhor, whenever it felt right, which of course had no rhyme or reason to it. Maybe I was hoping to incur some positive grace from the giving.

Part of the fascination of the whole scene was the varied traditional outfits worn by the pilgrims, nomads, and locals. A woman with a small child sat in the gutter eating what appeared to be raw meat from a yak bone. She and the child would hammer the bone on the ground to loosen it up, and then go back to gnawing on it. She was dressed in what looked like an old army coat, but it was draped off one shoulder and had the traditional Tibetan extra-long sleeves (called "chuba"). In her hair were bits of turquoise and she wore felt shoes on her feet. Her baby had a bare butt on the cold sidewalk. Many people wore western outfits. The men sported slacks, vests, sport coats, or leather jackets. The women were in slacks, blouses, and coats. As I spent more time there and came to recognize the vendors, it became obvious that folks had only one set of clothes, at least for their work, because they wore the same thing every day.

Other traditional outfits for the women consisted of a dark skirt, a bright woven apron, dark sweater, and a variety of earth colors for handbags. I never saw flashy or revealing clothes. Some of the younger women wore miniskirts but nothing provocative to my mind. I saw other women with strings of turquoise in their silky-black hair, with bracelets, woven shawls holding babies, and black skirts. Most of the clothes were dark, but with the turquoise, red, and yellow beads that accented the shiny black hair and radiant faces, there was color galore.

My first road trip was a warm-up for my mission; visiting the deepest canyon in the world. I had been approached to join several others for a three-day, two-night trip. I figured it would be good training for what was to come, so I said count me in. Jenny, the woman studying Chinese; Yetta, an Aussie woman; and Alan, a Brit; plus a driver and our guide made six of us in the Land Rover. Our goal was to visit Nangartse, near the sacred lake, and then Samye Monastery. Our ride was up and over a 15,000-foot pass, a dusty and dirty road with long tight switchbacks up and down the mountain. We stopped at the pass and were rewarded with an incredible 360-degree view and a multitude of prayer flags flapping in the breeze, sending their prayers up to the gods. Walking around at that altitude was okay, but I would hate to be on the road crew we passed, breaking rock with hammers to fill in the potholes and using wheelbarrows to haul rock. The Chinese idea is to employ many people because machinery is not available.

We arrived and checked into the guest house. There were five beds in a room, with no heat. The room did have linoleum square tiles with flowers, a battered table in the center of the room, a west facing window and a TV the guide said didn't work and was there for decoration. The walls were cement, blue to the mid-level, then three thin stripes of red, blue, and green, and then white to the ceiling. There were three huge, very cliché posters: kittens in a bowl, an American-style house, and a picture of a huge meal. There was also a large thermos of hot water, a few cups, and a washing basin.

The bathroom was down the stairs, across the courtyard and up a few jerry-rigged cinder block steps; the men's to the right and the women's to the left. An oblong slot cut in the cement floor was the target. Just aim and/or squat, and do your business. There was plenty of evidence showing that some of the aims were not as good as one would have hoped for. In addition the ceiling was low and I could not stand up straight in the space.

Our guide instructed us to stay together, so we took a walk back in time. If the cars and motors disappeared, I would have guessed that most of the locals would not be impacted much. If the power wires were removed, things would look as they did for centuries before power was available. Horses were still driven to chafe the barley, wooden handmade rakes were used to toss the barley in the air, and sieves were used to strain the finer barley. We walked through this scene enjoying the leisurely pace. We were at 14,800 feet, so as long as we walked slowly we were okay. The scenery on our way back to the guest house included brown mountains, blue sky, and white clouds. We dined at a café, claiming it was an "elegant situation." This particular elegant situation included windows that let in the cold, mismatched tables and chairs, torn table cloths, and, for the final touch, a plastic dispenser with toilet paper for our napkins. After a tasty vegetarian dinner, we repaired to our room and went to bed.

The next morning we headed back the same route, up and over the dusty, dirty, pass with its amazing views, eventually coming to the ferry to Samye. The Samye Monastery was founded in 779 A.D. The monastery mixes Chinese, Tibetan, and Indian construction styles. The first floor is Tibetan, the middle Chinese, and the top Indian. The monastery has a room with 9000 Buddhas. Monks chanted, incense burned and yak butter lamps illuminated. It was all fascinating but probably the highlight of this part of the trip was the ferry ride.

When I think of a ferry, I conjure up the Alaska Marine Highway system, which ferries between small southeast Alaska communities; or the boats that run between Seattle and the San Juan Islands, or around the harbor in New York City. You know, ferries made of steel that can ride out most storms, with berths, showers, a café, and a lounge. Not so for the ferry to Samye. This was a more rustic affair and possibly my first legitimate method of "hard travel" on the trip so far. The boat was a wooden affair, thirty feet long, maybe ten feet wide, three feet max for the freeboard, and flat-bottomed. The rear three feet had a platform where the engine was mounted; it looked like a small tractor engine with a shaft leading directly into the water, a tiller, and the driver perched alongside the motor. Forward were thwarts placed every four feet. Some of the ferries had extra poles crossing the width with bags of supplies piled high, or in our case, pilgrims. The ride to Samye was about two hours against the current. We had about 100 bags of cement (or some white substance of a chalky nature), and a dozen passengers, so it was a relaxed cruise with plenty of space to stretch out and enjoy the scenery. The river ran smooth and our driver, apparently the son of the driver of the ferry running next to ours, amused himself by playing bumper tag with the other boat, continuing to do so even after knocking a few of the upper planks loose.

Our return ride, shorter, as we went with the current, was more typical. I counted at least 70 heads, and we four were the only westerners aboard. The rest were the multi-hued pilgrims, local residents, and monks. The scenery was again the brown barren hills, blue sky, white clouds and the chrome river, mixed with the red, turquoise and other bright colors of the people, a stunning tableau. Without the engine and without us, it would have been a scene that was as old as the Samye Monastery. This was one of the few times as an outsider in Tibet I wasn't constantly being stared at, maybe because I was sitting down, or maybe because we were all pilgrims in some sense and the real pilgrims granted us that fantasy.

My height (I'm six-feet six in bare feet) constantly drew looks, stares, and double takes. There wasn't a day that went by when I wasn't followed, stared at, or stood next to so the monk or pilgrim or nomad or other citizen could compare our heights. If it brought a smile to someone, what a nice and easy gift to bestow; if they were mocking me, I didn't know it; the eyes and body language didn't say that. I was having a great time, and happy to provide a bit of amusement.

We returned safely from our journey but with at least one moment of concern. Our driver, when awake, was a skillful and careful driver. However, when he fell asleep at the wheel he tended to neglect his duties. I was sitting right behind him and was watching. I thought his head had nodded a few times, but I wasn't positive. I did notice Alan sitting next to him and Jenny next to Alan keeping a sharp eye on him. When the driver did doze off, Alan would give him a sharp elbow to awaken him. Once he fell asleep and the car slowly came to a stop, almost as if it were falling asleep too. We called for a break, and asked if we could drive. Our guide said, "No, no, everything is fine." As we got closer to town, the driver did seem to regain his alertness. This experience gave me enough cause for concern that in all future deliberations for transportation I would insist that the driver stay awake as part of the bargain.

The ride back was scary, but also interesting for the view of home life of the locals. I was also slowing down. While I had been gone only two days, it seemed like longer. Was this due to the many ancient connections and connotations, or to the constant use of body English to dodge all the road hazards? All along the narrow road, cows, sheep, pigs, and goats were wandering, with no fences to keep them in. It was truly astounding good luck that we didn't hit one. People who lived along the road were also a hazard. They seemed to be camping on the side of the road, or working on the road, or literally living on the road, using it to cut firewood, chafe barley, comb their hair, or sit in chairs and enjoy the afternoon sun. There were donkeys with hay bales, women doing laundry, nomads walking, and pilgrims on pilgrimage, and us, all on the road, lost in our own murmuring, or maybe muttering, thoughts of the moment.

Back in Lhasa it was time to focus on getting to the Yarlung Tsangpo Valley. One of the travel staff, a concierge of sorts, at the Snow Land Hotel told me the gorge was "forbidden". Okay, how about the village of Pe located 30 miles from the deepest part? They would know in a couple of days. Meanwhile, they recommended "a guy" up the street in a different travel agency. When I approached him, he told me Snow Land was trying to get him caught by the Public Security Bureau (PSB), one of the many types of Chinese police. As he could not get me a permit, here was the first inkling that Snow Land was in control. According to him and others, Snow Land controlled 90 percent of the travel permit business, and once you were connected to them through the original Traffic Hotel hook-up, you had to stick with them; that was the Chinese way. It was suggested that I go to an outdoor gear store and ask them about transportation to the gorge or Yarlung Tsangpo.

So plans were hatching. I found the backpacker equipment store. They said come back on Monday, and when I did, they had a car and driver ready to go right then and there. I begged off, telling them I was sick (actually I didn't want to go as yet because I was still waiting to see what Snow Land, could pull off). I received an e-mail from Richard Fisher telling me Pe was the right place to start. This brought relief. At least I was aiming in the right direction. Pe was about thirty miles from the deepest part of the canyon, as I understood it. From Pe there was supposed to be a 4x4 road about fifteen miles into the canyon and then another fifteen miles of trail to Gyala. I am not sure if that is the deepest spot, but thought it was pretty darn close from the information I had at that time; close enough for my purpose anyway.

Jon, the muse, had also given me the name of a travel agent he had used. I tried to find and call the woman, to no avail. Later, checking the map he'd given me, I noticed she was just up the street, but while it was the same building that he had been in less than two months ago, they claimed to never have heard of the woman with whom he had dealt.

Meanwhile I was still enjoying Lhasa. One morning I found myself using the e-mail and drinking yak butter tea, compliments of the establishment, once again a combo of old and new. I was standing on the street waiting to meet the man that Snow Land had sent me after -- the one who told me Snow Land was trying to get him in trouble - and he was late, and the pilgrims were passing, nomads too, the monks chanting in the old part of Lhasa. I was standing in spit and urine, excretion odors wafting about, old carts rumbling by with wooden wheels on them, cyclos passing, and a man came up to me with a cell phone, saying, "It's for you." It was the man I was supposed to meet, calling to tell me he'd be a few minutes late! It left me scratching my head

One feature of Lhasa was the openness of the other travelers and expatriates, Hayden, for example. This is his story. He had been living in Lhasa three years and was a rug "runner," a person who doesn't own the shop, but buys and sells old woolen Tibetan carpets along with any other old stuff he could find. He is kind of a middleman for the bigger dealers in old Tibetan things. I observed several transactions where people brought him various items. Mostly (in a British accent) he said, "this is shit, shit, shit, shit. Here is five Yuan for trying, come back with old stuff old, old, old." Once, according to him, while riding and showing off, he fell off his horse and was dragged through the village, never to live it down. He'd left England at sixteen, went to Greece and lived in a cave, where he caught squid and traded it for food. Then he moved to South America and eventually the Caribbean, where he lived and worked in casinos for twenty years. He finally had to leave due to what he called "politics." Then it was off to the U.S., where a friend of three years ripped him off. That sent him packing, and he ended up in Lhasa, but not before a Cuban adventure in which he smuggled rum and cigars into Florida. These tales kept me amused while waiting for news of my canyon quest. I wondered if I would be part of what Kerouac calls, "a world full of rucksack wanderers, Dharma bums refusing to subscribe to the general demand that they consume production and therefore have to work for the privilege of consuming all that crap they didn't really want anyway." This seemed to describe the nomads and pilgrims much more accurately than we travelers.

The next day came; I arose to the cold and incense aroma that floated from the Barkhor into my room. I had my usual two croissants, butter, jam, and tea and walked to the Snow Land travel agent. She said come back at noon. At noon she told me to come back at four. At four p.m. they had an itinerary: day one to Bayi; day two to Pe; day three Pe; day four, Bayi; day five and back to Lhasa. It would cost $1000 Yuan for them; $2,400 Yuan mileage at three Yuan per kilometer; $750 Yuan for the guides at $150 a day; $300 Yuan for the permit; $4,450 Yuan or about $550 U.S. total. Sounded okay to me. Sure it was a bit spendy, but if it got me to the canyon, that was fine with me. I figured once I got to Pe I would wander downstream as far as I could, and if they had to wait for me for a day or two, well, so be it.

Next thing was to find company for safety and to help offset the expenses. I dutifully made signs to hang up at the other backpackers; this was the normal way to find folks to help share a journey. My sign said: "World's deepest gorge, Depart Nov 8 or 9, 4 nights – five days. Yarlung Tsangpo. Contact Jeff at the Snow Land room xyz."

At dinner that night I ran into Jim and Maggie, from the original Chengdu group, sitting with Kate, from Australia. As word of mouth is the best publicity, I talked up the trip and asked if any were interested. Kate, a healthy young hippish looking woman with strawberry blond hair said, "Maybe." So did Sophie, from the Isle of Skye, short with dark hair and an impish smile, and Dan, from Quebec, dark with a quick smile. I said, "Sleep on it. If you are interested I will be at the Snow Land restaurant tomorrow at 8:30 am for breakfast and we can discuss the future." So off I went to sleep on it too, hoping at least one of them would join me on this dance.

I was still enjoying the street scene around the hotel, Jokhang, and the Barkhor. Families with bundles, long lines of pilgrims and nomads thronged throughout the area, amber-skinned, with dark, etched lines in their faces. In the crowded streets and alleyways, every tribe and group had its own distinct garb, some tall and regal and proud with long hair braided and tied over their heads in red bandanas, Tibetan women with the turquoise shining in their thick black hair. Others were listless and ragged with dark skin and runny noses. They were both young and old, some with new clothes and others in clothes that could have been centuries in the wearing. Buddhist monks, cripples, beggars, prostrating pilgrims, beautiful, rosy-cheeked women, and a parade that went 'round and 'round the Jokhang and Barkhor. Stall owners sang about their wares, the devout muttering their prayers, prayer wheels humming as they spun around and around sending their prayers to the wind and gods, all of us walking 'round and 'round and 'round. For me, just digging the scene, each circumnavigation brought me closer to a feeling of comfort and ease with my surroundings, watching and being watched, getting into the meditation of the Kora and losing track of time in this timeless arena.

Despite my enchantment with the surroundings, I was still anticipating the breakfast meeting. I was there at 8:30. At 8:45 I was bummed out and resigned to going by myself on this canyon dance. Then in walked Kate, the Aussie woman, raised in Tasmania by hippie parents, and shortly after Kate, Sophie and then Dan! I laid out my plan: we get to Pe, sprint as far down the trail as we can, and then return by dark. We all gave up our passports to the Snow Land travel agent; it was now a matter of deciding between a Thursday or Friday departure. I knew we had taken a step: whether it was in the right direction remained to be seen.

I spent a very pleasant lunchtime with Kate, Lee, an Irish lad, and several others. Two things occurred. First, I realized after thirty-seven days of travel, I wasn't in any hurry. I had no meetings to rush off to, no phone calls to make, no appointments, no deadlines, and no paperwork to turn in. Ahhh, I was slowing down. This was about right, a month plus to wind down after almost six years of work. Second, I did not necessarily feel old; although I was almost twice everyone else's age, I was taken with the people I was hanging with. Their acumen, skills at travel, wit, and education were obvious. I felt a bit out of my element, but also fortunate they accepted -- or was it tolerated -- my company.

The sun continued to shine with pleasant daytime temperatures. I was checking in often at the Snow Land travel agency. They told me I didn't need to check every day. I let them know it was my duty to teach them a new American word or concept; "to bug" was my choice of words. It got a laugh. I had an epiphany during lunch. I had absolutely nada, nil, nothing to do aside from get to the canyon, and wasn't that just grand!

Except the next day, I actually did have a few odds and ends to do. I had to change hotels. I had been spending about 150 Yuan a night at the Snow Land. Most everyone I knew had moved across the street to the Pentoc, which had cleaner toilets and showers, and it was cheaper too. Plus they offered free movies at eight p.m. every evening. So I followed the group. It was 40 Yuan a night and I got one of the two "penthouse" suites, room 402, on the highest floor.

The bathroom was down one flight of stairs, and the shower, down two. The room itself was about cell-sized, seven feet wide by twelve feet long, with one single bed against the wall, and a small hassock at the foot of the bed. There was a three-drawer chest and a small end table next to that on the opposite wall. A window was in the wall at the foot of the bed, overlooking a Chinese hotel, its courtyard, and the distant mountains. There was a worn wainscot all around the room, a burnt brown color, with one-inch stripes of blue, red, and green above the wainscoting, and then dirty white walls, cracked and peeling, as was the ceiling. There was no heat. The carpet was dirty and stained a gray shade long ago, but with late afternoon sun streaming in, a reading light over the bed, and a thermos of hot water, I spread my stuff out and it felt like home.

My curiosity about how this canyon dance would turn out kept me on edge, but the street scene gave me respite from those concerns. On a walk to one of my e-mail spots I took notes every thirty or so steps, and this is what I saw: a three-wheeled bike cart with a dozen used, rusty propane tanks attached in a haphazard way; garbage all over; broken glass; plastic playing cards (these appeared one day, all over the street and for the rest of the time in Lhasa they were a part of the trash). Street sweepers, men and woman, with long branches of leaves acting as brooms, came through and swept the place up, dust and all. Then there were vendors, either in ten foot-by-ten foot shops built into the bottom floor of the building, or on the sidewalk selling from carts or blankets laid on the ground, or from three-wheeled bikes, selling clocks and watches, belts, socks, shoe liners (though not in my size, much to their merriment when they looked at my feet). There were butchers selling all kinds of meat, lying on the sidewalk, on shelves, or hanging from hooks. There were tailor shops, with only men's or women's, or bolts of cloth, all with odd bits of cloth scraps scattered about on the floors. Alleys were lined with more vendors, peddling their specialties: beads, animal skins, prayer flags, prayer wheels, incense, yak butter, yak meat, and bowls made from human skulls with silver inlay called "kapala.". There were barber shops, hair washing shops, liquor stores, cigarette stores, and kid vendors selling the same on the sidewalks. There were shoe stores, army surplus stores, purse stores, pharmacies, sweets stores, toy stores, bike repair shops, carpet shops, bakeries, toilet paper shops, and eyeglass shops. There were three-wheeled carts piled with apples, bananas, oranges, nuts or berries and fruit I did not recognize. The streets were filled with taxis, pedicabs, pedestrians, buses, bikes, motor scooters, motorcycles, and the sounds of honking and bells, but not in anger, just, "Look out here I come". And this was just half a block of walking, and then the same menagerie of shops would start all over again, repeating itself. And the people! There were throngs of them: women with colorful pork pie or flat-top hats, dark suits or skirts, woven colorful aprons and sashes and sweaters. Men with black hair, ponytails tied on tops of their heads with red scarves, woolen coats to their knees with sleeves the same length, one shoulder off and wrapped around the waist, dark pants and boots. School kids in tracksuits. Monks in red robes, sashes, and various footgear. Chinese men and women in their ill-fitting army, police, PSB, and other unknown officialdom uniforms, were abundant in all areas of Lhasa as well as the Jokhang Temple and Barkhor. I liked the place more and more, not so much the military presence.

In front of the Jokhang was a courtyard about as wide as two football fields, and easily as long. A ten-foot stupa stood in front of the monastery just a bit off center, burning incense that wafted over to my hotel room every morning and woke me. The Jokhang itself is three stories, topped with a golden stupa. Stupa or "Chorten," were originally built to house the cremated relics of a famous Buddha, Sakyamuni, and have become a symbol of Buddha and his teachings. There are five levels and they represent the four elements and eternal space. Atop the Jokhang is a large golden Mandala with deer facing it on either side. There are various spires dotting the rest of the roof. The building is whitewashed, with dark trim around the windows. Vendors were selling lots of things, including pictures, but not of the Dalai Lama. Why? My guess is the Chinese feel it will create disturbances. Tibetans with a picture of the Dalai Lama were in for a rough time.

In the center of the courtyard, a few Chinese police set up a table and kept the crowds from gathering too close to the temple. It seemed rather arbitrary -- the farther away from the Jokhang, the less they seemed to care -- but if too many people gathered close by they would move them along. I had heard there was a law that no more than four people could congregate, so that was the excuse the police used to keep them moving. When a traveler named Jess, a juggler and a good one too, juggled at the Barkhor, a rather large crowd gathered and police would disperse them. At the farthest corner from the temple itself, a few carnie types set up "games of chance" (throw a hoop over a can of coke and win the coke). They, however, seemed immune from the crowd rule.

While the crowds and vendors and pilgrims and nomads and everyday street life drew my attention, I still went back to the Snow Land to get an update. The next report wasn't so exciting. They said they could not get a permit to Pe, the small village at the head of the valley. So that was the bad news. The good news was we could go to Bayi, and then Miling (sometimes spelled Meling), which was across the bridge that went over the Yarlung River. If that didn't work, I was told we could go to the PSB in Bayi and ask for a permit to Pe.

At that point I was still naïve. I thought we could just go to the bridge (it is named the Congga Bridge) and cross it. I didn't know the police were there, armed and checking permits. The cost for this canyon dance was adding up, while the plans kept on a-changing. It was at this point that the idea of adding an incentive, a gratuity, a special consideration, a gift to the powers that be, might be an option. Keith, another rug salesperson, said the real deal is if your guide wants to get there, then you'll have a better chance, but having some cigarettes, booze, and money won't hurt either. In the meantime, a part-time guide, Tsering, overheard our conversation and offered to take me, saying he had been there before. So we went across the street to Snow Land Travel, and to my surprise they said okay to Tsering as the new guide. At that point I had decided money wouldn't stop me from going and giving it a try. The options seemed to be: Snow Land and their guides, the travel agent up the street, who was still trying, and the outdoor store. I was still hoping to get to Pe and hike, or to Bayi and ask the PSB, with what I hoped were the correct incentives, to get to Miling and then to Pe, but nothing was certain, that is for sure. I wasn't entirely sitting on pins and needles waiting to see what would happen, but I was curious for sure, or "nervous in the service," as my dad would say. Or as we used to say in Ohio, I had the buck-aggers.

Finally we four were to meet at five p.m. at the Snow Land to pick up our permits, get our passports, which we had given up for processing, and meet our new guide, Tsering. I was betting that the Snow Land would throw us a curve. At five-forty p.m. the curve came: Pasang a thin older man was a more established guide, so Tsering would not be our guide. The permit was only to Bayi (not even in the guide book). When we got there we would need to go to the PSB and see if we could get to Miling and then on to Pe. There was a definite possibility of getting turned back. Pupu was to be our driver, and would meet us at nine am. I rehearsed the three things I wanted the guide to know and understand: 1. This was an all-out attempt to get to the deepest canyon on each continent, 2. Please tell the police that, and 3. If possible I wanted to talk with the police myself. I hoped that I might be able to charm the people in charge.

I was still beating myself up for spending so much money, but it was the plan, and the only one at that point. Just to be safe, I had started on a just-in-case, backup plan. Tsering, who was to have been our guide, was checking to see if we didn't make it, whether perhaps we could go without a permit.

Part II
A First Time for Everything

"So I continue plugging away as if by following this way of suchness one could prepare the infinite room for that which cannot be contained."

Thank you and OK, by David Chatwick

On the 10th day of November 2000, at nine a.m., after ten days in Tibet, we were off to see the Yarlung Tsangpo Valley. Leaving Lhasa, we headed east. Of the ways to arrive in Lhasa, three main ones are to fly from Chengdu, come from the west overland on the Freedom Highway from Nepal, or fly from Katmandu. So it was new to all of us, including Pasang, although Pupu the driver had been a truck driver and so had been this way. Leaving Lhasa and the wide valley in which it resided, we began to pass through the brown mountains along a two-lane paved road. We had the normal number of near misses with cattle, pigs, goats, bikes, pedestrians, and the ever-present blue trucks hauling all types of cargo, from pilgrims to produce to pigs. The valley gradually narrowed and we started to climb. Soon we were on a dirt road. The scenery got better and better. Jagged and ragged saw-toothed peaks rose to greet us. The river got narrower and shallower and ice began to form near its edges. We kept climbing into that perfect cobalt blue sky. After several hours, we were at Mila Pass, about 15,000 feet. A teeming galaxy of prayer flags flapped there, green, blue, white, red and yellow, letting the wind carry their karma to the cosmos. We stopped for a stretch and pictures, with 360 degrees of outstanding scenery, the Himalayas off in the distance, as well as other snowy peaks unknown to our guides.

Back in the carryall, a Toyota four-wheel drive, with three in the front, three in the back, and gear-in-the-rear storage area, we headed down the river valley to the start of the Kongpo Nyangchu River and its headwaters. It was narrow enough to easily step across as we descended, a hop and skip would get you across and if you missed the jump, you'd only get your feet wet to the ankles. It was a pleasure to follow the wide valley out of Lhasa, see it narrow, see the headwaters of the Lhasa Valley appear across the pass, and see it all in reverse. There was one difference. As we descended, I started to notice green, a few shrubs here and there, the spectacular azure blue sky, rushing turquoise water, white clouds and now and then a dot of green. This was not the case on the Lhasa side, at least that time of year. As we descended, the greener it became, until I was ready to concede at least three-fourths of the view was green, pine trees with real pine needles. There were trucks with logs passing and buildings made of wood; not so on the Lhasa side. There was even a hint of red and yellow fall colors. After eight hours of this uninterrupted beauty, we hit Bayi.

By most standards, Bayi would be considered a podunk town. There were three-and four-story buildings in the central part of town, but even to our untrained eyes it looked very much Chinese, and not at all Tibetan. As it turned out, it was mostly Chinese, with most of those residents there working for the government. The Chinese relocated people, giving tax and business breaks to encourage a strong Chinese presence.

Our first stop was the Public Security Bureau (PSB) to let them know we had arrived. The PSB is the same as the police, uniformed or not. According to the guidebook, their jobs included "suppression of political dissidence, crime detection … and enforcing regulations that concern foreigners." If we disobeyed the laws, we might get our hands slapped, but the guide and driver could really catch hell, or at least that was what we were led to believe. At first we could not get out of the vehicle, but after our guides had been interrogated, officials came and got us and we were escorted into the PSB building. The room was clean, although a bit of dust had settled on the furniture since the last visitors. The tile floor, however, gleamed from what must have been a rigorous and regular waxing. Our seats were a new-to-me furniture style: wood with shiny polished black lacquer, intricately carved arms and legs, and slats for seats and back. The walls were bare; a window looked out from the head PSB official's office.

ROUND 1. We were informed we could not go past Bayi, a forbidden military area. I felt like I had gotten a quick punch in the kidney, but shook it off to survive the round. Also pondering how gullible a naïf I was.

ROUND II. We all talked at once with the PSB interpreter, a young Chinese woman with a neatly pressed uniform, quite possibly hand tailored. "All we want to do is see the river. We're trying to visit the deepest canyon in the world. I've had no problem in Africa and Europe. Please, please, please, can you try again, won't you please try again, please, please, please." The judges called round II a draw.

ROUND III. Our young interpreter went back into the headman's office. There were ten minutes of loud talk, laughing, and then quiet. I was nervous. What were they saying? Judges didn't count this round; if anything it went to the PSB.

ROUND IV. Our interpreter came back: "OK, you can go to the bridge, 30 kilometers away, 200 Yuan each." I went to the vehicle to get my money; the round was a tie.

ROUND V. I was invited into the headman's office; it had a heater in it, the first I had seen in Tibet. The floor actually glittered, it was so heavily waxed and buffed. Two desks with cloth covers and a modern lamp adorned the room; everything else was bare, save the low-slung couch I was seated on, putting me significantly lower than the two of them in chairs. I was unsure if I should look relaxed or be the nervous guy that I was. Again, I explained through the interpreter what we were trying to do. It was the first time in a long time that I felt that if I had been clean cut, I would have a better chance of success. At the time I might have agreed to a haircut if it would have gotten us to the valley. Round to PSB.

ROUND VI. Here was the final deal: for 200 Yuan I could go to the bridge, not over the bridge, not take a picture, and not get out of the car at the bridge. But I could see the Yarlung Tsangpo River that flows under the bridge that leads to Miling that goes to Pe that takes the trail to the deepest canyon in Asia and the world. So? Had I lost the match? Not yet. It looked as if the PSB was winning so far, and despite all the boxing, we still needed a place to stay for the night.

We had two options: the very expensive hotel, and the not so very expensive hotel. We opted for the not so expensive hotel, which turned out to be a three story Chinese truck stop, as evidenced by the jammed parking lot with the blue and green Chinese trucks, and nary a car to be seen, other than our Land Rover. We dickered and bickered with the hotel staff. We all wanted to stay in the same room for money saving and safety reasons but that was "forbidden." Finally we talked them down to 60 Yuan a person, which we felt was expensive. Dan and I went to our room, only to find that the bathroom had at least two inches of standing water. Back to the front desk we went. They took us to the next room which looked okay at first glance. At least there was no water on the floor. But when I went to pee and glanced into the bathtub, oh oh, turd's in the tub, (or as Dan liked to say, "Shit in the shower." We showed the staff, again, and, with what we took to be embarrassment, but a haughty embarrassment, they took us to room three. Room three had tall ceilings, with the wall crawling with mold, a bit of mildew, and fungi for texture. There were a variety of scrapes, scratches, and peeling wallpaper mixed with unknown substances. The floor was tile and faded, and torn curtains tried in vain to hide the broken windows. The furnishings were two single beds. Dan found two different colors of hair on his sheets; I didn't look. A few chairs and two thermos bottles finished off our room. The ceiling looked to be the cleanest place to me. The bathroom door had no doorknob, and two bare wires leading to the light bulb, which was hanging from a broken fixture. The tub, while turdless, was too scary with growth to contemplate.

Our next adventure was dinner. We were originally seated among the local populace, but apparently we were too distracting and were removed to a private dining room. We ate an okay dinner and then returned to our minus star hotel for a game of cards and then the lights went out.

ROUND VII. I met our driver, Pupu, at 7:50 a.m. for the drive to the bridge and river; the others opted to save the 200 Yuan. We drove for an hour and came to the bridge over the Yarlung Tsangpo River that leads to Miling. The ride was beautiful. We quickly left the buildings of Bayi and were in the country, on a dirt road, along the edge of the river, but not the Yarlung. We passed small lumberyards, pigs, cows, yaks, and goats. People and children scattered as we drove past, horn blaring. The mountainside of the road was green, sprinkled with yellow and orange fall colors. On the opposite side the mountains rose to 18,000 feet. The road was tree-lined, forming a canopy inviting us further along. The cloud level was about 18,000 feet so I could not see the peaks of the two 21,000-foot mountains on either side of the canyon. We bumped along in silence, both of us awed by the beauty. Finally, around the bend on the Congga Bridge to Miling, soldiers paced back and forth. The river was running, but a wide valley remained. I could guess which of the valleys in the unclear distance would be the Yarlung and lead to Pe. It was beautiful, but I knew it could not count as having been to the valley. The round and match went to the PSB. I had lost the bout. We didn't even get out of the car, just turned around and headed back to Bayi. I was disappointed, yes, but not ready to throw in the towel. I later rechecked the map and noticed on the east side of the river, directly east of Pe, was a village called Mainri. Maybe it was possible to reach it since we didn't have to cross the bridge to Miling.

On the last night, Dan, Pasan, Kate, Sophie and I played cards by candle-and-flashlight, and Pasan told us his story: When he was 13, (he was 27 at that point), he had been at a demonstration against the Chinese at the Jokhang Temple. He was arrested, clubbed, had his hand broken, and ended up spending eight months in jail, one of the youngest to be imprisoned. He was told upon release that if he were caught again he would spend the rest of his life in jail. However, he did go to more demonstrations, but started thinking of his parents' concern for him. They sent him to Dar Eslam in India to stay out of trouble. There he learned English and then returned to Lhasa. Pasan answered our questions. Tibetans, he said, knew that other countries were aware and concerned about what was happening in Tibet. Tibetans were not allowed to form groups in the Jokhang temple area; the police kept them moving. I realized I was clueless. I have never lived in an occupied country and have no sense of what it must be like. The Dalai Lama left in 1959; he is gone but clearly not forgotten.

Our adventure wasn't over yet. I had seen the bridge, the river, and the direction in which I wanted to go. Being a Buddhist area, perhaps there was a Zen lesson to be gleaned? Was I missing the koan? So close to the canyon, yet so far. It felt like being at the entrance of a world-class museum and only seeing the outside.

I harkened back to my through-hike of the Pacific Crest Trail, all of California, Oregon, and Washington; six months and 2,600 miles. I had plenty of time to think and daydream, and wait for "visions" to find me. They did, nineteen "lessons" that "came" to me. I listed them:

Be nice to & enjoy Mother Nature.
Be nice to myself & others & recognize when people are nice to me.
Nobody is perfect.
Be positive.
Keep it simple.
Check in with my senses & emotions no matter how briefly.
Be Happy
Be Healthy.
Be honest.

Keep my sense of humor.
Be humble
Family is a priority.
Don't give up.
Don't waste.
Practice the Golden Rule.
Watch where you are going, in every sense of the word.
Be thankful.
Seek the truth.
Appreciate the miracle of how "it" all fits together.

Not always, but often, when I was trying to figure out what to do I would review these and see how they fit. I figured this might be a time to review my list of "enlightenments" or "credo" or tenets, I learned many of them had relevance to this particular canyon quest, with "don't give up" the most obvious one to focus on, the crux. What was I willing to do to get back and try again?

The highlight of that attempt, aside from the incredible scenery and actually seeing the Yarlung Tsangpo, was our stop at a Tibetan guesthouse where Tibetan truck drivers stay in the Village With No Name. The village was a row of buildings, maybe ten on each side, and that was it. Our guesthouse was two stories. The first floor was about 20 feet x 40 feet. Windows on the street side let in the afternoon sun. There was a communal sleeping room, with three beds along one wall, end-to-end. The short side of the room had three beds end to end also, and the far side three more beds, plus a shelf and a door that led to the back of the building and the toilet (enough said). The other short side of the room was occupied with some type of appliance and shelving. In front of each bed was a table and in the center of the room a wood-burning, or yak chip-burning stove and a water barrel.

According to tradition, the ceiling had red-painted planks running the long way, and then purple round timbers spaced six to eight inches apart running the short length of the room. Thin yellow and blue stripes with bands of pink and green were near the ceiling in a wavy pattern that looked like a curtain fluttering in the wind. The next three feet down were painted pale yellow, and then another series of small stripes, red, blue, and yellow, wound 'round the room.

The rest of the wall was aqua green to the floor, which was made of eight-inch-wide planks about six feet long running the length of the room.

The support beam was outstanding, running down the center of the room. It was yellow, green, blue, and pink pastels and adorned with dragons and floral patterns in vivid green, yellow, and orange. Holding the crossbeam was an orange, red, green, purple, and blue dragon on timber with numerous prayer scarves tied around it. This room was like many of the Tibetan rooms I was to see, gaudy by western standards, but it worked for me.

We turned out to be the evening's entertainment for the locals. We had already gathered and dispersed several groups of children. Now it was the adults' turn. I climbed into my sleeping bag at nine to go to sleep. I drifted off to a variety of voices coming and going, not sure if I was dreaming, or if new folks were coming to stay the night or visit with friends. When I awoke at one in the morning the lights from the generator were still on. My eyes were met by the Tibetans' watching us sleep, sitting by our beds looking at us, intently commenting now and then, much the way a TV is watched. The room was smoky from burning yak chips, but smelled no worse than a wood fire. The next morning we awoke, ate the chipatas, and headed back to Lhasa.

On the way back, after the normal narrow misses of pigs, goats, people, yaks, sheep, and pilgrims, we decided to stop at the Ganden Monastery. This monastery is up a long and steep dirt road with a great view of the Kyi Hu Valley. A monk who settled there to preach and create the Gelugpa sect founded the monastery in 1417. The monastery was under artillery fire from the Chinese in the 1950s and early 1960s, but is now being rebuilt and is considered to have the most precious artifacts. Apparently, in 1996 there was trouble when the Chinese cracked down on pictures of the Dalai Lama that were found there.

We finally returned to Lhasa and decided to celebrate, so we went to a Chinese disco. It was a deafening, screeching, unintelligible din, and smoky too. After finally leaving there, we caught the end of a Tibetan cultural show across the courtyard, with authentic music, dance, and singers. Later we waltzed with the dressed-up and serious Tibetans, getting what seemed to be appreciative nods for our ability or effort.

Part III
Cloak and Dagger

"A man never goes so far as when he doesn't know where he is going."

OLIVER CROMWELL

Back in Lhasa, I went looking for people to help plan the second attempt on the Yarlung Tsangpo. Entering one small-but-crowded cafe, I announced, "I am going where I'm not supposed to go, anyone interested?" And that is how I hooked Mike.

Mike Hansen is an ex-marine, ex-Mormon, and current sketcher/artist and student. He was on a four-month trip getting college credit for taking pictures and preparing a report on how the trip influenced his art.

Mike was good a companion. His senses of the absurd and enjoyment of cosmic goofing was borne out in his sitting on the sidewalk in front of the Pentoc, feet in the gutter, with the monks who were chanting the "Om mani padme hum" while Mike "chanted" something that sounded like "oh give me a home." He begged with them, the monks all in dusty red robes, and he in full military motif, head to toe. It was an arresting site. I thought Mike a great partner.

In a brilliant stroke of strategy, we, - Mike, our drivers and guides and I - left in the middle of the day from the busiest part of the city. Mike and I met in front of the Third Eye Restaurant where all our previous clandestine meetings were held. Not once did we ever see a customer in this café, strange for such a great location, but the food was rumored to make one quite sick. All along we were constantly aware that we must be as discrete as possible. No one must know where we were going or whom we were going with! A vehicle with tinted windows was even arranged. A cover story was developed: If we were stopped we'd disavow any knowledge of our three accomplices: Tashi, our burly middle-aged driver, Tesring, our young twenty something guide mentioned in the first attempt that was discharged by the Snow Land travel people, and Tenzin, another twenty something but more serious minded friend of Tesring. We were to say we were hitchhiking and they were to say they couldn't speak English. The price was set, too high, in my eagerness to achieve this elusive goal. To Mike's credit and bargaining skills, our friends would only receive half the amount if our final destination was not reached.

It was risky for our Tibetan friends, a permit-less trip to a forbidden area, with at least one outlaw, me, according to the Snow Land travel people. While trying to get my second permit the agent was told I had "caused problems" on my last attempt. The Chinese authorities felt I caused problems; I did get a rosy glow of pride when the agent told me that.

The area is forbidden for many reasons. It is close to the border of India, swarming with military, too strategic to let goofy tourists roam around. Richard Fisher notes in his *Earth's Mystical Grand Canyons*, "First the canyon is unfortunately located right on the border between China and India and while we in the west have not yet chosen to see how important this is to the Chinese, this is a primary and overriding blockade to exploration and travel. The Yarlung Tsango is a very tightly closed military control zone, and is almost impossible to obtain permits which are extremely expensive." Also there is gold there, as well as rare plants that the Chinese do not want disturbed, too precious to have big-nosed clods like me tromping around. And finally two years ago on a National Geographic-sponsored trip to try and be the first to kayak the gorge, one person was killed. There were irregularities in permits, or the visitors didn't apologize correctly, so the canyon was closed.

I went to one of the few travel agents not swallowed by Snow Land and asked a travel agent if I could get to Pe, and told him my quest. The man seemed to think it would be no problem; we even made a bet, one Yuan, on it. It would take a few days. The agent confirmed that I had "caused problems" on my first visit. When he turned in my name and passport, several of the bureaucratic layers had "red flags" go up. He had to deal with the PSB, the military, foreign affairs, and the tourism bureau. He indicated that several of these groups had heard of me. I had already been to the area and, again, had "caused problems." What could I do? He said to get a note from Snow Land Travel stating I had not caused problems. I traipsed down the street and found the woman who is the travel fixer for Snow Land. She dutifully filled out a note that said, "Jeff Budd did not cause problems." I took the note back to the agent, who said he would forward it to the authorities, but enough was enough. The problems were not defined, but I could not go to Pe.

So we started hatching the next plan which was to go to the opposite side of the river, directly east of Pe. I counted Pe as getting there, and then I could walk from there. Perhaps reaching the village of Mainri on the opposite shore might be just the ticket. Getting an accurate map showing topography was not possible, at least from my attempts. General maps were around, but nothing specific. All I knew from looking at the map was, Mainri was directly east and across the river from Pe. During the first trip I thought I'd seen the valley that Pe was in; it looked steep and narrow to me. This would be a trip without permits into an area with roadblocks checking for permits, PSB checkpoints, and military checkpoints. According to Tsering, there were village "coordinators," who, if they see a westerner, report them to the PSB. A large sum of money, by Tibetan - and my - standards, was agreed upon for what turned out to be two days, one night, and a marathon of driving. When I asked why Tsering would risk so much, the answer was, "for life."

Mike and I were to meet Tsering, Tashi, and Tenzin, in front of the Third Eye at three p.m. In the meantime I was already packed. And that is why Mike and I, loaded with our own backpacks, me sticking out like a 6'6" sore thumb, and he in his camo military gear, both with pony tails and beards, came to be leaning on the rail outside the Third Eye awaiting Tsering. Tsering leaned out of the door of the Third Eye, glanced around at the throng of people, and motioned for us to come inside where nobody could see us. We were again reminded, "No one must see us." And instructed to follow Tenzin, single file, keeping an interval between us so as not to be too noticeable. We went out the front door, passed the Barkhor courtyard of the Jokhang temple filled with tourists, pilgrims, nomads, military, and cops of every stripe and style. We threaded our way through the vendors, beggars, seekers and searchers, school kids, pedicabs, taxis, bikes, spies, and business people. It was a good thing we were tall so we could see Tenzin who was a tad over five feet tall. Then, right in the middle of the teeming street, there was the car. The rear door was opened; we tossed our packs in and were quickly ushered into the car. Nobody saw us except the driver from my first attempt at the canyon, who I stopped and shook hands with, and maybe 10,000 others who were watching these two Americans looking furtively over our shoulders while three Tibetans looked nervously around and kept us moving. We slammed the door and were hushed as we slowly drove through the multitudes.

Our first stop was around the corner where we parked right in front of a policeman who studiously ignored us, while one of our guides ran into the alley to buy some snacks. Then we were off.

The first checkpoint we passed was at the city's edge. Tsering riding shotgun ducked, I pretended to be asleep, and Mike pretended to read. Tashi drove and Tenzin tried to block the view of the back seat by leaning toward the middle of the front seat. The vehicle we were using on this covert operation was a very new Land Rover, cream colored, tinted windows, leather seats, buckets up front, bench in the back, a very posh rig by any standard. The critical piece of equipment, however, was the Bayi license plate. According to Tsering it would cause less attraction. A Lhasa plate would raise eyebrows, so we exhaled after the first checkpoint. I got to know when we were approaching a checkpoint: Tashi would start chanting before and after we had safely made it through, and then clap three times.

The drive to Bayi is awesome in its beauty. We passed several more checkpoints that I had ignored on the first trip when we had a permit, but now I was tuned in to them. We slid on by. Either they were looking the other way or smoking or just didn't give a damn. We just cruised along enjoying the scenery. As we descended from the pass, the landscape got greener and darker. We passed a military checkpoint just outside of Bayi and entered the city in darkness, which was part of the plan!

Next, we pulled into a crumbling section of town and were told to "rest" by Tsering. Our guides disappeared. Every now and then it would cross my mind that this was some kind of great scam being run on us. I had heard good things about Tsering and liked him right off, but still … About fifteen minutes later, Tashi returned; we parked under a street light where men were peeing against the nearby building and were told again to "rest" by Tashi. We snacked and chatted another fifteen or so minutes. Tesring returned. "okay, we can eat." Both Mike and I were under the impression that we were not to be seen under any circumstances. For the last eight hours we had been instructed to duck, pull hats over our faces, and not let anyone see us. So under cover of darkness, abetted by the bright street lamp, we entered a hole-in-the-wall café and were served a delicious meal of rice, spicy onions, mushrooms, and veggies. After seeing me eat with chopsticks the owner brought me a spoon. We somehow attracted a few beggars and several other street characters, but we finished up the meal, with several people following us and watching as we snuck back into the car.

Next we drove around to get lost, or we got lost driving around. We crossed from the pavement to bounce along what seemed like a riverbed, but finally pitched up at a new construction site. After much Tibetan discussion amongst our two guides and driver, the proper road was found and we headed for Mainri. Along this country road, according to our guides, we would pass several military camps.

We hit the dirt road with more military camps and an occasional light from a building off in the distance. We stopped at one house with a light on and were told not to speak English, as it was the house of a "neighborhood coordinator," a person who reports to the Chinese the goings-on in their area. Tesring said that we were pilgrims wanting to make sure we were on the right road. If English were heard it would arouse suspicion. I thought it strange that pilgrims would be driving a new Land Rover in the middle of the night, but that was just me. At that point we had been told many times not to speak and that if someone saw us they would call the PSB and report us on the phone, because there were in fact phones out there. We didn't say a word and took off towards our goal.

Finally, after bouncing and jouncing and bumping and thumping we came to an old Chinese military camping area with broken glass, bottles, cans, cow shit, shoes, springs, plastic, you name it. But it was also our camping spot. Somehow Mike found and cleared a semi-level spot, and with numb hands on an incredibly cold and starry night, we put up the tent, climbed in, and went to sleep. Sort of. While I slept warmly, I didn't sleep much.

Before dawn we heard the pilgrims passing by in the dark. Our guides rousted us out, telling us we needed to knock down the tent so as not to be conspicuous. With even stiffer hands, we shivered and got the tent down and were told to huddle in a ravine so that no one would see us. Except the car, of course, stuck out in this traditional space like a rocket ship in the middle of a dark-ages flea market.

That was as close as I would get, when I walked down the ravine to the river that lead to the world's deepest canyon. I was at the river; I saw where Pe was across the river. I saw the two 7,000-meter peaks, where the river runs between them. I picked my rock and I could see where I wanted to be, but I knew I would not get there on this trip. My one month Tibet visa was almost up and I had way overspent my Tibet budget.

I had done the best I could with my time, money, and resolve. I walked down the frozen earth with deer and cow prints, plastic trash, old shoes, and gazed towards my goal, pilgrims chanting in the background. I know I did not succeed, but neither did I fail. In the gully out of sight of most of the pilgrims, our guides boiled water for tea and tsampa (a traditional Tibetan meal made of roasted barley flour mixed with water), and we nibbled gorp. Finally, our guides signaled it was time to head back, time to face what we had covered in the darkness now in the bright reality of day. Slowly, defroster blowing, we made our way back towards Bayi, passing more and more pilgrims, some with the heavy smocks and thick slipper-like gloves who stood, bent, knelt, and slid prostrate in the dust, shit, rocks and cold, only to stand and repeat the same motion over and over again, a faith and devotion that remains beyond me.

We rolled past military camps and, as always, ducked for cover or feigned sleep. There were more pilgrims, the locals waking up, kids on the way to school, yaks being taken for their walks to pasture, pigs snorting through garbage, ducks waddling along. The narrow road was tree-lined, and gradually the sun shone on the mountain peaks. We stopped several times for pictures but were always hurried back into the car at the sound of approaching people, often reminded there were phones here and if the civilian spies saw us they'd call the PSB.

We entered Bayi, re-traced our path through the new Chinese development, drove along the main avenue, and past one of the few gas stations in Bayi. We slid right by the next military checkpoint -- the officer was looking in another vehicle, a huge sigh of relief and three quick claps by all of us. At the very last gas station, we drove in and were ordered, by Tsering, to cover our heads and pretend sleep. Tashi refueled in Indy 500 style and we were off. We sped past another military checkpoint, set up about a mile from town, consisting of a card table, two chairs, and two soldiers on one side of the street and one on the other. We didn't even slow down, again a sigh and three claps.

As we headed back towards Lhasa and the pass, we knew there were two more critical checkpoints to pass. Our story was altered to having hitchhiked into Bayi with a truck and having been picked up by these three fine civilians for a meager 200 Yuan each. We were now being driven back to Lhasa.

At one of the checkpoints the road crosses a bridge in a good-sized village to traverse the south side of the river. The checkpoint had soldiers, but our luck was holding up, they were busy with other vehicles, and Mike and I pretended to sleep. Tashi chanted, and we flew right through, horn blaring, to move the pedestrians, cyclers, children, sheep, and yaks aside. We all clapped three times. Despite the knowledge that Mike and I could get in less trouble than our guides, we still had a nervous edge about what would befall us if we were stopped and asked for a permit. After each checkpoint, we both sighed with relief.

On we drove through world-class scenery, 15,000-foot peaks, green forests, a turquoise river, grazing yaks, sheep, goats, and cattle and the occasional nomads plodding along. We stopped beside a road kill that had almost 100 vultures waiting their turns at the carcass. We could approach within ten feet before they nervously hopped away. Back in the car we were getting sloppy. We flaunted ourselves as trucks passed, no more ducking for cover at the approach of any vehicle or person.

Onward we drove, up the pass, and we entered a small town where we were finally pulled over. The soldier pointed to where he wanted us to park and walked briskly up to the driver's window. Mike was busy reading and I was looking wide-eyed through my frosted/tinted window right into the young soldier's eyes. He issued a very crisp salute and asked Tashi for his license and registration. He looked these over, stepped back, smartly saluted again, and motioned for us to proceed. There was a collective silence as we pulled away. With the window safely rolled up, we all cheered. Tsering said we were 95 percent out of the "danger zone." We continued up the pass where we ran into another roadside kill, a yak this time, which was eaten about down to its hooves. This time the vultures were standing three deep on each other to get a piece of the yak. We drove on and finally reached the pass where we stopped among the bright prayer flags flapping in the wind, the 360-degree vista, one of the best I had seen. We loaded up and headed downhill towards Lhasa. We still needed to waste some time, according to our guides, so that the last Lhasa checkpoint would be reached in the dark, or better yet, closed down.

Down from the 15,000-foot pass, we stopped in a small village with about ten "shops" on each side of the road, and selected a guesthouse to hunker down in for the wait. The sun was shining through the window, yak butter tea was served and the guides ate some yak soup while I nibbled on a piece of bread. It wasn't until later that I wondered at the wisdom of this. The proprietor threw pieces of yak dung into the stove and then handled the round bread, turning it over on top of the wood stove, which then reminded me that I had drunk tea water fetched from the stream; it had boiled, but just barely. I thought myself going a bit native or getting lax in my diligence in staying healthy. We waited for dusk to arrive so it would be dark in Lhasa when we finally returned. We kidded with the children that westerners always seemed to draw and then it was time to take our final chances as we headed towards Lhasa.

The rest of the trip was uneventful, unless you count trying to pass the pale blue, two-and-a-half ton trucks that were everywhere, all driving in the middle of the road like a Southern California orange grove widow in her big old Cadillac. Two or three minutes of constant honking alerted the truck driver that there was someone behind them who wished to pass. Another couple of minutes honking, and they would move over so they could just be passed. Some liked to pretend they were moving over and then rapidly swerve back into the passing space. The record for this type of feints was five.

Other excitement provided by the driver included approaching a village at speed, applying the horn and then cruising through, still at speed, narrowly missing children, cars, trucks, adults and a wide variety of animals. He also liked to go around blind corners in the middle of the road only to meet another driver doing the same with the bonus excitement of a bicycle rider and boulders strewn across the road. There was more than scenery to make the trip exciting.

Finally the Potala hove into view; we crossed the bridge, no soldiers, passed the usual checkpoint and were soon back on the busy streets of Lhasa. Our new story, if we were asked, was that we had been to a mountain, Kailash, and didn't know our driver or guides. We were never to tell anyone their names, unless of course we met some foolish westerners like us who wanted to go for a ride.

We had made it, at least gotten close to our destination without a permit, which was possibly a significant accomplishment. At least our guides thought so. As I carried my gear back to the Pentoc Hotel, up the stairs, arriving among friends who had just returned from their own adventures, I was tired. I had had enough driving adventures, too many close calls and paying too much for these Tibetan canyon attempts. It was time to cut my losses, recognize I had done what I could, and move on.

I searched for a way to describe my feelings. Long, long ago, way back in the early '70s, as a young YMCA youth director in Dayton, Ohio, one of my jobs was to lead high school students on educational and cultural excursions. We planned one for Washington, D.C. One of the youthful passengers had to ride on the transmission hump in the center of the back seat, which was uncomfortable and hard to see from, not to mention hot, and miserable. One girl, Debbie F, always ended up in that spot. Finally, after five days enduring the spot from hell, she exploded. "Damn with a capital fuck!" she yelled. My sentiments, exactly. Damn with a capital fuck!

But, but, but ... despite the giant blue diamond of disappointment, there were gems that kept the scale even: the holy smile of the little girl at the guesthouse with Pippi Longstocking braids, soot-stained coat, and dirty pants. The goal had been to get to Mainri, east of Pe, and without adequate maps there was no way to know that it was just a broad part of the river valley. But we did get there and back without a permit, a plus for the good old U.S. of A.

Trust. My brother Mike emailed me before I left, wondering how was it that we would put our lives in the hands of strangers, but didn't even know our next-door neighbors. Our guides, while paranoid and melodramatic, took good care of us and delivered what they promised. That I paid too much was my problem.

Scenery. Enough scenic gems to fill a treasure chest of pirate loot. The beauty almost made the trip break even -- almost -- but not quite. And isn't that a hang up to be so focused on the goal of getting to the canyon that I almost didn't see the beauty and missed the journey as the destination.

Watching the vultures with their ten-foot wing spans close up; seeing the pilgrims walking and prostrating towards their destinations, though I still cannot fathom the devotion, gave me a feeling, that by just driving by I might add a tidbit of good karma to my own bare tote-board. So powerful was their aura it could penetrate our steel-hulled vehicle and pass a few good random vibes my way. And goodness gracious, great balls of fire, I was alive, on top of the roof of the world, and it was an adventure, and hopefully there would be more! I had stopped and smelled the roses, and the scent was good.

My friend Jennifer, in an e-mail said, "Wherever you are, wherever you go, remember we are all looking up at the same moon." So with those words, I knew it was time to leave Lhasa. I had a few more meals with the "gang" and we shared our stories (I learned a new expression: being "as pissed as a fart," meaning drunk). I made my reservations, packed my bags, did some last minute shopping and inadequate bargaining for gifts for friends and family and took my last perambulation around the Barkhor. The next morning I was up and off. The local bus drove us back in the dark along the Kyicho River, and just like my attempt to get to the valley I could not see the river for the darkness, a fitting goodbye.

Jeff Budd

Index of photos

DARWIN
Northern Territory
Western Australia
Queensland
South Australia
New South Wales
Victoria
Tasmania
PERTH
ADELAIDE
MELBOURNE
SYDNEY
CANBERRA
BRISBANE
HOBART
N

Four

Australia

Better to see something once, than to hear about it 1,000 times.

Asian Proverb

"Sometimes before I take a big trip, I look forward to having the time to contemplate the answers to life's big questions, but a good trip is when you are so much at peace that you cease seeking the answers and forget there ever were questions." Yukon Wild by Beth Johnson

"If you don't know where you are going – any road will get you there." Lewis Carroll

Part I

I arrived in Sydney, Australia on the 23rd of November, suffering only a bit of culture shock. Leaving Lhasa, I flew to Chengdu and then on to Beijing and its neat and tidy airport, which rivaled the airport in Singapore for cleanliness. I flew out of darkness into the Australian light, and before I knew it, I was riding in a taxi at 60mph, on the opposite side of the road, windows down, birds chirping, the weather balmy and palm trees whizzing by. And I was at sea level, quite a contrast to where I'd been just thirty hours ago: freezing at 12,000 feet surrounded by dusty mountains, and listening to a totally unfamiliar language. And yet the residue of Lhasa stuck to me, in the form of a persistent hacking cough and itchy and dry skin, as did the frustration of not getting to the canyon, both of which lingered for two additional weeks, keeping me connected to Tibet even as I began the Australian canyon dances.

A plethora of canyons, valleys, chasms and gorges in Australia were thrown in the way of my quest, along with the nagging question of what the difference was between them. Maybe it is time to define these terms with the help of Mr. Webster:

> Canyon – A deep narrow valley with precipitous sides characteristic of regions where downward cutting of the streams greatly exceeds weathering.
>
> Chasm – A deep opening (as in the earth): A narrow steep walled valley, gorge, or canyon.
>
> Gorge – A narrow passage or entrance as a: defile between mountains; a range of steep rocky walls; a narrow steep walled canyon or a particular narrow steep walled part of a canyon.
>
> Valley – An elongated depression of the earth's surface commonly situated between ranges of hills or mountains and often comprising a drainage area – compare to canyon, gully, and ravine.

So they are all related. I have been taught not to use the word I am trying to describe with that word. I cannot say a canyon is a canyon, but Webster says a canyon is a valley. A chasm is a valley, gorge, or canyon, and a gorge is a part of a steep walled canyon. A valley can be compared with a canyon, gully, or ravine. Readers may decide on the differences to suit their purposes; for mine, they are all about the same. The Grand Canyon is not the Grand Valley, but that doesn't mean that Webster wouldn't define it as such.

I was pondering these definitions while experiencing more culture shock, having gone from the unheated, smoky spartan Pentoc to an upscale B & B with a view of the ocean just outside of Sydney that was recommended by a family member who knew the owners. My task, once and for all, was to identify Australia's deepest canyon, valley, gorge or chasm. I had some ideas. I had looked over guidebooks, read Australian travel accounts, and asked literally hundreds of Aussies, "What is the deepest canyon in Australia?" But none of them knew. Can you imagine an American being asked about the deepest canyon in the United States and not knowing? I forged ahead. The Sydney Public Library Research Librarian told me her answer: the Stanley Chasm. I had not even considered looking for chasms. She assured me that she knew that Stanley Chasm was it, as one of the Australian TV quiz shows had used this very query as a contest question. I added Stanley Chasm to the list. Then I went through the phone book and called some other sources: the University of Sydney Geology Department, the University of Sydney Geographic Department, National Mapping, Maps Unlimited, the Mining Department in Sydney and Canberra, the Sydney Museum, the Australia Geography Society, and the Surveyor of Land & Property. My notes indicated I made sixteen long distance calls from Sydney trying to chase down the correct canyon. After two days of calling I had narrowed my list of potential candidates to the following: Stanley Chasm, Simpson Gorge, and Kings Canyon, all of which were near the Alice Springs area, also known as the Red Center of the country; the Grand Canyon of Australia, Kanangra Walls, and the Grose Valley in the Blue Mountain area; Kowmung, Tablelands, Katherine Gorge, and Franklin Gorge in Tasmania, and the Geehi Valley in the Snowy Mountains.

I called the Stanley Chasm ranger who was flattered by the notion of being the deepest, but said the Grose Valley or Kanangra Walls were definitely deeper. I finally got through to my Richard Fisher contact, Mr. Jamison, who said the deepest was the Geehi Valley in the Snowy Mountains. So with eleven canyons to choose from, I'd narrowed my choices down to Stanley Chasm, Simpson Gorge, Kings Canyon, Grand Canyon of Australia, Grose Valley, Kanangra Walls, and the Geehi Valley. What to do? What to do, indeed? I had a plan: take the train to the Blue Mountains, fly to Alice Springs, and then the Snowy Mountains. If I went to all of them, surely I would get to the deepest!

1. The Grand Canyon of OZ

"Remember that not one shred of evidence exists in favor of the idea that life is serious."

Brendan Gill

The Blue Mountains are not far from Sydney, about 60 miles, and are part of the Great Dividing Range thought impenetrable by the early Sydneysiders. My guidebook noted that some of the early convicts thought China was just on the other side of the mountains. Aboriginal people lived in the Blue Mountains for many years, at least 14,000 of them, as evidenced by axe-grinding grooves and rock engravings, but most of them had been wiped out by disease by this time.

The name Blue Mountains was derived from the haze caused by the oil from the eucalyptus trees, or effects of light and weather. Lord Rayleigh was the first to investigate the phenomenon sometimes called "Rayleigh Scattering." The Blue Mountains National Park consists of 218,100 hectares (about 539,000 square acres), made mostly of sandstone deposited by rivers more than 250 million years ago. There are also layers of red and gray shale between the sandstone. At the deepest parts of the valleys are shale, fine sandstone, and black coal seams.

The train ride from Sydney to the Blue Mountains takes about two hours and costs about $6 U.S. I selected Blackheath, a small town of about 3,000 people, as my first destination, as it was a great jump-off point for the Australian Grand Canyon. Directly across the street from the train station was the Gardner Hotel, reportedly the oldest in the Blue Mountains at circa 1832. But just as there is more than one deepest canyon in Australia, there are also several Blue Mountains towns that boast the oldest hotel. No matter, I checked in and tossed my gear into my room. I was still carrying everything I had with me, which was a load and a half, the 9000 cubic inch pack and my daypack. The walk to the rim of Grose Valley, of which the Grand Canyon of Australia is a small part, was just forty-five minutes away, so I strolled over for an evening look-see from the rim.

The next morning I was back, with day pack, sunglasses, water, maps, and a wide brim hat. Down and down the trail went. It was steep, so steep in places that a railing had been installed. If one can see nose prints on steep climbs out of a canyon, the converse must be butt-cheek prints going down; I know I left a few.

This Grand Canyon was tree-covered with eucalypts, gum trees, mountain oak and ash. There were also incredible ferns, lush springs, creeks, falls and parrots and cockatoos chirping, trilling and squawking. It was like a Garden of Eden. The fauna included water dragons, bigger than lizards of our own southwest, Yabbies, which were orange, fresh water lobster looking things, and a lone goat with a chain around its neck. Moss and lichen were greener than green. There were also birds I had never seen: the lyrebirds and polot, the yellow-tailed black cockatoos, and a few king parrots. A steep climb and six hours later, I had hiked the Grand Canyon of Australia. I am not sure of the exact depth of this particular "deepest" canyon, but I do know I left a gallon of sweat on the trail.

On the walk back up I met a woman from the Bay Area named Susan. She told me about a small Buddhist Vinrah near the hotel, and invited me to attend. The service was attended by three monks, one in red, one in yellow, and one in orange, along with a third westerner, a woman from the Midwest with dreadlocks. The monks chanted for 20 minutes and meditated for another 40. I sat quietly and reflected on the lushness of the hike and the peaceful serenity of the small monastery. It left me with a serene feeling about this quest. The Grand Canyon of Oz is nothing like the Grand Canyon of the U.S., but I had already decided not to compare, and appreciated the time to reflect; it allowed me to remember this lesson, brought home while sitting quietly.

2. Kanangra Walls

It was probably good that I sat for an hour of silence, for the next day offered great challenges and danger! Not from hiking or even the snakes. Australians, like people everywhere, like to tell the scary animal stories; the only thing is, in Oz they can be true. There are more dangerous snakes and poisonous things in Australia than anywhere else according to two of my guidebooks, and some were said to be at Kanangra Walls - exactly where I was heading. Many snakes, feeling a hikers foot vibrations, will hide. Oz boasts snakes that chase you. There are also the funnelweb, redback and whitetail spiders whose bites are treated like snakebite. As for other insects, there are the infamous "mozzie" or mosquito and the outback fly. These bugs are the inspiration for the stories of people driven off the deep end. As for crocodiles, well I didn't expect to see any, nor the box jellyfish, but that didn't stop me from worrying. But this fear I speak of wasn't from any of the deadly critters, it was of … driving. I was going to rent a car and check out the Kanangra Walls, about a two-hour drive away and at least 1,000 meters deep. I called Katoomba, what I thought of as the "big city" of the Blue Mountains area. Thrifty Car Rental drove out, picked me up, returned me to Katoomba to sign papers, and gave me a driving lesson, including these valuable pointers: keep the line on the right side of the car, and always look twice. I took possession of the car and promptly drove on the wrong side of the road right into oncoming traffic. But I quickly corrected and headed for Kanangra Walls.

The scenery was of a ranch type, no crops but herds of cattle dotting the rolling green hills, with an occasional house and barn. The road was a nice two-lane blacktop, winding up, over, and around the hills and dales. I kept to my side of the road and the other drivers kept to theirs.

Arriving in Kanangra Walls was a bit anticlimactic. I was still sore from the six hours of hiking the day before, my thighs pleasantly aching. I had brought little water and only Tevas to walk in. I wasn't prepared to hike down, and in the back of my mind I knew this wasn't the deepest canyon, maybe 1000 meters, about 3,000 feet. I parked at the end of the road in the shade (it had to be close to 100 degrees) and walked a short way, first to the waterfall, and then an overlook. The view was a lush, green, verdant valley, thickly covered with trees. It sported a bit of a cliff on the edge of the rim. I could see the river gleaming in the sun far below me. I decided not to hike it, took the look and headed back.

Kanangra-Boyd is a national park with some interesting history. Early aborigines settled here and left axe-grinding grooves, campsites, and rock art. The first Europeans came in 1796 and 1802. Graziers, or cattle herders, brought their stock in the 1870s. Later, mining became part of the history and brought more people. As early as 1891, Kanangra Walls was recognized as a special area, to the extent that the Kanangra Tourist Resort was founded. An early bushwalker, Myles Dunphy, said, "It is beyond description the most interesting, wonderful, wild beautiful, weird place I ever saw."

Highlights of being in Kanangra were seeing, for my first time in the wild, kangaroos that were lying like big lumps by the side of the road and working on their tans. Upon returning to town, I found an e-mail from Richard Fisher. He essentially said, "If Mr. Jamison says that the Geehi Valley is the deepest, it is the deepest." That was good enough for me, but the next day I planned to hike down the Grose Valley, just to be sure.

3. Grose Valley

I would have gladly slept in, but by seven a.m. I knew I was awake, and so was the Grose Valley, so I figured I might as well do it in the cool of the morning. This is a bit confusing – the explanation is I was off to another section of the Grand Canyon of Australia in the Grose Valley, which has many side canyons. After going through my morning rituals, I grabbed a banana, some water, and my daypack and drove the eight kilometers to the starting point. The book *Walks in the Blue Mountains* by Neil Paton contains an interesting comment about this Grose Valley: "The Grose is not so familiar to the public at large and yet is probably more deserving of recognition than any other part of the Blue Mountains. It is quite arguable that, if Australia has a Grand Canyon, it is right outside Blackheath in the form of the Grose Valley."

There were at least three indicators that should have given me pause, but did not. Two came from the above guidebook, in which the author writes, " … it is one of the steeper tracks in the Blue Mountains," and, "I have not had the dubious honor of going uphill along this track, since I have always made it a point of avoiding it: it is not recommended, especially for backpackers."

The third was the sign I saw along the way, which said it was two kilometers to Grose Valley, but that it would take five hours to get there! Four kilometers round trip is less than three miles. Five hours? It must be steep! However the car was parked and I needed to redeem myself for only looking at Kanangra Walls yesterday, so I set off. The trail head seemed like a diving board. I walked to the edge of the canyon and jumped in.

It didn't take long before my big toes were bumping the front of my boots. They were screaming, barking, and whining to the point that I began debating with myself: If I hear the river does that count? If I make the effort does that count? I had driven to Kanangra Walls but this was different. I knew I had to get to the bottom for this one to count, so barking dogs and all, I kept on going. Later I dropped the daypack, hoping that losing its weight would help, and I think it did. About 15 minutes later I reached my destination. I touched a few of the Blue Gum trees for luck, stuck a finger in the water to test the temperature, and started back up.

The walk up was beautiful, and mercifully, easier on my toes, but still sweaty. I had missed much of it on the way down while trying to ignore the pain. The valley floor was thickly covered in duff, occasional startling purple or red flowers shining through succulent green, and pine trees with absurdly long needles. The birds made shrill, mysterious new sounds. I finally saw the yellow-tailed black cockatoo in the trees, black with white chest that was making the *wooo eeee* sound in the trees. I kept hearing bells, too, most likely from a goat or sheep.

I topped out of the Grose Valley three hours after starting down, leaving me to ponder, am I in better shape than the average hiker? More likely I was so obsessed with getting down and back that I took no time to stop and smell the roses, let alone dangle my sore toes in the cool stream.

After returning the car, I settled into another backpackers in Katoomba, the big city of the Blue Mountains with its 17,500 people and Art Deco atmosphere. That evening I went to an IMAX-like theater to watch a movie about the rediscovery of 40 Wollemi pine trees. The Wollemi pine trees were alive around the time of the dinosaurs. In my search for the deepest canyon in Australia I had talked with David Noble, one of the discoverers of the Wollemi pines hidden deep in a Blue Mountain valley off in some very hard to reach obscure valley, kept secret from the general public. I liked that I had made a connection in my research. I was looking for the deepest canyon and came across a man who had been part of discovering some of the oldest trees, or at least their distant relatives. The pine trees were in their heyday 100 million years ago, when people were the size of mice. There are now more of these trees growing in the laboratory than in the forest.

My time in the Blue Mountains was over. It was worth the time and effort. My adventure included three canyons, a car ride on the wrong side of the road to me, kangaroos, old hotels, and some of the oldest plants, although on screen. Next stop: Alice Springs.

Sydney Interlude

My next stop would be Alice Springs to visit Stanley Chasm, as well as Kings Canyon, but I had a few days before I was to leave. I found a backpackers in Sydney that had been a nunnery and which had more false stairs and doors than the Winchester House of Mystery in San Jose, California.

At this point a brief discussion is in order about "backpackers." In Australia, as well as the rest of the places I went, a "backpackers" is the same thing as the American version of a youth hostel. If you say "backpacker" to an American, we think of a person hiking, but if you say backpacker to a German, African, Chinese, or Australian, you are talking about a place to stay. They are generally low budget dormitory rooms with a shared kitchen, shower and bath down the hall. I usually got a private room, rarely en-suite, for about $20 to $30 U.S. a night. I found that backpackers were generally peopled by the friendly and diverse twenty- and thirty-something crowd. I stuck out like a sore thumb, age-wise. It brought me to an internal discussion of my own mortality, feeling sorry for myself as I watched all the young people parade by, healthy, hale, fit, full of life and energy. I suppose since I had been on the road for a month or so I was a bit lonely, but it was a fleeting thought. I was well tolerated.

Sydney, Australia's oldest and biggest city of four million people, was not my cup of tea, but I did manage to find my way around. The backpackers was located in the city center, surrounded by upscale shops Tino Lanz, Bulgari, Louis Vitto, Loeme of Madrid, Chanel, Gucci, Armani, Bally, Carte-Juaillers-1847 Paris-London-NY-Genona. Not bad company, but not affordable on my budget.

The Sydney streets were good for people-watching. The people wore everything, from short hair to dreads, wing tips to Tevas, tie-dyed to three piece suits. They were young and old, but very, very few overweight folks, which was the case throughout Australia.

I had one memorable encounter on this Sydney stopover. It was World Aids Day, and while walking to the Post Office I saw this very tall woman. When I got close, I realized this was a man dressed as a woman, and very well dressed, I might add. He was tall, with nice makeup, stylish hair, and high heels so high he was taller than my 6'6" self. He was soliciting donations for the World AIDS Day cause. Being the good liberal I am, I got out some money to contribute.

He said, "Thank you, and do you want my knickers?"

I stammered, "Um ah well er ah, no thanks that is okay."

He said, "No, no you really do!"

So I said, "Okay, I do."

He pulled out a red refrigerator magnet shaped like a pair of men's Jockey shorts, with "World Aids Day" printed on it, and said, "Put this on your icebox … and every time you put something in your mouth you will think of me."

I am sure my face gave away that I had been got. To this day, the magnet resides on my icebox at home.

My other major task on this Sydney stop was to mail home four boxes of stuff I was originally sure was critical for my survival during my round-the-world sojourn, including tent, ground cloth, stove, extra water bottles, winter clothes, summer clothes, mid-weight jacket, extra rain gear, extra flashlight, first aid kits; you name it, I had extra. This exercise lightened me up literally and figuratively. I was now down to one backpack and one day pack that would serve me very well the rest of the journey. I made a reservation for Alice Springs; I was ready for anything.

Alice Springs, Outback Red Center

It was a three-and-a-half hour flight from Sydney to Alice Springs, which looked flat, flat, flat and brown, white, orange, and splotchy, kind of like the desert wearing camouflage from 30,000 feet. As we neared Alice Springs, also known as the Red Center due to the extreme heat, it got greener and greener, which I found puzzling! I deplaned to a hot and windy day. As I exited the airport, I was hit with a blast of heat that felt like an oven set on 350. Add the glare, and I could tell this was not a place to mess around with; there were serious consequences for not being aware of the elements here.

Alice Springs started as a station for the Overland Telegraph Line and didn't have more than 200 people up into the1930s. The town is in the middle of Australia. I am tempted to say the middle of nowhere, but I like it too much to say anything mean-spirited about it. There are about 25,000 residents and some Americans on a military base in the vicinity.

I took a cab to the Alice Lodge, which I'd chosen from the myriad backpackers listed in the Lonely Planet Guide book because it did not boast a bar. I figured this might mean it would be a bit quieter, suitable for my fuddy-duddy life style. The Alice Lodge had four small trailers, and several dorm-type rooms, a shared kitchen space, and large bath/shower rooms, with picnic tables scattered under a welcome awning. My trailer had a double bed, table, chair, patio, and most important --- air conditioning.

The office walls were lined with brochures and photos of tours around the area, and I noted one that left in half an hour for Stanley Chasm. I called and made reservations, figuring I might as well get started. After waiting a half hour in the sun with no one showing up, I returned and called again to see what the deal was. You can imagine my surprise when I learned there is a 1½- hour time difference between Sydney and Alice Springs. One-hour difference I could fathom, but the extra half an hour was another example of Oz's quirkiness.

Keith, our guide, and the other passenger, a 73-year old retired architect from Japan, picked me up. We got the royal treatment. We stopped at a monument for Dr. John Flynn, the founder of the Flying Doctor program, and then proceeded towards the Stanley Chasm. The chasm was named for

Mrs. Stanley by the Aborigines, in recognition of her good work in the area. According to the guidebook, it was "gouged into tough sandstone by floods, over untold millions of years" and is a "deep red cleft crowned on either side by craggy slopes that rise 80 meters above the floor."

The Stanley Chasm certainly has its own beauty. It took 20 minutes to walk from the parking lot to the Chasm and back. It was okay, but that it was the deepest canyon in Australia, or even the deepest chasm, I found hard to believe. If I'd had a bit longer reach I could have stretched my arms from one side of the chasm to the other, and I could have thrown a rock to the top of the chasm if I had a good throwing arm. It is steep and narrow, that I will give it. They say that the sun only shines for fifteen minutes a day to light the bottom. I suppose the highlight was seeing wallabies in the parking lot and hearing flies buzzing with an echo that sounded like a didgeridoo. So much for the canyon the Sydney Library claimed was the deepest in Australia.

Back at the Alice Lodge it was time to choose between the multitudes of tour outfits for my visit to Kings Canyon. All the brochures featured a trip to Ayers Rock, or as the Aborigines call it: Uluru. Truth be told, they all were about $100 Australia per day, including transportation, lodging (tents), food, and guide. All I needed to bring, I was assured, was a toothbrush, towel, pillow, water bottle, flashlight and swimsuit. I ended up bringing a change of clothes, camera, sleeping bag, etc., and was glad I did. My itinerary involved a drive toward Ayers Rock, with a stop at a camel farm, sunset at Uluru, and camping in a tent. Day two, a visit to Ayers Rock at sunrise, a climb or circumnavigation of Ayers Rock, then Kings Creek for a camp-out. Day three to Kings Canyon and back to Alice Springs. My only hesitation with these tours was the fear of being tossed in with a group of twenty-something partiers, but I was also game to try it.

Our "Outback Tour" was to commence at 6:10 a.m.. At 6:15 the twenty-two-passenger bus, towing a trailer, picked me up and proceeded to gather up the rest of the flock, or "mub" (mob) as our driver/guide called us. He pointed out that Mob is from the Latin *mobile vulgus*, "rabble on the move."

My fear of the busload of twenty-something's was not to be. Our group consisted of one Russian, two Latvians, three French, one Argentinean, four

Italians, one Aussie, one Yank (me), two Swedes, three Brits, one Scot, and one Irish. We ranged in age from twenties to fifties. I was polite and did not ask the gray-haired woman her age: we were close. Our guide/driver, Bret, said he spoke "Strain" (AustSTRAINian), and if we didn't understand that, well too bad 'cause that was all he knew how to speak.'

The bus was almost comfortable. On one side were two seats while the opposite side had just one, so I camped on the single seat side so I could stretch my legs whenever we were moving. The air conditioning worked well, the tune box was adequate, and Bret kept us moving.

This trip was going to be, it seemed to me, one of super superlatives. Our first stop was Mt. Connor, 300 meters high and the second largest "table mountain" in the world. It was 30 kilometers around the base. I do not know if there is a difference between a "table mountain" and a "mesa," but it wasn't my worry, of which I had enough trying to figure out the differences between canyons, valleys and chasms. We all dutifully piled out and took the obligatory pictures, and burned our feet on the sand. It was over 100 degrees, Fahrenheit. By noon we got our first distant glimpse of Ayers Rock, or Uluru, and, as it turns out, the world's largest single rock monolith: six miles around, 310 meters tall, and 100 to 150 million years old.

We made a stop at the Olgas, an Aborigine sacred site, where it remained 38 degrees or 100 Fahrenheit, but mercifully we had a breeze. The Olgas are part of a trilogy, the Three Great Tors: Mt. Connor, Ayers Rock, and Mt Olga, survivors from the Cambrian age. The Aborigines call it "Kata tjuta," which means "many heads." I was definitely open to any magic that the site could offer, so I forged ahead and was rewarded with thirty seconds of alone time. The Olgas had a mystic sense despite the crowds. We were not the only tour group by a long shot, we had plenty of company. The magic was slowly reaching out to me when a couple from another tour showed up, loudly blew their noses, took a picture and left, and, soon after the hordes of my fellow travelers showed up. Similar experiences became a regular part of our group's tour, although we tried to beat other crowds with our early departures.

We also seemed to stop every few hours, thankfully, for a stretch, smoke break, water, and bathroom break. One such stop was a camel station.

Apparently, in the days before trains, camels were used for transport of goods. When the railroad was finally established, the camels, about 200,000 to 250,000, of them were turned loose, forming the world's largest herd of wild camels (back to those superlatives). They were now being exported to their original home in the Middle East. According to Bret, a camel's price could range, per camel, from $3,000 to $1,000,000, depending on the quality of the animal.

We re-boarded and headed off to watch the fabled sunset at Ayers Rock. We came to our campsite, pre set-up: twelve canvas tents, two cots inside each and a cooking and eating shelter. All the tour outfits had similar arrangements. Down the path were swimming pool, bathroom, and shower houses. We all grabbed our gear from the trailer and found a tent and tent-mate, threw our gear inside and then rushed off with the other 50 or so tour buses and groups to watch the sunset at Ayers Rock.

The postcards, pictures, and magazine photos I had seen displayed the vivid reds, oranges, and purples of the sunset on the rock. I have always been a sunset fan; you never can tell when you might see the Green Flash. When the sun finally set, I turned to look at the rock, and it, indeed showed a half-dozen or so different colors. When I got home, I had purple, orange, and red pictures of the rock, taken the same day and same place. But to be frank, it looked like a giant loaf of bread in the distance. As the reader knows by now I am very leery of being guilty of bad-vibing anyplace, and thereby provoking a superstitious karma kickback, and the next morning I knew I was going to either climb or circumnavigate it, maybe both, so I felt it best not to provoke the gods. We returned to camp, ate, and all pitched in to prepare and clean up after the meal. I was the only veggie and while I wouldn't give it an haute cuisine rating, I didn't go hungry or get sick.

The heat was still oppressive, so I dragged my sagging cot outside the heavy canvas tent in hopes of a breeze, which never really showed up. But the stars were outstanding. I finally decided the buzzing in my ears were not mossies (mosquitoes), just buzzing bugs. I flung a towel over my ears to try and reduce the bug noise and slept a fitful night until four a.m. when we were roused to watch the sunrise and climb or walk around Uluru.

Aboriginal law advises against climbing Uluru, though it wasn't disallowed. In the old days, people climbed it as it was thought to be a path of great spiritual significance. I opted for the walk around Uluru. I didn't need to climb the rock to get my spiritual fulfillment.

The morning sunrise was a bit better than the sunset over the rock. I circumnavigated the rock in the company of Ignacio, a student from Argentina, and the two Latvians: Inga, a doctor; and Solvita, a biochemist. The rock had its textures, fissures, and many signs placed by the Aborigines which read, "This is a sacred site, don't climb or take pictures." I couldn't get into the spirit of the place; it was too over-hyped for my taste, too many people. The sky was blue with nice puffy clouds and a pleasant morning breeze, but the spirit just didn't touch me, though I enjoyed the walk and the company.

The land, of course, has been Aboriginal forever. When white folks showed up, they built hotels and such right at the base of the rock. Recently, the land was returned to the local Aborigines, the Anangu, who now "re-own" the rock and area. They signed a 99-year lease with the government to run and operate the visitor industry. There is a governing body, with a board of directors with six Aboriginals and five whites, so the balance of power is with the traditional people. There was a complete and impressive cultural center, the Kata Tjuta Cultural Centre. If a person could take time, I sensed there was much local history to be learned, but we were on a timeline, and took off shortly after our visit began.

We returned to camp, ate lunch and then loaded up to head to Kings Canyon, our next day's destination. Our guide told us the Kings Canyon story. Forty-plus years ago a man named Coltier showed up in Alice Springs to be a mechanic, which he was for a bit, until he met the owner of Kings Canyon Station, or ranch (the average Australian ranch is about 3,000 square kilometers). He went out to the ranch to check it out, and apparently was so struck by its beauty that he proposed they become partners, with his role being to run the operation and build the road and buildings. And so a deal was struck. Coltier and his family went through hell to build the road and get ready for the first tourist season, which they assured all the booking agencies they would be ready for, and they were, by a day or so. Over time their hard work and the beauty of the area saw them succeed and grow. Before they knew it, thirty years and the lease had come and gone and the two original partners had passed on. It was assumed that all would continue for another thirty years. But the daughter of the original owner, an attorney, gave the "hired hands" thirty days notice to vacate. In the best bush tradition, a final bash to celebrate was scheduled. All of the guests were issued sledgehammers and the ranch and its thirty years of work were completely demolished. Finally it was bulldozed into a ditch. The owner showed up to discover nothing but a lone gas pump sticking up like a middle finger. She re-built, only to go bankrupt two months later because no one would work with her due to her treatment of her father's partner. She remains in Alice Springs, working on Aboriginal rights. The latest story is the Aborigines went on strike because she was too hard to work with. Meanwhile, the Coltier family bought a station nearby, and the family continues to work in the area.

I slept outside again the next evening, with not much better success, but we did get to sleep in until 4:30 a.m., before we were off to Kings Canyon. Kings Canyon is located in the Watarrka National Park. We arrived early, with only a few other tourists about. I headed off in the middle of our mub, but somehow I was the first person to reach the 300-foot-high canyon edge. We actually climbed up to the rim edge and took a circular route back to our starting point. I forged ahead and was lucky to spend most of the three hours there by myself, trying to absorb the spirit of the spot. I sat and cooled my feet in the "Garden of Eden," a permanent pool surrounded by palms, ferns, and a small flock of ducks. After refreshing my feet, I traipsed off to spend a solo half-hour at Kestrel Falls, not named for the birds themselves but rather what falls naturally from them. I sat and contemplated and watched the scene, the red canyon walls, blue sky, white and gray clouds, and the yellow of the acacia trees.

The group returned and we re-boarded and headed back to Alice Springs. Inside the bus, the twenty-two passengers were splayed out in various postures of repose, mostly sleeping. I reflected. Hanging out with twenty odd strangers was not burdensome after all, and I had seen some sights, gotten some private time, made a few friends. Truth be told, the outfitter, Sahara Outback Tours, did a very nice job: it had been fun.

Later, back in Alice Springs, I met up with Inga and Solvita for dinner. Inga ate a kebab of camel, crocodile, emu, and kangaroo, while Solvita had the rabbit. I stuck to a veggie burrito.

"The future is not a fate to be mastered, but a destiny to be embraced." My brother Mike sent that quote, which it seemed appropriate to ponder on, as I blithely or blindly or blatantly blundered ahead, trying to tick off each canyon. I was still trying to get another permit to visit the Yarlung Tsangpo, and the travel agent at the Pentoc sent me a possible itinerary. It looked good to me, but it was a nice reminder of how little control I had on the future or my fate, and to stop and smell the roses.

It was upon my return to Alice Springs, after our Ayers Rock et al. tour, that I learned of my friend Leonard Jackson's death. Leonard and I go back to 1985, when I started work at Ketchikan Youth Services in Ketchikan, Alaska. He was the youth drug and alcohol counselor, and he'd put us on the map, so to speak, as a credible agency. Later he was recognized as the Counselor of the Year for the State of Alaska, which was much deserved. Leonard had been on my mind. A few weeks earlier I had e-mailed my daughter, Amelia, and asked her to give him a call and say hello. Leonard is one of the few people I would call a friend, one of the few I ever confided in, and even rarer, one of the few the people whose advice I listened to. Saying he was one of the best doesn't cover it. Leonard was, and is, my friend, and I miss him. I am not good with the death and dying stuff, but I thought, if it was me who died, what would I want my friends to do? Live life, count each day as a blessing, and go for the gusto. Leonard did that and more; he left the places he'd been and the people he knew better than before. When Amelia was having some difficulties in her personal life, it was Leonard I talked with first. He reminded me that he had known Amelia since she was four years old, that she was a good person, not to give up on her, to hang in there, and she'd come around right. Leonard always wondered, aloud, how such a sweet, smart, attractive, bright, active child could come from the likes of her mom and especially her dad. One of his favorite expressions was calling nutty people "fruitcakes," which I picked up and still use. In fact, my journey to Alice Springs gave me a few opportunities to use that term.

Ordinarily, Alice Springs is the "Red Center," but due to the recent record-breaking rainfall, locals jokingly called it the Green Center. Alice Springs had so much rain that the road was actually cut off for three days due to flooding. I spent a few more days just hanging around Alice Springs, thinking about what to do next, and how. I also had my most interesting encounter with an Aborigine.

Aborigines – Thoughts * News * Who Knows

I was sitting outside the biggest backpacker in Alice Springs, which had more than 300 beds and my favorite e-mail station, enjoying the dry heat, catching some 100-degree rays, and waiting for the e-mail place to open, when my first and last interaction with an Aborigine occurred. Jimmy, thirty-something, I'd guess, wearing ragged, holy jeans, a torn t-shirt, no shoes, and with bad teeth, had two of his paintings to sell. I am certainly not a connoisseur of aboriginal art, but I know what I like and don't like. My knowledge of this art style is limited to peeking into a few of the galleries and cultural centers and shops. I have not really been taken with the style. I enjoy a didgeridoo, but had decided not to drag one around on this canyon quest.

Jimmy told me he had two kids to feed and the paintings were $50. I tried to explain I did not have the $50 for a painting (not true, but I didn't like either of them, and decided that we didn't know each other well enough for me to share that). We chatted a bit; he was a bit difficult for me to understand, as I must have been for him. He asked me where I was from. I told him the United States. He shrugged his shoulders and with a perfectly timed pause .... said, "Never heard of it." He made no more sales pitches and we chatted some more about our kids, and then he ended with a pleasant, "Oh well, have a Happy Christmas and a g'day mate." I wished him the same, and that was that.

With the limited contact I had, and mostly from distant observations, it was my sense that the Aborigines were not in a big hurry, unlike most of us non-Aborigines. We all live busy lives, go to meetings, take the kids to soccer, get to church, rush off to accelerate to the next stampede or buying frenzy, and then hurry up and wait. My sense was the Aborigines were on a different time continuum, and had learned that we are all going to get to the same place sooner or later; they didn't have the urge to acquire all the toys or to rush pell-mell after them.

I had been in Australia about two weeks, read the papers almost daily, and absorbed a half-dozen books about Australia. Occasionally, I overheard the odd white local or tour guide talk about the Aboriginal "situation." No one had been overtly racist, and most felt there were two types of Aboriginals: one was the stereotypical drunk, unemployed, lying under a shade tree, drug-using, unproductive, smelly, no good type person. The second was the hard working, sober, trying-to-assimilate Aborigine. Therein lies at least part of the crux. Aborigines are pastoral nomads, and have been for up to 40,000 years. They have been moving around forever, living off the land. I don't have a clue if the Aborigines sitting under the shade trees in the parks and river bottoms were stone drunks or just on holiday. Why should Aborigines, or anyone for that matter, have to conform to a nine-to-five? They, like the natives in many countries, were caught in the cultural bias or no-person's land, living in a dominant culture but having their own culture that could be traced back 40,000 years. I am sure there are whites that understand and accept the black culture, and Aborigines who understand and accept the white culture, but generally a strained relationship seems to exist, a sense of each tolerating the other, living and letting live, but with a kind of look-down-the-nose attitude by many white Australians. From the Aborigines, an attitude existed of, "Who are you to tell me how to live," all the way to, "How could you even begin to understand me?" But that is from the perspective of a Yankee who had been in country only a week or so.

I did hear and read that there was a drug problem. These issues, drugs, violence, sex abuse, run across cultures. True, the lines outside the bottle shops are 100 percent aborigine, and the angry shouts I hear up and down the street are from the aboriginals, but lord knows some of the white Aussies haven't had a beer can out of their hands in years.

The local newspapers were reporting on a ten-year process of a committee made up of blacks and whites, The Council for Aboriginal Reconstruction, which began in 1991. The committee was operating under the assumption that the Aboriginal had not gotten a fair shake. Over the ten-year period more and more Australians seemed to agree. One paper made the comparison to the U.S. Civil Rights movement, but said a greater percentage of Australians (500,000 out of 4,000,000 Sydneysiders) were involved and supportive.

There were two main sticking points: the government at that time, 2000, did not want to apologize for "The Stolen Children," aboriginal children who were removed from their homes and forced to live in boarding schools and foster homes between 1947 and 1972; two, the government doesn't want to sign a treaty, mostly because the politicians don't want to accept blame for the sins of their fathers. As I left Australia, these issues were still not resolved.

There are similarities between the situation of Alaska Natives and the Australian Aborigines. In both places, "mistakes" were made, that is certain. And in both places dialogue has begun, sometimes, seemingly unending dialogue. Suffice it to say that any solution will take time, dialogue, compromise, and action.

My next plans were coming together while I hung out in Alice Springs, e-mailing, sunning, and walking around trying to figure what to do next. I decided to fly to Canberra and make my way to the Snowy Mountains, my destiny being the Geehi Valley, Australia's deepest canyon and valley. My budget had long since been shot down, so I would try and be thrifty on my way to the Geehi Valley.

Geehi Valley (gee, like in gee whiz, and hi like in hello)
Canberra – Latvians – Hospitals - Mission Accomplished

I knew I wasn't in the outback any more, as if being in Canberra, the capital of Australia with its 300,000 residents and 12 million and counting trees weren't evidence enough. There were wide, leafy boulevards, high-rises, and many sidewalk cafés surrounding my backpackers hotel. While seeking an Internet café, I passed an "art theater" showing the movie *Himalaya*, which I later saw. I spent an hour in the core area "Civic" looking for Christmas gifts to mail home to Amelia and her mom. I finally found a souvenir store and bought a few aboriginal designed tee shirts, earrings, and a small wooden turtle and platypus.

My plan was to check with my Alice Spring friends, Inga and Solvita, who were planning to go to the Snowy Mountains and Thredbo, the village I was heading for. We met for a walk; they had friends, an older couple, one German and one Latvian, who had been in Australia for 20 plus years, and who were excited about showing off the Snowy Mountains, and yes, they had room for me. We agreed on a starting time, and said we'd meet at the museum the next morning.

At the National Gallery of Australia the next day I was reminded of my American, or perhaps just my own penchant to sometimes jump to conclusions, with the resulting fall that the jump precipitated. I was marching through a forest of 100 or so didgeridoos, figuring there must be some symbolism. They were taller than the didgeridoos I had seen and a bit wider also, and spread out as if in a forest. I walked through several times trying to figure out what they signified. I stopped to read the information. Oops! They were actually 200 hollow painted log coffins used by some of the Aboriginal groups to keep their deceased clan members. More perusing of the National Gallery of Australia, located in the old Parliament Building, turned up Picassos, Monets, and Rubins.

Over coffee in the morning I had been enjoying the Australian headlines. For example, under the headline, "Name ruled offensive, passport cancelled," there was this summary: "The Administration Appeal Tribunal upheld a decision to cancel a passport issued under the name Mr. Prime Minister John Piss The Family Court and Legal Aid. He was John Zabareth until 11 Nov 97 when he lodged an appeal but he is still the above name – Mr. Prime Minister John Piss the Family Court and Legal Aid on his driver's license, medicate card, Bank Key Card, and National Bank Visa Card."

At 7:55 a.m., Sigfried and Valdis, friends of Inga and Solvita, showed up. We loaded up our gear and headed for the Snowy Mountains, but we didn't get far. We stopped at Lake Jindabyne, an artificial lake that had flooded the original town, to take a rest and enjoy the view. When we pulled over, Solvita started throwing up blood, a whole bagfull. I am no doctor, my area of expertise being blisters, but while the four of them were talking in Latvian, I was kind of flapping around, thinking "Shit-o-dear! Throwing up blood is serious business." Inga however was a doctor, so I felt sure they were having the same conversation. We stuffed Solvita,(she was almost 6'3" tall, so not an easy task) back in the car and took her to the EMT in Jindabyne. They put her in the ambulance and took her to Cooma, where the hospital is. But Cooma, while having a population of almost 10,000 (and boasting of being the home of the Snowy Mountains Hydro-electric Scheme Information Center, which indirectly allowed me to get to the Geehi Valley), did not have a doctor on duty. One did arrive shortly however. We were told to come back in an hour or two while they checked Solvita out.

Meanwhile, Valdis related stories of his half-brother, long lost for 43 years. Apparently, Valdis' father's unit - fighting on the side of the Germans during WWII - was told to; hold an area against the allies against pretty steep odds. Somehow they did, but it was near the end of the war and his outfit was told to surrender. Valdis' father and a few others did not want to surrender, however, so they went into hiding in the local forests. For four years! They may have had some contact with American espionage, but got little help. They did get assistance from the farmers in the area who helped hide them. The dad fell in love with a farmer's daughter (he had divorced Valdis' mom) and a son was born. After four years, they were discovered, and he was sentenced to twenty-five years in Siberia. After ten years he was released, only skin and bones, and died four years later. Later, Valdis, living in Australia, was looking for relatives, not knowing he had a half- brother, when out of the blue he got an e-mail from his half brother living in Germany, who had found him. He journeyed to Australia for a great reunion.

After lunch we returned to the hospital and learned Solvita possibly had a stomach ulcer, would be getting a transfusion, and would be in the hospital for a few days. We spent time visiting and trying to cheer her up, and then decided we would complete our plan and go to Thredbo and find a place to stay. I found a guide as there were no rental cars to take me to Geehi Valley the next morning, and the others were going to take the ski lift up the mountain to hike around.

It was there in Thredbo, the evening before the trip to the Geehi Valley, within the Australian state of New South Wales, country of Australia, Southern

Hemisphere, planet earth, that at approximately 6 p.m. that I had my first taste of Vegemite, the quintessential Australian mysterious substance that all Australians seem to love. It is no doubt an acquired taste, for at approximately 6:00:001, same time, place, etc., I resolved that that would be the last time I would eat said Vegemite, forever.

The next morning at seven a.m. sharp, my guide David arrived and we headed for the Geehi Valley. We drove southwest around Kosciuszko, reportedly Australia's highest mountain at 6,000 feet or so. It is the west side of the valley wall of the Geehi Valley. On the way we stopped at one place with almost 100 kangaroos lying around like a herd of cattle.

David had been in the area quite a while; he was an avid skier and the Snowy Mountains, known as the Australian Alps, are one of the best areas to ski in Australia. He told me a little about the area in the early European days. The first white folks came in the 1800s to raise cattle, and by the mid 1800s "they really got fair dinkum with the cattle raisin'." In the summer they would take the cattle up to the mountains, and in winter bring them to the valley. It destroyed the original ecosystem, and in the 1950s the Australian government put an end to the practice.

We drove toward the Geehi Reservoir 6000 feet' Mt Kosciuszko came down to the 2000 foot Geehi dam and with a small hill opposite formed the valley, the deepest one in Australia. I stepped out of the new Ford Explorer with leather seats, tinted windows, and air conditioning, took a few pictures, looked around, got back in the car, and we headed back to Thredbo. It wasn't until we were almost back that I remembered that I forgot to get a rock.

Back in Thredbo I tackled, to my way of thinking, the most dangerous challenge of the day. I rode a ski lift, for the first time in my fifty-three years, up to where a two-mile hike in the Australian Alpine would take me to the peak of Mt. Kosciuszko. It was far more inspiring and beautiful than the valley I had just visited. There were patches of snow, great expanses of rocks strewn here and there, blue sky and clouds, and small, colorful wildflowers next to the creek running crisscross through the alpine area. I met my three companions and we headed back towards Thredbo, and then to Cooma to check on Solvita.

In Cooma we learned that Solvita had a stomach ulcer; the doctor gave her some adrenalin, and prescribed a few more days in the hospital. We did our best to raise her spirits and headed back to Canberra, my mission accomplished. The scenery was rolling green, with horses, cows, sheep and goats. Back in Canberra it was time to figure out what came next. What was next was Coober Pedy, according to the locals, said to be, "so hot you'll get sunburned through the car window even with number 75 SPF sun block on."

Coober Pedy
The Opal Capital of the World

One doesn't just show up in Coober Pedy by accident; one must want to get there. I suppose if you were driving from Alice Springs to Port Augusta or Adelaide and as you drove by, an overwhelming urge to mine opals came over you, you might wander off the bitumen (Aussie for road) to try your luck.

Coober Pedy is famous for its opal mines. The last hand mine was dug in the 1970s. Our bus driver from the airport told me that there were two ways to find opals: go outside, throw your hat in the air, and dig where it lands; or follow your dog, and wherever it takes a dump, dig there. He allowed as how the former was his preferred method as dogs seem to take their dumps on hard, rocky ground. It was my sense that he seemed to be talking from experience.

My own journey to Coober Pedy was semi-circular. Originally I was going to drive a rental camper van from Alice Springs to Sydney, $10 a day for seven days to deliver the camper, equipped with VCR, AC, tape player, etc., with a stop in Coober Pedy. But a suitable fan belt could not be found and would take more than a week to truck in. Alas, that plan didn't pan out. I flew from Canberra to Melbourne and then Adelaide, and then to the Columbia Dam (a gold, uranium, and copper mine with 4000 people, average age of twenty-seven), and then finally to Coober Pedy!

The flight was bouncy over flat brown/tan/white camouflaged country with an ocean of dry riverbeds. As we neared Coober Pedy, I started seeing hundreds, then thousands, of small white circles with black dots smack in their middles. As we lost altitude, it was apparent that these were mineshafts, dug straight down - hence the black, and the sand around them, the white. For some strange reason, the circles scattered randomly about reminded me of an Aboriginal painting gone wild. Aboriginal paintings have bazillions of dots, often forming shapes.

We bumped to a landing and were greeted by 100 degree temperature and a light breeze. I had been told by one advisor, when I mentioned I was going to Coober Pedy, "It is so hot there that you could fry the proverbial egg on the sidewalk, along with home fries and a cup of coffee, too."

My time in Coober Pedy was well spent. I wanted to visit it for its quirky reputation, the underground businesses, and of course, because I had not been there.

My residence while there was in the Radeka's Dugout Accommodation, a backpackers, thirty-four stairs down, cool, and, for the most part, quiet. I took a stroll down the five blocks or so of the main drag and noted the following underground businesses: The Opal Cave ("come browse underground"), Underground Dream House, Underground Accommodations, De Bro Underground, Desert Cave Hotel, Underground B & B, Underground Art Gallery, Fay's Underground House, Underground Café, and Underground Pottery. I wanted to believe there was also an underground drive-in theater, an underground gas station, and underground golf course.

If you were to drive through Coober Pedy, the only way you'd know about the underground is by the advertising signs or by taking a tour. I am not the only curious one. The 3,000 Coober Pedians host 100,000 visitors a year. With just four inches of annual rain, it is a bit dusty and dry, and looks like a burned out southwest American town. Several of the Mad Max movies, Priscilla, Queen of the Desert, and other films were shot in the town and local area.

My tour was called The Desert Breakaway Tour; we got to go fossicking -- or noodling -- the term for looking for opals, see some of the Dog Fence (world's longest fence), visit an opal mine, and drop in on the "infamous" Crocodile Harry and his underground home. When we got there, Harry was asleep on his bed. We walked on in, looked around, and walked out. The females were warned about Harry's agility and practice of trying to take a few liberties, but as noted, he was asleep, so we all got off without mishap or adventure.

There were about ten of us who jumped on the bus and took off on this guided tour with a nineteen-year resident as our guide and driver, and a most excellent guide she turned out to be. We learned there are 45 different nationalities represented in Coober Pedy, many coming after WWI and settling there. They had been used to digging foxholes and trenches, so when they came, mining became easier, as did living underground. Coober Pedy is the bastardization of the Aboriginal word for "white fella live underground." Potch (meaning common opal) Gully was a neighborhood of 300 underground houses. They have all the amenities of an above-ground house except for air conditioning. It costs about $17,000 Australian to dig a nice-sized three-bedroom underground house, which, with all the finishing touches, came to about $60,000 Australian, still cheaper than building and living above ground.

There are six underground churches in Coober Pedy, and we visited two of them. Both had very nice stained glass windows, letting light in from above to the congregation that would, I'd guess, feel a bit of the spiritual, given the light from above and the earth all around them. Or maybe they thought they were in a coffin. Anyhow it was cool, as in not hot.

We learned there were about 800 Aboriginals living in Coober Pedy. We also went fossicking. While I found one tiny rock, I will not be retiring anytime soon. We would run to our guide, showing her our finds, secretly hoping this was going to be the big one, the mother lode of opals. Other people had this dream come true. Millions of dollars had been dug out of the local mines. Our guide explained that just as there is gold fever, so there is opal fever. Once you've found a vein it is very hard to quit; the urge to look just once more, just one more pit, keeps a person going back.

The world's longest fence, when first completed, was about 6,000 miles long. Now it's about half that. It is not an ornamental fence, but is meant to keep the dingoes (wild dogs), on one side of the fence and the sheep on the other, and is aptly named the Dingo Fence, or dog fence. For all intents and purposes it has worked well. Dingoes, until they breed with a domestic dog, cannot jump.

I have to say, Coober Pedy touched me, and not only my funny bone; it was filled with mad characters, but also very friendly. The café owner and grocery clerk waved when I walked down the street, calling out "g'day" to me, and I liked, as well, the hot, outback, weird, wild, wonderfulness of this barren place. The barren sandy golf course had a 'keep off the grass' sign, and old cars had their trunks filled with dirt that became cactus gardens.

My flight back to Sydney was uneventful, save for what I perceived as a large cloud bank way in the distance, on the horizon, which, as we drew closer, turned out to be a state sized salt lake.

Surf Lesson

You can't stop the waves, but you can learn to surf.

Jon Kabat-Zinn

The first time I remember surfing was on a college Christmas road trip, 1967. It was forty-eight straight hours of driving from Ashland, Ohio, to L.A., with a good chunk of it on old Route 66, in a friend's sister's 1960's- era Austin Healy 3000. We were supposed to deliver it to her Laurel Canyon Blvd. house, near where it was rumored some of The Mamas and Papas lived. I smoked my first banana. It was said if you peeled some of the inner skin off and put it in the oven; you could then smoke it and get high, but that was years ago. Anyhow, my friend and I borrowed a surfboard and took it to the ocean. No one else was around; it was a flat gray winter day. We took turns taking the board out. I stood up on the board, only to have it sink straight down under my weight.

Thirty-four years later, I was going for my first lesson. Pines Surfing School, ("Quality surf education for all surfing levels") would instruct me. They had levels from one to nine, nine being for the "Elite surf training, visualization, priority surfing, obtaining and maintaining sponsorships, video analysis, speed surfing, controlled tube riding, preparing for competing abroad, achieving goals, high performance winning maneuvers, using psychological advantage, how to handle elite profile and keep an edge on surfing." At level one we would be taught "surf awareness, board handling and paddling, how to escape rips, ocean and beach knowledge, surfboard stance and coastal environmental protection." I was hoping for a pre-level one class. My instructor, Carman, a twenty-something female, tanned and not hard to look at, was my teacher.

Here is what I learned. Surfing takes strength, balance, and timing, much of which can be extrapolated as some of life's lessons. My instructor was patient; I guess I wasn't the worst student she ever had, but I had to be in the running.

First Carman explained how the waves were made, something about the angle of the beach, wind blowing the water, and the water having nowhere to go. Water going out, some of it coming in, at an angle, causes rips which give a very strong pull, sometimes life threatening. She said something about jellyfish, and something else about poison, and then something about stingrays, her voice muffled by the pounding surf, and then "they really don't bother people too much." Reassuring words, given that I'd missed all the gory stuff she must have been talking about.

Carman demonstrated the correct manner to lie on the board, and in one swift movement, jump to one's feet and ride the wave. I tried it. She told me I was goofy, a bit early to intuit that I am a disaster waiting to happen. But it meant that I preferred my left foot forward. I then graduated to the ocean, where I rapidly flunked. I was to lie down on the board and paddle out to sea. Just before a wave broke, I was to push up on my arms and let the sea slide between the board and me. Yeah, right. I could hardly balance long enough on the board to get one arm in the water before I fell off, let alone get in two strokes or a third. I fell off, again and again and again. Finally, Professor Carman decided that maybe we should try going toward the shore. Again the drill was to lie on the board and paddle, using a type of swimming stroke, right hand then left. I was so green I thought you used both arms at the same time, but was gently corrected.

I did manage to get a semblance of balance, only attained while paddling. Next, I was instructed to jump on the board, just as the wave was breaking. I was expertly parked by Carman and told to "Paddle, paddle, paddle!" Just as the wave crashed and that huge churning water reached me, I would lift up, get to my knees and then jump up into the goofy position and surf on in. Once, just before I hit the shore, I started pushing to my knees, but that was as far as I got with my first surfing lesson.

I got an inkling of how and why the phrase "perfect wave" originated. Indeed. In my one-hour surfing lesson, I at least felt the possibilities of the perfect wave. Later, at home and reading a magazine article on happiness, I came across what psychologists call "flow." It is, as noted earlier the "single minded focus of athletes and artists, scientists and writers, or anyone doing anything that poses a challenge and demands full attention. People in flow are too busy to think about happiness, but afterward they think of the experience as incredibly positive. And it's followed by well-earned contentment."

What did I learn? The way to get to be a surfer is practice, practice, practice. I recommend it heartily.

My time in Oz was running out. A newspaper article was taking Queen Elizabeth to task for apparently not quite speaking the Queen's English anymore. A speech professor had been analyzing her Christmas speeches for almost 40 years, and said she was starting to speak more like a commoner. If the Aussies were getting this stuffy, I figured I had better head on out.

I was in Australia from November 23 through December 27, just over a month's time. I did six out of the seven main Australian canyons I had learned about, although I never did sleep in any of them. I spent enough time in Sydney, Canberra, Alice Springs, Blue Mountains, Snowy Mountains, and Coober Pedy to feel like I had gotten to know them as places. On the whole, the Australians I met were friendly, helpful, warm, sincere, good folk. The ideal of "No Worries" is more than a catch phrase there, it is a practiced philosophy. All I can say is "good on "em." I left happy, and would find myself whistling at all kinds of odd moments, just happy to be there. Also, I didn't get eaten or bitten by snakes, jellyfish or sharks either.

Following is the account, by my friend Cara, of our time in Australia; she arrived six days before Christmas.

The Travel Partner Who Wasn't There

By Ms. Cara

It was Mark Twain, I believe, who said "There are three sides to any story – his, hers and the truth." This then is the second side to six days in Australia.

In October, 2000, I was living well above the Arctic Circle in Barrow, Alaska, on the edge of the Arctic Sea. I had arrived on August 1, when daylight still lasted 24 hours, and the children played outside at midnight. By mid-September it was too cold to walk one mile from my apartment to the school where I worked.

When I began receiving e-mails in September from my friend Jeff, who had undertaken a seven continent round-the-world journey, I enviously read his e-tales from Germany, Namibia, Greece and Tibet. He had tempted me with invitations ("Come join me") and compliments ("You'd be an awesome travel partner!"). At the time, I naively disregarded the thought that these solicitations might have been universally bestowed to other e-mail recipients.

Australia had never been high on my list of travel destinations. I had lived in San Diego for seven years while attending graduate school and during my initial teaching years. The warmth of southern hemisphere beaches was irrelevant then to someone living in southern California. But to someone just beginning to experience eight-plus months of the severe cold and darkness of an Arctic winter, Australia became a desirable destination to fantasize an escape to during the end of December. That, and the daily e-mails from my friend, enticed me to persevere and find a last minute ticket to Sydney during the busy holiday season. So I found myself arriving in Sydney, Australia (from Barrow, Alaska, by way of Anchorage, Seattle, and Honolulu) a few days before winter/summer solstice in December, 2000.

I had not traveled with Jeff before. Indeed we had only shared several lunch meetings when I had lived in Sitka, where I had met him six years earlier and then occasional dinners later when I lived in Juneau, and he might be passing through. I reasoned that we had seven years of friendship between us, as well as nearly three months of daily e-mail correspondence. The least I would enjoy would be a welcome hot weather escape with a friendly travel companion, with the further appeal of a few good Scrabble games. Beyond that, it was up to fate and/or our own choices.

I arrived in Sydney, where Jeff met me at the airport and adroitly maneuvered us to the train station, and onto the train to Wolloongong, a few hours south. There we stayed at the Novotel, with a balcony view of the sand and sea, and the sound of waves crashing all night – a most heavenly arrangement to one shortly arriving from a bleak, frozen moonscape. We spent a leisurely first two days as I adjusted; Jeff took his surf lesson, and the first of many-to-follow Scrabble games began.

The third day, we rented a car and drove through the rolling countryside to Minemurra Rainforest (and the Buddaroo National Park), where we took a short walk to a waterfall site. The sound effects were wonderful, with birds screeching and twittering in the leafy canopy. At one point, as we stood on the wooden walkway, Jeff quietly said, "Don't look now, but there's a large lizard behind you." Yeah, sure, I thought. But I turned around and he was right. A two-foot long lizard was sitting there, blinking and posing for pictures.

On the drive back to the Novotel we stopped at the largest Buddhist temple in the southern hemisphere -- Nan Tien Temple -- and wandered around the grounds and buildings. The weather was hot and sticky; what a contrast to a week before. We made a point of trying to return to Wolloongong in time to see the sunset on the ocean. But as we headed in that direction, it eventually dawned on us that the beach and ocean were not to the west, and we would need to drive up a nearby hill to see the sunset in the opposite direction. When you have lived much of your life near the West Coast of the U.S., you come to expect the sun to always set over the ocean, no matter which way the ocean might actually be.

Next day we took the train back to Sydney and changed trains to head west to Katoomba and the Blue Mountains, a pleasant enough touristy area.

The first night we stayed at Guerin Hotel, a cheap dive near the train station, which was very noisy, especially since our room was above the bar and band. A lumpy bed and scalding hot water in the shower down the hall completed the scene, one of those budget traveler's experiences.

During the afternoon we had walked out towards the end of town, past eucalyptus trees and occasional cockatoos, to see the cliffs and canyons. Along the way we passed by a hotel/restaurant overlooking the canyon, and inquired about dinner for the next night. It looked good and we made reservations. After the semi-sleepless night at the train station, we decided to splurge the second night and stay at the dinner place, which was Echoes Guesthouse, a former nurses' living quarters. It was a bit extravagant for budget travelers -- $185 each in Australian dollars for one night, with dinner and breakfast included. Was it worth it? To me, yes, yes! The Dawes room was a mini-suite. It had a huge bed with big fluffy pillows, a couch by the TV, private balcony, fluffy white robes and a dual-headed shower in the bathroom. There was also a private spa room with hot tub, sauna, and candles, which could be reserved, and we did.

After we settled in we walked to Echoes Point/Three Sisters lookout and over to the scenic railway, where we descended by railcar and hiked back up, past a trickle of a waterfall. Back at the Guesthouse, our dinner was followed by a game of Scrabble in the leather-couched lounge area upstairs. Jeff was losing at first and started to pout (which he now denies), but he won the game in the end. As we passed the receptionist in the lobby he gloated, "Guess who won?" and I countered, "Guess who let him?"

The next morning we had breakfast on the veranda with morning sun smiling on the Blue Mountains. Then we took the train back to Sydney, where we checked into the Albert Park Hotel. It was listed in the guidebook as "budget quality accommodations" but Jeff mentioned that it was really "quality budget accommodations." It was very hot and sticky in the city. I lounged while Jeff took a taxi to say goodbye to his Latvian friends, who he had met earlier in Australia. Afterwards, we took an Inner Harbour ferry ride past the Opera House and the Bridge, out to Mossman Bay. Sydney reminded me of a sunny Seattle vista. Mossman Bay was dotted with older, wooden houses with balconies and tasteful gingerbread situated on hillsides with steps going down to the boathouses and decks on the bay.

Just as I was getting used to the warmth of the country and the company, my six day winter escape to Australia came to an end the next day, as Jeff headed off to Tasmania and Antarctica, and I headed back north – way north, as far as you can go. Our final Scrabble score was 3 to 2, in Jeff's favor, but that was just the initial tournament. And how was it to travel with this friend? This "awesome travel partner?" All in all, it was not bad, quite fine and fun. For two "loners," we seemed to tolerate and enjoy each other's company quite well.

On the last night Jeff brought up the question "Okay, where do we go from here?" and we discussed meeting up again in Mexico (which didn't happen), and in Juneau, Alaska (which did), and the possibility of me spending time in Sitka the next summer (which also did happen). But these are all other tales to tell – or not.

In retrospect I think I was the only one of the "awesome travel partners" (other than his brother and daughter who traveled with him to Mexico) who accepted the invitation. Imagine, then, my surprise and dismay to find out a year later that when the Canyon Dance chronicles were written, Jeff had left out this six-day interlude. When I asked why, he replied, "I don't know what to say. If you write your account, I'll include it."

So I did, and now we'll see if he keeps his word.

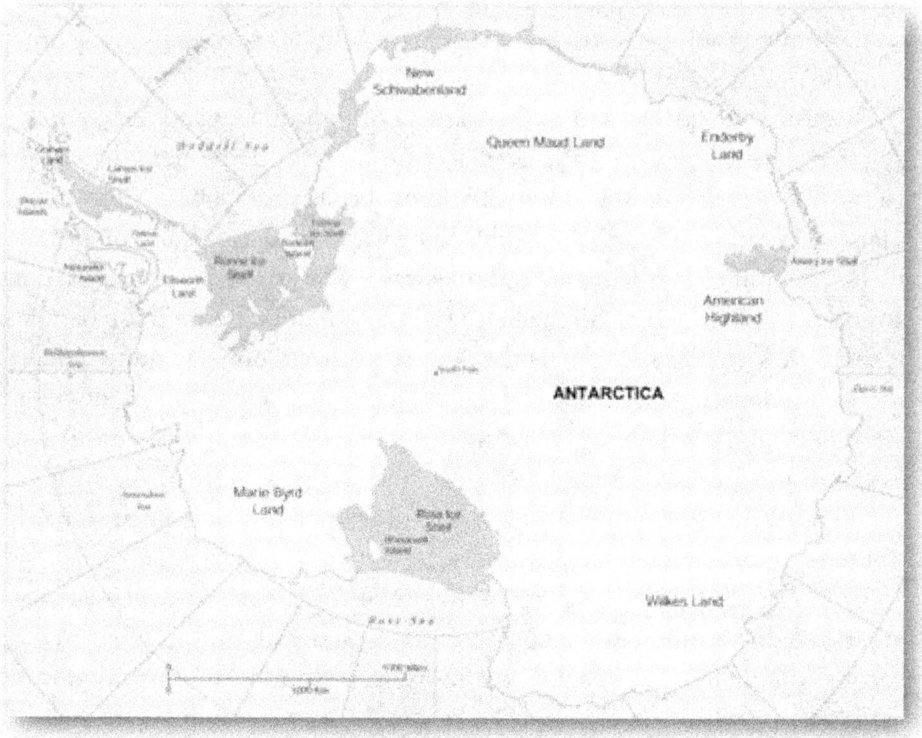
New
Schwabenland
Queen Maud Land
Enderby
Land
American
Highland
ANTARCTICA
Marie Byrd
Land
Wilkes Land

Five

Antarctica

"Love many, trust few, and paddle your own canoe."

From an anonymous 1850 poem, or an English or American Proverb

There were horror stories from the start. Before I left home, I had heard of passengers on cruises to Antarctica who were injured by the pitching and tossing of the ship. The day before the ship set off, I met two of the lecture staff from the *Kaptain Klebnikov*, Harry and Rob, both Kiwis, who got my blood pressure fired up with their stories. Both men had been on this ship and had sailed my destination. On a previous Antarctic cruise, our Russian icebreaker, the *Kaptain Klebnikov*, was turning starboard when a rogue swell caught the ship and really sent it for a pitch. Many passengers were injured, and it was quite the scene according to Harry and Rob. Later, my sister-in-law, An, confirmed the story. While on a cruise in China, she met a doctor who told her the Antarctica ship was met by ambulances, and all the booze in the bar had been used as painkillers!

Rob and Harry had other scary stories, too. A ship pitched so hard, it put a woman's head through a door. The lower part of the doors to the berths was made to break away in case of an emergency. If the ship fell over or was sinking, or the door became jammed, it would allow people to break through. They also mentioned disasters that could befall the entire ship, like whiteouts and being frozen into the ice. There was a true story going around about the Australian Antarctica ship, the *Polar Bird,* which had just returned after being stuck in the ice for two weeks. Harry told me about a ship that would not run forward, due to some engine room mishap, and could only go in reverse, three knots an hour for days on end! Our ship's bird expert told of the time when a huge wave rocked his ship just minutes before an elaborate Christmas meal, sending the entire meal to the deck and resulting in one broken arm.

So this canyon dance to get to the Dry Valleys, Antarctica's deepest canyon, had a resonance, a familiarity that added to my case of the buck-aggers (nerves), but was also slightly familiar, and thus in a strange way, sort of reassuring. All the canyons had their dangers: snakes, tigers, baboons, bandits, jellyfish, spiders, and salt-water crocs. Now I had wind, waves, swells, ice, cold, wild seas, and seasickness to envision.

Along with the new fears on my agenda, I was going through a bit of culture shock, again. I was coming from a typical Australian backpackers, with sparse room, worn carpet, bathroom down the hall, view of a brick wall out the window, and a superior sagging bed. On my way to Antarctica, I found myself in Hobart, Tasmania, in the Hotel Grande Chancellor, where Quark Expeditions, our outfitter for the Antarctica polar excursion, booked us for the night prior to embarkation. It was a four-and-a-half star hotel with an incredible view of the harbor, bathroom in the room, bar, TV, chair, bathrobe, the whole deal.

At the hotel I met my roommate, Gary, from the Bay Area, who worked for the San Francisco Bay Conservation Society, a mid-forties environmentalist with a great sense of humor. We had some free time, so we checked out the pier and met a few of the other travelers. Our walk along the pier brought us to other icebreakers in port, a veritable armada of ice ships. In the group were the *Aurora Australis* and *Polar Bird,* Australian ships: the *Italica* of the Italian Antarctic program: and the *Astrolabe,* a French polar ship.

After Harry and Rob's stories, I bought a variety of seasickness pills and gadgets, including an acupressure wristband, and naturopathic ginger pills, western medicine pills, and several other remedies touted to prevent seasickness. We saw a double rainbow, which I took to be a good omen for the upcoming journey. On the 28th of December, the local paper noted, "there were three days before the anniversary of the circumnavigation of St Basil the Great." With that and the rainbow, it was an auspicious time to leave. By eight p.m., we were rocking to twenty degrees!

We were 94 passengers on the *Kaptain Klebnikov*. I'd read it called "a block of flats on a barge," and thought of dubbing it the Kamp KK, as we were to be at sea for twenty-three days. Our crew consisted of eighty staff, Russians running the ship's bridge, helicopters, maintenance, engine room, and wait staff. The cooks, including the baker and pastry chef, were also Russian but were coordinated by a German. The Quark staffs, contracting with Russia for the ship, were almost all Aussies or Kiwis, with the Expedition Leader, Werner Stambach, a German. The passengers hailed from the USA, Finland, Switzerland, Australia, the United Kingdom, Tasmania, Israel, and Canada.

As we left port, I counted a crowd of thirty-one gathered to see us off. The crowd included eight Scottish bagpipers (Tasmanian police), who played a medley, including, "Its a Small World" and "Yankee Doodle." There were more passengers waving goodbye than folks to see us off. As the ropes were relaxed, the bagpipers piped, the sun peeked out from below the clouds, and we headed up the Derwent River for the open ocean.

We were given our one and only lifeboat and safety drill, which was well attended and done in a quick and professional manner, albeit a bit disconcerting. First, we all grabbed our life jackets and met at the muster point. Next, we tried to squeeze into the micro area that would be the staging area if the ship did call for us to abandon it. This gave me a flash of the pandemonium possible in the case of a real emergency. Later in the evening, we attended our first briefing and met the staff. It was also to be the beginning of numerous superlatives of which we were informed as we traveled toward our southerly goals.

<u>Superlative</u> - The Kaptain Klebnikov is the only ship ever to circumnavigate Antarctica, or as we would begin to call it, The Great White Continent.

Maybe not a superlative – The daily ship's newsletter we all received noted, "Please take great care of our rather delicate vacuum toilet system."

The staff certainly exuded enthusiasm and even love for the Great White Continent; it was most affecting. So, with wrist acupressure bracelets in place and seasickness pills swallowed, I went to bed knowing I was in good hands, looking forward to facing some big seas, more sunlight, and lots of things new to me. And, also wondering, would I get to this canyon? I remembered there were no guarantees of landing at the Dry Valleys: it was weather dependent, and that worry would dog me for days.

The next morning we were in the Southern Ocean. I had survived my first night at sea. By surviving, I mean I did not throw up; but I didn't get much sleep either. Our cabin on the eighth deck was about ten feet wide by fifteen feet long, with a small head which included a toilet, sink, and shower. The cabin had two bunks and a settee, which could be turned into a bed for a third person, a closet, and desk. There was space to hang gear and clothes near the door, and a lone porthole over the settee. The bunks were perpendicular to the fore and aft of the ship. The first night, I slid down my bed, every three or four seconds due to the pitch and yawl of the ship, bumping my head on the bulkhead. Then I would slide back to the railing at the bottom of the bunk as the ship rolled back the other way. Every three or four seconds. All night long. When the ship was level, I could see sky out of our porthole from my lower bunk. When we rolled or pitched starboard, I could see ocean. When the waves got wild, the entire porthole view would be water at a forty degree leaning. Every three or four seconds for two and a half days, I would clunk my head-- slide -- clunk my feet -- slide -- clunk my head -- slide -- clunk my feet, every three or four seconds! I ended up getting a sheet burn rash (which is like a rug burn) from all the sliding back and forth on the bed.

While it is true that I was worried about getting seasick, I was strangely unconcerned with the ability of the ship, even if it was a Russian ship. I harbored no Titanic anxieties, unlike some of my shipmates, even after our chilly mandatory lifeboat drill.

The ship was made by Finnish ship builders, for the Murmansk Shipping Company, a Russian business, and launched in 1981. Her purpose was to keep the northern Russian ports ice-free. She had six diesel engines that could put out 24,000 total horsepower. The real deal is the torque the diesels can provide, thanks to the electric generators which turn the three screws. The ship could go both forward and backward due to all this engine power. The front of the ship had two more feet of reinforced steel. She was 430 feet in length, 88 feet in breadth, 157 feet in height, and 12,000 tons.

When Russia collapsed in 1992, the Kaptain Klebnikov, along with other ships of its kind, went idle for lack of funds. The story I finally pieced together of how we tourists ended up on a Russian icebreaker in Antarctica went something like this: a long-time tour guide and Zodiac driver named Mike McDowell, without a penny to his name, thought, "Hey, those ships are just sitting there; why not take them to the Arctic and Antarctica with tourists?" He approached a wealthy businessman who had just sold a business and had two million dollars lying around. They put the money in a big, black suitcase and went courting the Russians. They figured their odds were slim to pull it off, but the potential rewards were also great. The suitcase and contents must have opened the right doors, because they came away with a deal. The Russians' idle ships were working again, with Russian crews making U.S. dollars. A win-win situation for both sides. Later, McDowell sold his share, but he had made his money and Quark had an excellent reputation for meeting client expectations and thensome, being a leader in eco tours, and for working with the Russians. Quark now has a five-year contract and I believe a few more ships, too. Rumor had it that McDowell bought a spot on the Russian space station ride home for two million dollars, and then sold it to a rich American businessman for twenty million. We were also told he had contracts with a Russian bathescope that they used to dive on the Titanic for a mere $75,000 a pop. We all missed meeting him and his family as they were on the previous tour.

To keep the passengers busy, the Quark folks presented a few lectures every day. The first was on The Heroic Age in Antarctica, 1893 through 1918, an overview of Scott, Shackleton, Amundson, and the rest of the explorers of that time. Another lecture was a video documentary, "Mysteries of Ocean Wonders," which was about the wandering albatross. As interesting as the lectures were, we were in the thirty-sixth hour of being on the Southern Ocean with a non-stop rock and roll, pitch, sway, plunge, buck and snort. I was starting to feel like I was in a wash cycle, or maybe in a blender on mix. But as we were to hear over and over, the 40 mph winds we were experiencing, and the 45-degree rolls (we had waves up to the sixth deck) were normal, so not to worry. My stomach did not feel normal.

Before I knew it, we had passed the forty-eight hour mark, and still, every three or four seconds, we were pitched hither and yon. I wasn't bored, but I had been forty-eight hours inside. It was deemed unsafe to walk outside, and to take a shower was too dangerous. Most of the other passengers missed my potential defining moment, when I commented to an almost empty room, "Tossed salad," as the huge bowl of salad was thrown off the counter. Even taking a pee was difficult, but the old hands continued to tell us this was normal. The Great White Continent was well worth all this bashing about, discomfort, locomotion, vomit, and queasy stomachs. We saw a wandering albatross fly by, a good sign that we were nearing Antarctica, according to the old hands.

Superlative – It has been estimated, that on average, 130 million cubic meters of water per second are continuously on the move in the Southern Ocean, four times that of the Gulf Stream, and 400 times that of the Mississippi.

Day three at sea, we were in what is called, without irony, the Furious Fifties. We still had forty-knot winds, and the portholes up on deck eight got sea spray flung at them. All this accounted for the constant roll to the port side, as my feet bumping the rail, two or so seconds passing, rolling to the starboard side and my head clunking the bulkhead, bump and clunk! Bump the feet, clunk the head, bump the feet, slide, chafe the skin, and clunk the head, literally ad nauseam for some of us. Later, I was to discover the trick of wearing Tevas while in bed to protect my feet from the bumping, and an extra pillow to protect my head from the clunking. Other passengers swore that sleeping on a damp towel or wearing clothes to bed slowed down the sliding a bit; getting duct taped to bed or Velcro PJ's worked for some. Werner, our expedition leader would say with his German accent, "Un hund for zee sheep and vun hund for zee self." In other words: Hold On! A couple of times after almost smashing into a bulkhead or other ships part, I saw the wisdom of his words. Our daily reminder put it this way: "Please remember to hold on to the handrails and don't leave swinging doors free."

<u>Superlative</u> - Antarctica is the largest wilderness in the world.

<u>Maybe not a superlative</u> - In 1822, a Captain Douglas had this to say about the Macquarie Island: "The most wretched place of involuntary and slavish exilium that can possibly be conceived; nothing could warrant any civilised creature living on such a spot."

<u>Another point of view</u> – "The Island is dreadfully dreary to the ordinary observer, but to the naturalist it is full of fascinating interest." JR Burton, 1900, Macquaraie Island.

I figured the weather was calming down a bit when, on the evening of the third full day, I saw faces I had never seen before. I had been lucky with just a queasy stomach, but some had gone to the doctor for seasickness shots!

I was learning to read the weather by gauging how the ship reacted. If the ship gave a little extra shudder and shimmy, I would anticipate a steep rock and roll. To be fair, by day three, I was getting my sea legs. The swells were not as extreme by then, nor was the pitching, thank goodness, because the next day was New Year's. We parked, or anchored, near Macquarie Island, our first destination. For the first time in years, I stayed up until midnight, and was rewarded with an international collection of people, Russians, Kiwis, Aussies, and Yankees, all of us watching Gennadiy Antokhin, the Russian second Captain, set off seven Chinese flares. A few oohs and aahs, and that was the Happy New Year celebration for me. The real revelers were in the ship's bar, and they took care of the rest of the festivities.

Day four brought an epiphany: while I like to spend like a sailor, I do not like to sail like one. A member of the crew told a story about a passenger whose goal was to visit a specific set of remote islands. He stayed in his cabin until they got to the island, went ashore, and then re-isolated himself back in his cabin. I could identify with this, as far as being goal-oriented. I was just pacing myself and rummaging through my brain for what good juju I knew of that would get us to the Dry Valleys. On the last trip, folks were weathered in at the Dry Valleys for a twenty-four hour period. I knew getting there was weather-dependent; I would need some strong magic. As the seas were calming a bit, we were again treated to a few lectures, the biology of whales of the polar oceans, a slide show about Antarctica, and a lecture on the branding and tagging of seals.

The next flurry of activity came when we were informed that, if we wished to have mail stamped from the Great White Continent, we had to get the mail into the mailbox by X time. Later we learned it would stay on the ship until we reached New Zealand because none of the stations we visited would take mail.

I'd started to feel pretty blasé, biding my time until we got to the Dry Valleys, but I decided, okay, I will play the game and go ashore to see the penguins. What's the big deal? We went down the gangway, waited for the swell to lift the Zodiac up, and, one at a time, eight of us hopped in and were driven to shore. There we experienced what they call a wet landing; that is, we would get out of the Zodiac, and wade through the water up to the beach to see the penguins, seals, sea lions and elephant seals. My first impression knocked me for a loop. In a half-football field-size area were 5,000 to 6,000 penguins, the taller Kings and the shorter Royals, jammed up and jelly tight, honking and squawking and doing their Charlie Chaplin waddle, feathers in the air like snowflakes in a flurry, penguin poop all over like a carpet, and the aroma filling the rest of the available space. Even the old hands were awed by the sheer numbers. The rule of viewing was to stay five yards from the birds, but if you wanted to sit down and wait, and they decided to come and check you out, that was fine. The birds, not afraid of people, would come up and stare right back.

The penguins stole the show, but the drowsy seals and elephant seals, burping, belching, and farting while lying in piles of two, three, four, five, or six, and more, right side up and upside down and sideways back-to-back, belly-to-belly, like a zombie jamboree were a sight, too, and could teach relaxation techniques to Bing Crosby.

We reboarded the ship and had two days until we got to the 60th degree latitude of the Southern Arctic Circle, and our first view of the Great White Continent. As the day ended, Werner came on the intercom and said, "Ve vish you a great even ink." The day had indeed, been great.

The next morning he woke us with what became a daily wake-up call, which went something like this: "Goot morn nink, itz 7:10 a.m., 10 minutes after 7. Dis isss your vake up call. I hope you have had a pleezant sweep and art wested." My roommate Gary could imitate Werner to a T, and it made for many an amusing time.

By day four we finally crossed the Antarctic Convergence. The Antarctic Convergence is a natural boundary between the warm sub-Antarctic surface water and the cold Antarctic surface water; in other words, the warm seas meet the colder seas. The water south of the convergence is often referred to as the Antarctic Ocean, about 13,500 square miles, or 10 percent of the world's oceans. Scientists claim this area governs the climate of the world.

The weather then began to get colder and foggier, and, mercifully the seas began to calm, but we still had 400 nautical miles to go. We had a briefing on helicopter procedures. We were divided into groups of six and reminded not to walk backwards once we got out of the helicopters, because we would only make that mistake once due to decapitation by the rear rotor blade. More lectures on ice, penguins, and history were presented for our edification, and to my surprise and delight, I enjoyed the lectures.

Superlative - Antarctica covers about 5.3 million square miles, an area larger than the United States and Mexico.

Superlative – The total weight of krill in the world's oceans is thought to weigh more than the whole human race. There are 85 kinds of krill of which 11 are found only in the Antarctic waters. The largest is two inches long.

In addition to enjoying the lectures I was also not having trouble skipping any kind of regular exercise, and in partaking of the three dessert opportunities each day at lunch, tea, and dinner. I think the first day or so we had tea there were actually little sandwiches, but after that it was always cookies, cake, and pie. Dinner, like lunch, had four courses: appetizer, soup, salad, choice of three main dishes (usually a vegetarian one among them), and, of course, dessert. So, while we had been battling seasickness, we also had to confront all the food available. There was an exercise room, with even a pool "it was empty", and a sauna "but it wasn't much", a few free weights and an exercise bike, and really that was my only criticism of the ship.

I have to say at this point that Antarctica had not yet cast a spell on me. I was liking things, but not going gaga like many of the others. I was focused on the mission -- getting to the Dry Valleys -- and pondering the rationale of twenty-three --plus days at sea, and $10,000 to get there.

Almost six days out, we finally hit the pack ice, which is not to be confused with fast ice, ice bergs, tabular forms, pinnacled berg, slushy bits, growlers, pan ice, bay ice, brash, frazil, or any of the other myriad types of ice that those in the know know. The pack ice is about one foot to two feet thick and is in all kinds of odd shapes. The ship just plows right through it, and this evokes exaltations much like those reserved for the Fourth of July fireworks.

Icebergs are something else. The *USS Glacier* saw a berg that measured 335 kilometers long by 97 kilometers wide, about the size of Belgium. Tabular bergs, like the one just mentioned, are huge pieces of floating ice shell. The ice breaks away from the shelf and can float around for years until it melts or reattaches to the ice shelf. Berg comes from the Scandinavian and Germanic languages and means mountain. But not all bergs are tabular; there are icebergs too. Icebergs are pieces of ice of any size, which have calved or broken off the ice sheet, ice shelves, or glaciers, and are floating in the sea.

<u>Superlative</u> – Antarctica is the coldest, windiest, and driest continent.

On January 17, 1783, Captain Cook was the first to cross over the Antarctica circle; we did it on January 3, 2001. This accomplishment was celebrated by hot wine on deck. Slowly, some kind of Antarctic magic was getting to me. Standing on the bow of the ship watching the Kaptain Klebnikov ram, bash, battle and smash the ice and bergs, brought the kind of thrill one gets when demolishing a building.

Then came Cape Adare. Out the portholes were 50,000 to 100,000 Adelie Penguins. The entire site boasted more than half a million! How do you describe 500,000 penguins in a rookery? It is a veritable clamorous celebration of life. The smell was pungent, a musty poop smell, but sort of refined. The sound, like a party favor that uncurls with a bleating sound, with a radio set to static on full amp in the background, multiplied by 500,000. The visual, black and white as far as the eye could see, 1,000 feet up the side of the hill. All over the place. The penguins filled camera lenses, wide angle or not.

Maybe penguins appeal to us because they are cute. It is easy to anthropomorphize penguins; they stand up straight, look like they are dressed for a formal dinner (one that would be fun to attend, given their antics), walk like Charlie Chaplin, have flippers where arms would be, and stand around in groups as if at a cocktail party. Apsley Cherry-Garrard had this to say about penguins in *The Worst Journey In The World*: "Whatever a penguin does has individuality, he lays bare his whole life for all to see. He cannot fly away. And because he is quaint in all that he does, but still more because he is fighting against bigger odds than any other bird, fighting always with the most gallant pluck, he comes to be considered as something apart from the ordinary bird - sometimes solemn, sometimes humorous, enterprising, chivalrous, cheeky – and always (unless you are driving a dog team) a welcome and, in some ways, an almost human friend." It was my thought that the penguins looked like they would enjoy being picked up, cuddled, and sung to.

<u>Superlative</u> – "Who would believe in penguins unless they had seen them?" Connor O'Brien

While walking amidst a half-million penguins was beneficial for my soul and attitude, what I also really liked was getting back to earth, feet on the ground. Six days at sea was a record for me; of course, every day was a new record. On shore, the penguins surfed up to the beach, stood up, and then waddled off at water's edge. But to watch them land on the edge of an iceberg that was two feet or more above the water line, that was the best show in town. The water was calm, except for the odd little bullet of penguin traveling about ten mph, exploding out of the water head-first like a jack-in-the-box or a cork out of a popgun, sailing through the air, as high as eight feet. Then, without so much as a look-around for applause – much deserved for that show of acrobatics -- they would land on their feet, look left, look right, shrug like it was no big deal, and start walking off with a very purposeful manner. It was close to seeing poetry in motion; their exit from the ocean to land combines speed, grace, acrobatics, balance and surprise, all rolled up into a twelve-to-sixteen inch ball of tuxedoed fire. Barnum and Bailey and Cirque du Soleil both come in a distant second to these little guys.

As I walked the beach with the penguins, I got caught up in the dancing forces of nature. The Great White Continent was a bewilderness. If I looked toward the sea, it was awesome, a distant scenery of ocean and white mountains. The problem was, which way ought I to look? 500,000 penguins, snow-covered mountains, or ocean?

Superlative – "I have often had the impression that, to penguins, man is just another penguin – different, less predictable, occasionally violent, but tolerable company when he sits still and minds his own business." Bernard Stonehouse in *Penguins*

We were now in the area where much of the "heroic era" of Antarctic exploration occurred, mainly by the British. The Ross Ice Shelf was named by James Clark Ross, who explored the area in 1841 and had this to say: "We might with equal chance of success try to sail through the cliffs of Dover, as to penetrate such a mass." Four of the thirty-four historic sites in the Ross Sea area have huts, which were used by the early explorers as bases for their expeditions. Two of them are at Cape Adare and were used for wintering on the continent; such was the case of the hut at Cape Adare, which Carsten Borchgrevink, a Norwegian, built in 1899 during the British Southern Cross expedition. In February of 1911, six members of Captain Robert Falcon Scott's Terra Nova expedition also used it while building their own hut. This was the Scott expedition that attempted to be first to reach the South Pole. They got to the South Pole only to discover that Roald Amundsen had beaten them. Scott and four others perished on their return from the pole.

Cherry-Garrard describes the hut they built in his book, *The Worst Journey In The World*: "The hut was a roomy place, 50 feet long, by 25 feet wide, and 9 feet at the eaves. The insulation, which was very satisfactory, was seaweed, sewn up in the form of a quilt. The sides have double (match) boarding inside and outside the frames, with a layer of our excellent quilted seaweed insulation between each pair of boardings. The roof as a single match-boarding inside, but on the outside is a match-boarding, then a layer of 2-ply ruberoid, then a layer of quilted seaweed, then a second match-boarding, and finally a cover of 3-ply ruberoid."

The hut was made of interlocking boards and had a double floor, and walls insulated with paper or felt. The supplies were still there, the cans and bottles with inscriptions, the doodles of the guys who wintered over, and even the smell of things rotting. In one of Scott's huts there are still marks made by his ponies pawing on the floor. The horse dookey still had a faint smell to it and there were improvised blubber stoves and blubber lamps.

All this was interesting, but I couldn't escape the feeling of too much humanity. I could handle a half-million penguins, but being with 90-plus human companions during this visit was a different story. I left after one hour. Maybe I wanted the scene to myself. Nassen, an early polar explorer, said, "Life has no meaning. There is nothing called meaning in Nature. Meaning is a purely human concept which we put into existence."

A piece of magic was catching my eye. While taking the Zodiac back to the ship, the blue of the ice began to work its spell. It was in the cracks of ice above water and just below. I was to spend the rest of the voyage trying to pin down the color, the neon aqua- blue coloration.

Superlative – Cape Adare is the world's largest nesting of Adelie penguins.

<u>Superlative</u> – 90% of the world's ice and 70% of the water in the world is in Antarctica and it only gets two inches of rain a year.

I liked that the sun was now up now up twenty-four hours a day, and I noticed some of my fuddy-duddyness leaving. I had enjoyed the day, the penguins, the scenery, the smashing of the ice, even the one-hour lesson at dinner with the Aussies attempting to explain Cricket, a game that begs for forgiveness from a Yankee point of view. And if I thought trying to understand cricket was tough, that afternoon, three New Zealanders we had picked up after three weeks at Cape Adare lectured us. They were comparing the mitochondrial deoxyribonucleic acid from living animals and from the bones of those long dead with samples from the same species from many different locations. Their findings indicated two genetically different Adelie populations, which are morphologically distinct. The rate of evolutionary development was also measured from analysis of the different ages of the deoxyribonucleic acid. Indeed.

In ship's parlance, you park on the ice, run the ship until it stops, and if done correctly and the ice is right, you can then say, "We are in the garage." They put the gangway down, and we got to walk on the ice the next day. Of course, we didn't just go tramping around. The staff went first, putting out flags to give us direction so we wouldn't get lost on the Great White Continent, with its white-on-white color scheme.

As I became more captivated by Antarctica, I sensed no artist could paint it, no photographer could capture it, and no poet or writer could describe its blue mystery, and its magic. Roald Amundsen, the first man to the South Pole, had a go at it: "Glittering white, shining blue, raven black, in the light of sun the land looks like a fairy tale. Pinnacle after pinnacle, peak after peak, crevassed, wild as any land on our globe, it lies, unseen and untrodden." Yes, some of the Antarctica magic was getting through to me, the endless undulation of the ocean, the immense and tiny, odd pieces of iceberg, the birds flying along with the ship, skimming the water, including South Polar Skuas, Snow Petrels, Antarctic Petrels, and the flightless Adelie Penguins. Other animals around included Weddell seals, dolphins, Orcas, Minke whales, and the seemingly countless penguins doing their own dance to the waves. And then there were the colors, the white on white on white, very subtle. The shadows and shapes kept things changing. The white was brilliant when the sun was shining, and it wove a dull gray pattern when it disappeared along with the cloud cover.

Superlative – Cape Royds has the most southern Adelie penguins in the world.

After eleven or twelve days at sea I was a bit antsy and apprehensive about getting to the Dry Valleys, but I also was starting to get into the rhythm of the ship: awaken, go to breakfast, walk the deck for half an hour or so to get a bit of exercise, attend a lecture, do some reading, eat lunch, take a walk around the deck again, attend a lecture, read, go to tea, maybe visit the bridge briefly to check on the Captain and crew, read, go to dinner, read, go to bed. Not too strenuous, so imagine my surprise when, within a twenty-four hour period, we visited Cape Royds -- a one mile walk there and back -- and the 4000 nesting pairs of Adelie Penguins, visited Shackleton's hut, and the Taylor Valley, the Dry Valley I was hoping for.

To start the day we helicoptered to Scott's 1911-13 Terra Nova hut, a cold and windy spot on Cape Evans. I had availed myself of the ship's library and so knew of the race between Scott and Amundsen to the South Pole from Shackleton's book *Endurance*. I learned that Amundsen was not afraid to put his hut near the Ross Ice Shelf. He didn't seem to be worried about the calving of the glacial ice, as Scott and Shackleton were. This gave him an advantage; he was 100 kilometers closer to getting to the South Pole. Also contributing to his victory were the sledges pulled by Greenland dogs, skis, and his meticulous planning. The cold, dry climate has helped preserve the huts, along with several restorations.

Next we went to McMurdo base via the ship's helicopter. McMurdo has the U.S. research station, including the National Science Foundation Headquarters, and the largest population on the Great White Continent with about 2,000 people, 600 of them support staff for scientific efforts. This trip included an opportunity to visit the research station and the historic hut, aptly named Hut Point. It, too, is part of the 'historic era,' and another reminder of the incredible conditions that those early explorers endured. We also got to climb Observation Hill. At the peak is a carved motto., *To seek, to strive, to find, and not to yield.*" It's a memorial to the five men from Captain Scott's expedition, who died during their return from the South Pole in 1912.

I joined a group at McMurdo and saw the aquarium, but in the building housing the ship's store (read souvenirs), I also espied the e-mail center. On the ship I could send e-mail for about $4.00 a message, but I could not get into my e-mail list, as the ship did not have the capabilities. Never expecting that, I did not bring a list of e-mail numbers and felt quite incommunicado after all the access I had in the previous countries I had visited. At the e-mail station I quickly hacked into the system -- thanks to the signage that explained how to access the mojo machine – and did my emailing. After my successful web time I rejoined our group for homemade chocolate chip cookies and coffee at the recreation hall. While relaxing, I picked up the McMurdo paper and enjoyed a quote from one of the service staff in building 155 who mused, "The floor is my canvas, the mop is my brush." After these tours we returned, via helicopter, to the Kaptain Klebnikov for our dinner.

And then abruptly I was standing at 77 degrees, 37 seconds, 163'336', which is the Taylor Valley, one of the Dry Valleys. It had already been a full day for staff, crew, and even passengers, what with McMurdo, Scott's hut, and all that, but at eight p.m, the weather was clear and Werner came on the horn and said, "Veer goink to the Why Walleys tonight." He then gave us an order to muster. I was in one of the last groups, but here it was, what I had spent all this money and time on the ship for, almost within reach.

The Taylor Valley itself was awesome in its own right, probably eighteen miles or so in length, three miles wide, glacier carved with each side about 2,000 to 3,000 feet in height. The Dry Valleys cover somewhere between 2,000 and 6,000 square miles, (which is less than two percent of the entire continent), almost all of which is without snow in an otherwise white color scheme. Features different from the other canyons included the walls. One side was gently sloping with round peaks, but the other side had jagged alpine peaks, and the Canadian Glacier, as well, for one of its walls. The shapes were wind-sculpted glacier moraine, a mosaic of a different sort than the other canyons I had visited so far. This was as lunar a place as I had ever seen. For the past thirty years, NASA has used the area for space landing training. In view were gray, black, tan, rocky, and rusty slate, rocks that were 500 million years old, the darker of them having come from deep within the earth's core at one time. The peaks were splotched with snow and almost lifeless.

Scientists don't like tourists tromping around in the valley because of the rare moss, lichens, and other tiny soil organisms, so valuable and precious are they that staff asked us to do our best to avoid stepping on them. We were asked to step on rocks so as to leave as few footprints as possible. However, the scientists were free to chainsaw the hell out of it all to study the "crypto-endolithic communities of lichens, fungi, and algae."

Robert Scott – the man who found the Dry Valleys – said, on his first trip to Antarctica in December of 1903: "It is certainly a valley of the dead: even the great glacier which once pushed through it has withered away."

So I got there, to the Dry Valleys. I was awestruck and relieved. But again, I felt strange, due to the lack of physical effort of the accomplishment. The canyons where I expended some sweat equity -- the Fish River Canyon, Vikos, and the Grand Canyon of Australia -- I liked because there was effort, physicality. The others, the Dry Valley and Yarlung Tsangpo, where I just showed up, spent the money and got lucky, or not, left me feeling as though something was missing from the experience.

I also discovered one of the reasons they are most likely called the "Dry Valleys." We came upon a mummified seal (there were rumors of others, but I only saw the one), and it certainly was dry. But the Dry Valleys are not completely dry, as there are rare mosses and lichens, and a small snow melt stream. Scott said the Dry Valleys display "all the indications of colossal ice action and considerable water action, and yet neither of these agents is now at work." Another source called the Dry Valleys a "miniature rainforest," because hidden in the grains of rocks are all those microbiological elements.

The Dry Valleys are also interesting to scientists because there they study global climate changes. Yes, the earth is warming, some scientist say, but others say Antarctica is the only continent that is cooling. Researchers fuel these debates from as far afield as the Polar Desert Research Center at Florida State University and the Pew Center for Climate Change in Arlington, Virginia.

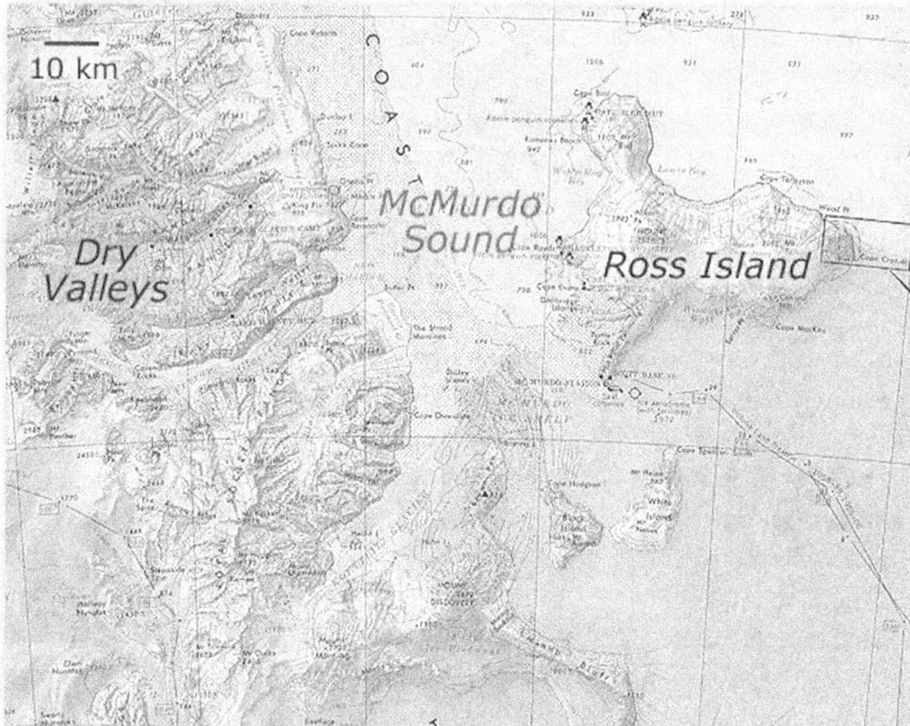

Tourists stomping around Antarctica are a legitimate issue of debate for the future. Presently there are about 500 visitors a year who get to where we were, the Ross Sea, and about 15,000 who reach the other side, the Peninsula, which is less expensive and easier to get to. The Antarctic Treaty, which has been signed by more than 50 nations, regulates, among other things, tourism in Antarctica. It's sort of an Environmental Protection Agency, if you will, for Antarctica. Any tour outfit that wishes to operate in Antarctica has to consider the questions: What do they plan to do? Will it cause "minor or transitory" impact? Quark, to their credit, had their permit reviewed by New Zealand and the United States. They even had a Kiwi observer from the New Zealand Department of Conservation on-board ship with us. We were not even allowed to tinkle or poop during any of the landings; think about that during a five-hour walk!

Tourism to the Great White Continent was first recorded in 1882; ships seeking to locate castaways or shipwrecked mariners would take paying customers to help offset the expenses. The 1970s really started the serious onslaught of visitors. Some felt visitors would see the beauty and go back and push for more preservation of Antarctica's animals, historic sites, and land. It is a double-edged sword. The more people, the more it can get loved to death. What Werner felt needed to happen for preservation follows:

a. Define where folks can and cannot go and enforce the rules.
b. Limit the number of people per site.
c. Set specific limits on impact in regards to the "minor transitory effects."
d. Send scientific observers with each ship (ours was Robb of the NZ Conservation Department).
e. Set specific times and dates of visits.
f. Restrict how close visitors can get to animals.
g. Manage the system consistently.
h. Have methods to check whether companies are in compliance.
i. Limit ships to 150 passengers.
j. Limit visits to only ships that have ice-strengthened hulls.

Superlative – Quark is the only tour outfit in the world allowed to go to the Dry Valleys; it is a specially protected area.

Something needs to be said about our Quark staff and their expertise. I wasn't singing Hallelujah because I got to the Dry Valleys so easily, but that doesn't diminish the efforts of our staff to pull off the trip. The weather can play havoc with travelers; the last tour group spent an extra twenty-four hours in the Dry Valleys due to the Katabolic Winds storming down the valley. While I took a short helicopter ride to the Dry Valley and pocketed my canyon, the staff was the unsung force allowing all of us to get there so easily. All I did was get in line, ride the helicopter, not get my head chopped off by the rotor as I got off, and walk a bit. And then … there I was, mission accomplished.

The staff, on the other hand, went into overdrive. They got 90 people aged ten to eighty-plus from the ship to the Dry Valleys and back via helicopter. But first they had to load the helicopters with about 1,000 pounds of safety gear, tents, sleeping bags, food, first aid supplies, radios, buckets of tools, whatever we would need to overnight on a windswept valley in Antarctica. Then they staked out the mile loop hike we were to stay on, put us back on the helicopters, making sure we didn't run our heads into the rotors, and flew us twenty minutes to the Dry Valleys, throwing in a great side trip up to the head of the valley and back to the glacier. Then we landed, and again the staff saw to it that we didn't decapitate ourselves, a feat that, I was told, at least one tourist would try to accomplish on every trip, without fail. They led us to the Dry Valley muster site, took our life vests, which we always wore on the helicopter, and which they used for counting purposes, and then took us on our tour of the Dry Valleys, with all the advance preparation that involved.

We were lucky to have, among our group, a PhD in Geology, Dr. Harry Keys, who used one of the three ways to say glacier. The Kiwis' pronounced it glass-see-er, the Aussies said glaze-sure, and we Yankees called it a glacier (glay-sure). However you say it, it was spectacular. While we were lucky to have Dr. Keys with us, I am not so sure how lucky he was to have us. Following are some of the questions he was asked: "Harry … is that glacier made of ice?" "Harry" … (for some reason we always paused before we began the question), "Harry … how old is that glacier?" "Harry … does a glacier move?" "Harry … is ice cold?" "Harry … how old were you when this glacier was formed?" "Harry … do glaciers freeze?" "Harry … is the B-12 glacier where we get our vitamins?" Harry was incredibly patient, and luckily for us, blessed with a sense of humor.

After our tour, we looked at the Canada Glacier from arm's length, avoided the precious lichens, skated on thin ice, saw the petrified seal … no, oops, I was corrected. It wasn't petrified, it was mummified. Petrified was how we felt flying in the Russian helicopters that shuttled us here and there. One theory held by staff was the "stupid theory," which held that some seals are so stupid that they take a wrong turn heading for the water, heading inland, and meet their doom that way. The Quark operation was smooth, professional, and relatively painless. To move the ninety individuals with grace, poise and patience was a skill and an art; their staff had it in aces.

So I got to the Dry Valleys, good on me! To my surprise, lots of staff, including the Russians and passengers, knew of my goal and patted me on the back, which was nice. Days later I still hadn't shaken the "it-was-too-easy" feeling, but hated to even contemplate not getting there.

Superlative –The B-15 iceberg is the world's largest iceberg. It takes six to eight hours to sail past, and is 90 miles wide and 20 miles long.

Superlative – During winter in Antarctica, ice mass increases by 11,000,000 square miles of frozen sea. The warm water of the Pacific, Indian, and Atlantic oceans meets the polar water at the Antarctica convergence, where billions of plankton and algae are released. These nutrients feed the krill (which are the world's largest) which in turn feed the 65 million penguins, 35 million seals and many other kinds of sea life, including the whales that hang out down there.

When the engine was running, standing on the rear deck, I swore the Russian crew was drumming on conga drums; such was the beat and rhythm. But no, it was the drumming of the diesel engines, with their electric turbines to help. Whatever the source of the drumming, it was definitely a danceable beat, as I proved whenever I boogied by on my circumnavigation of the ship. But when the ship's engines were off, it was nearly completely silent, the only sound being the lapping of water against the ship.

Really, what I was learning was how to slow down and accept that the journey was the destination, not vice versa. Ship's life was forcing me to accept it. I sure was not missing going to meetings, scheduling appointments, doing paper work. Those kinds of things had long ago slipped away. It was nice to realize that I didn't have any appointments. It wasn't as if I was being forced at gunpoint to have a good time; my goal was accomplished, but I'd decided that I would enjoy the rest of the journey.

One of the things I enjoyed was the onboard screening of the film, "*With Scott to the Antarctic - 90 Degrees South,*" a classic, filmed by Herbert Ponting, who was along on the expedition with Scott, and survived. One of our lecturers called Ponting a 'camera artist' rather than a photographer. Very true. It was a stunning film that vividly portrayed the hardships and beauty of the Great White Continent. I would posit that many of us who were watching were thinking, how would we have coped in those conditions, or could we have? A good question.

<u>Superlative</u> - Antarctica is the home of nature's harshest weather. No human groups have ever lived on this continent on a continuous basis (save some scientists), and the animals that live there feed from the sea.

<u>Superlative</u> – Weather and ice conditions were as unpredictable 100 years ago as they are today, presenting a constant challenge for every ship, even more so for small wooden boats.

Then we set the record! We set the record for the farthest south a ship has ever gone in Antarctica since the Historic Era, when Amundson got to 78 degrees in 1907. We were lucky; the B-15 glacier calved, migrating away from the coast and allowing our ship to slip in farther south than any ship had gone before. This was duly reported in the January 29, 2001, edition of *The Southland Times* of Invercargill, New Zealand: "The *Kaptain Klebnikov* … entered the history books last week [we had done this on January 11] when the Russian ice breaker ventured farther south than any other ship. The *Kaptain Klebnikov* had reached 78 degrees, 37 minutes south, 14.5 kilometers farther than the previous record set by Norwegian Roald Amundsen in 1911." We were about 682 miles from the South Pole!

<u>Superlative</u> – The iceberg designated B-15A is about 23 miles long and 54 miles wide. The C-16 iceberg is 11.5 miles long and 34 miles wide.

It took 90 years to break the most southern record. That was special for the passengers, and just to prove it, the staff wanted to lower the gangplank. They wanted to, but the ice was too mushy where the gangway would have gone, so we learned the fourth way to get off the ship, the first three being helicopter, gangway, and Zodiac. Now we found out about the CLO: the Caged Loading Operation, which actually had historic precedence. The Caged Loading Operation is a metal cage that lowers passengers to the ice, about elevator size, with a mesh wall, steel floor, and no roof. We were lowered to the ice, about eight at a time – then, so we wouldn't get lost or fall through a hole in the ice, ushered by our caretakers to a celebration of the historic accomplishment. This celebration included champagne, cookies, and the placing of flags representing the U.S.A. (Richard Byrd), Great Britain (Robert Scott and Ernest Shackleton), the U.S.S.R. (Petr Golikov, the captain of the *Kaptain Klebnikov* Captain), and Norway (Roald Amundsen), representing the four nations that have been to that point.

Later, an even better honor was bestowed, to my way of thinking, and I had a little bit more to do with it than just riding on a ship that got lucky with the weather. In this case, it was due to the calving of the B-15 iceberg. When the piece of glacier calved off, Dr. Harry Keys was mapping the new area, and asked for suggestions for names. While others contributed family member names, adding cash to sweeten the pot. I-- being a proud member of the Graceland Hiking Club -- suggested that Elvis Presley be recognized. Dr. Keys, accommodated my request by naming one of the fissures the Graceland Crack. To be fair I must report that a portion of the new area was also named Klebnikov Bight. The *Kaptain Klebnikov* is in good company with the King.

I was feeling my job of getting to the canyon was done. But it wasn't, not really. I still had a few loose ends to tie up, besides, of course, getting back. My task was to try to describe the blue that is a result of the combination of ice, the cracks in the ice, the depth and width of the cracks, and the water around them that result in a color to which I could not put a name. The shock of the blue that occurs in the ice cracks and just below the surface of the water; that exotic, near neon, pulsating, vibrant blue which mesmerized me. I stood on the bow of the deck as we cruised through the icebergs, mind and eyes glued to the ice and the blue, until a half hour or so later, my lips frozen, I came out of my reverie. I started a list: Electric neon blue, aqua blue, swimming pool blue, sky blue, sexy blue, sensual blue, the blue you see (if you see colors) when you climax, casting a magic spell blue, phantom blue, blue rapture, rhapsody in ice blue, blue ice blue, incandescent blue, breathtaking blue, wild beauty blue, impressive too blue, the blue color like no one is watching you dance blue, wow'd out blue, and blue beyond description. John Muir was also taken with ice and its color. In his 1879 *Travels in Alaska*, he wrote, "The whole front of the glacier is gashed and sculpted into a maze of shallow caves and crevasses, and a bewildering variety of novel architectural forms, clusters of glittering lance tipped spires, gables, and obelisks, hold out standing bastions and plain mural cliffs, adorned along the top with fretted cornice and battlement, while every gorge and crevasse, groove and hollow was filled with light, shimmering and throbbing in pale-blue tones of ineffable tenderness and beauty. The day was warm, and back on the broad melting bosom of the glacier … many streams were rejoicing, gurgling, ringing, singing, in frictionless channels worn down through the white disintegrated ice of the surface into the quick and living blue, in which they flowed with a grace of motion and flashing of light to be found only on the crystal hillocks and ravines of a glacier."

<u>Superlative</u> - In *Scott's Last Expedition,* he wrote, "… no art can reproduce such colours as the deep blue of the icebergs."

After two weeks I had come to another realization. Two weeks was a long time on a ship, and facing ten more days, well, I hoped I could do it. I was fine-tuning my routine now that the ship was more stable. Werner would still gently awaken us each morning, a little after seven a.m., "Goot morn ink, itz 7:05 a.m., five minutes after seven, vee vish you a goot morn ink. Breakfast iz be ink served." I would get up, do my business, take a thirty minute constitutional around the deck, getting a first-hand feel of the weather, checking to see if there were any new rust spots, and looking for birds and animals -- at sea or in the air – before heading down to breakfast. They did a nice job with the home-fried potatoes, which I am an expert at enjoying. They only served them three times while I was on the ship, but I always had hope. I would help myself to fruit, cereal, toast and juice and then our Russian servers, young women, mostly, and all pretty, would come and pour us cups of coffee. I would then pass the time chatting with my tablemates.

About nine o'clock, Werner would come back on and give us the day's schedule, even though each night a printed itinerary was slipped under our doors, with the same information, as well as a recap of the past day, and any additional news or changes. If there was no morning landing, then some lectures would generally be offered. The staff, which included several PhDs, were all informative and entertaining, and despite my nearly lifelong aversion to classroom settings, I learned a few things about Antarctica and enjoyed myself doing so. Several of the lectures I attended were about penguins, leopard seals, and Antarctic Art -- paintings and photographs by the sailors and visitors who had been there during the last 100 years or so.

Later I would find my way to the bridge to check our speed, direction, and progress, as well as sightsee from that vantage point. By then it would be lunchtime, so I'd head back down to a three- or four-course meal that included salad, soup, entrée, and dessert, all served by our capable but unattainable Russian waitresses. The wags among the ship were sure that they had been told, "Do not mess with the passengers!" They would hardly make eye contact with us, a disappointment to the more flirtatious among us. After being served and having the table cleared, it would be time for another walk around the deck. This would be followed by an afternoon lecture, landing or helicopter reconnaissance ride. I would then usually take a nap, read some, recheck the bridge, and chat some more with my shipmates. By four p.m., I had usually worked up an appetite for tea, which was really a second or third opportunity for dessert. That was followed by a bit more reading, writing in my journal, e-mailing, talking, or just gazing out the window. Before you knew it, it was dinner time. Again, everything was done for us. By the time we finished the dinner meal, our third dessert, talked a bit and finally waddled up to our rooms, the cabin steward had turned down our beds, placed a chocolate on our pillows, and cleaned up any mess we'd left behind. Then we'd go to sleep, so we could get up and do it all over again the next day.

We might not have been on one of those Holland America or Princess Line Love Boat luxury liners, but the only thing we passengers had to do was dress, feed ourselves, and bathe. Everything else was planned for us: when we ought to get up, and what to do. I understood the need for structure, but was surprised how easily some of the Type-A big shots got with the program. Every now and then I would rebel and not eat a dessert or attend a lecture. I showed 'em.

Time outside was enjoyable. They wouldn't let us outside if it was too rough, but when it was okay to go out and play, we'd go stand on the bow and watch as we plowed through and over the icebergs. It was a treat. The shapes formed by the ice breaking up were countless. Some of the ice ground beneath us, got pushed to the sides, while some just piled up on top of each other as we plowed our way through, leaving the crazy shapes and mysterious blue. If there was no ice to break, the horizon was still white, and the ocean was gray, black, or green. Sometimes we had huge icebergs for company, or just little bergy bits. Sometimes, as we nudged through, there would be a thin translucent sheet of ice that would push up onto another slab of transparent ice, leaving the effect of two pieces of frosted glass being passed over each other, with the ocean visible beneath the both of them. Now and then, a seal or penguin would be resting on the ice and would look up at our ship, and either go back to sleep or have a panic attack and rush for the water.

<u>Superlative</u> – At a lecture we were informed that the Quark trip had set a new record for the most lost camera lens caps found by staff on any previous trip.

The Great White Continent is Big Country with huge views. When it was clear, we could see to the horizon; other times it was ice 360 degrees to the horizon, with maybe a strip of blue to give a sense of color and scale towards the horizon, but otherwise it was BIG views for sure. The beauty was more accessible because there were few distractions. There were no trees, no rivers, no valleys, no hills, fields, or canyon walls, no fall foliage, no wildflowers, no cacti, no palm trees swaying, no grassy hills. This isn't a complaint, mind you. All that white, gray, and blue, ice and water, without anything else, made it apparent how big everything was. Ninety percent of the Great White Continent is snow and ice, and the bleakness, while huge in its expanse, leads the eye to the stark beauty and attractiveness, its "suchness" if you will, to use a Zen word I had picked up somewhere. Antarctica is the world's coldest, highest, windiest continent, and the forces of nature offer a vast and varied beauty, with all the sculptures made out of ice and snow and frozen water. It was like being in a gigantic outdoor art museum that focused on frozen water as the primary medium. Contemplating the powers of Mother Nature to fashion this art show was mind-boggling.

Speaking of water and ice and power, our ship weighed 12,000 tons, and when we ran into the ice, sometimes, even with all our power, the ice would have its way and shove us off course. So, navigating our way through the ice floes was no easy task. One might well wonder, then, how in God's name was I allowed to take the wheel, but I was. The answer is, it was easy. All I had to do was ask. I asked one of the captains, "Can I drive?" He repeated my question back to me -- "Can you drive?" -- looked me up and down, paused for effect, said, "Sure," and brought me over to the wheel, located in the center of the bridge. So there I was, nine stories up, sitting in the driver's seat, 200 lives in my inexperienced hands, tightly gripping the small, twelve inch diameter steering wheel of the *Kaptain Klebnikov*. There were icebergs to my port, icebergs to my starboard, and icebergs nearly dead ahead. I had sweat under my armpits: I could feel it dripping slowly, running down my body to pool up in the small of my back. My brow furrowed, my concentration totally focused. I wasn't outside slogging and pulling a sledge like Scott's men. I was driving the *Kaptain Klebnikov*, all 12,888 tons of it, and its 24,000 total horsepower, provided by six Wartsila diesels with electric generator adding extra torque, and a top speed of 15 knots. I was at the wheel, in the center of the bridge, sitting on a tall worn stool with a shorter step stool in front of me, with a leather-crisscrossed spot to rest one's feet upon, between the driver and the console. There were about thirty-five to forty feet to either side of the bridge, maybe twenty feet of space behind me, and the bow out the window, nine stories down. The bridge area was carpeted, and looked pretty clean to my eye. Except for the worn foot stool, everything seemed ship-shape. The bridge was totally surrounded by glass, except for the very back wall, where the stack ran to the top of the ship. On the far starboard and port sides were large, barbershop-type leather chairs with a box in front with levers for the engine speed on a large console, and a few lights indicating which engines were working. When it got really rough the pilots would be strapped into these seats. Behind the steering station ran a long table with charts, radar, all kinds of mysterious gauges, GPS, and lights, stuff for navigation, things a person like me, who was steering, didn't need to worry too much about.

In front of the steering wheel was a gyroscopic compass. On the outside edge it had 360 degrees of the compass points. Inside that area was another smaller instrument, showing just ten degrees. If the course was 345 degrees, the outside compass needle would need to be kept at 340 degrees. The inside line was for fine tuning to the exact degree, in this case, the five degrees to keep us on course. Of course, I was constantly checking to make sure we were still on 340 degrees on the outside ring. Below the two compasses in the same panel, was a small box with gray and red needles. The red needle pointed to where we wanted the rudder to be to gain our 345 degrees; the gray needle pointed to where the rudder actually was. After an explanation, I was seated and watched like a hawk by the officer. I guess I did okay. We didn't hit anything. I made no sharp swerves. After five minutes my brain started to seize up with the exertion of concentration, and my clothes were soaked through due to twitching nerves. I had to watch way in front of the ship, trying to pick out icebergs, while the color of the sky was gray steel and the water was gray slate. At times it was like looking through pouring, blowing sugar during a whiteout in a snowstorm. At the same time, I had to remember to look in front, to port, and to starboard, and to check the gyroscopic compass. The little gray and red arrow-like needles were constantly moving, causing me to keep readjusting the wheel. I just wanted to put it in overdrive and full steam it ahead.

After ten minutes I had had enough and requested to be relieved of my steering duty. Permission was, thankfully, granted. I don't know who was more relieved, me or the officer. Afterward, the captain took me to look astern at the wake. I saw a long, gentle arc glittering through the blowing ice crystals. This was the visual proof of my ship-driving abilities; how straight was the trail I had left behind? The captain said, "Good job." I swelled with pride, sported a shit-eating grin, and left to take a shower. After my stint driving the ship, all the other passengers were jealous, but apparently not enough to ask to drive, except for a ten-year-old boy who stayed at the wheel for more than an hour.

This experience brought another insight. Earlier, when I was questioned by the captain about my driving ability, he said he knew I could ride a bike because he knew I had a tourist bike business. I had only told a few passengers about my business, yet somehow, within two weeks the Russians knew everything. Apparently, we passengers were quite a source of entertainment for them, where we were from, how much money we had, what we did, and our habits. They cleaned up after us and literally did our dirty laundry, and then aired it out for all of them to see. No wonder the wait staff sometimes seemed to be looking at us with private smirks.

<u>Superlative</u> –Scott Island, which we passed, is one of the most remote of the peri-Antarctic islands. Since its discovery on December 25, 1902, until today, there have been only six recorded landings.

The crew moved the Zodiacs from the front deck to the rear, where they stored them for bad weather, a sure sign that we were going to be in for it soon. We were heading northwest, back into the Southern Ocean. Like Pavlov's dog, we knew what to expect. We had been conditioned to expect the rock and roll over the bounding waves. We were advised to secure all our belongings in our rooms. That meant putting away books that were lying around on a desk, glasses from past drinking adventures, toothbrushes, binoculars, anything that could be flung by a sudden movement. Oh yes, and commence seasickness pill-taking at once. Vomit bags came out, with "vomit" in four languages: "Sickness bags" for us English readers, "Spuckbentol" for the Germans; "Sacchettovomiti" for the French, and 'Sac Vomitovia" for the Italians. Fifty mph headwinds came with spray breaking up to the seventh deck. No one was allowed on the bridge or outside. We were old hands at this, but then, we had also had almost two weeks of a break from the old stuff.

I was approaching my 54th birthday, and used that as an excuse to think about the voyage so far. As I mused, I recalled an interest and aptitude test

I took in college in 1967, which said my number one interest was to be a youth worker for YMCAs and youth agencies, which I did for almost 28 years. My number two interest/aptitude, it said, was to be a ship's captain. Go figure.

We stopped at Campbell Island and took a stroll. The sea lions were still about, as were the albatross. The teenage sea lions don't get to mate, and were a bit feisty. We had walked about two-thirds of the way in low grass, where it is easy to see the sea lions, and where if they decided to charge us, we'd have plenty of warning. If we were charged, the drill was, to stand our ground, put our arms up, and look big. This is close to what we practice on Baranof Island, where I live in Alaska. We have anywhere from 1,200 to 4,000 Alaska brown bears on the island, (depending on which bear expert you talk to) for our 4,700 square miles. In other words, we have lots of bears. Conventional wisdom says, do not run, put your arms up, try to look big, and stand next to someone. Here, in the short grass of Campbell Island, we could avoid the sea lions by taking a wide detour, until we came to the tall grass, where it was the same drill, only now we couldn't see the sea lions until we had just about stepped on them. Our defensive strategy was to have a guide in front with a red flag on a five-foot marker pole. This was used to ward off the charging teenage sea lions, kind of like sword fighting. At one point, I looked up, and Robb, the Kiwi observer, was holding a teen sea lion at bay with a banana pointed like a pistol. We made the last half-mile having fended off several charges by the creatures, with no casualties. In the past, some of the tours had not been so lucky. Robb told a story of one tour, during which he was fending off a sea lion only to look up and see a half dozen Quark folks being chased, all running in different directions. He hinted that someone did get bit on the butt, but it may have just been his Kiwi humor.

<u>Superlative</u> – Later in the day folks were taken on the best Zodiac ride of the trip, according to Werner, who said it was the best tour he had seen in his twenty years on the Great White Continent, for wildlife viewing.

<u>Not so superlative</u> – I stayed on the ship.

While all this was going on and we kept steaming towards New Zealand and the end of the journey, Dr. Bob Hedland, a British historian who was on board with us, had developed and passed out a test. Depending how well we did on it, it could earn us one of the following degrees from the University of the Antarctica: PhD, Master of Philosophy, BA-Distinguished, BA – pass, fail, and MTV (Must Repeat the Voyage). There were eighty questions; the highest score was seventy-four, the lowest thirty-one. Of the ninety- plus passengers, twenty-six took it. I was one of them, and that is enough about my score. As Dr. Bob explained, some who took the test were "exceedingly serious," which aroused a chorus of boos. And then there were others who, "did not take the test seriously." Cheers. On the exam it was noted: "Be aware of possible idiosyncrasies, dubious humor, some subtleties, and a degree of cunning, and a little persnikityness." Here are some of the questions, along with a few of the answers that were reported:

> Q. How many letters in the Russian language? A. Only three I can recognize and one was back to front.
> Q. What is the green flash? A. A glimpse of American money.
> Q. Why are icebergs blue? A. Seasonal affect disorder.
> Q. Where are the most meteorites found? A. Antarctica. As an aside, the Japanese research station finds the most because they are in the rockiest area; in the snow they disappear. The real meteorites are called Meteorights, and the false ones meteorwrongs.

Superlative – "Strange: there is always sadness on departure. It is as if I cannot after all bear to leave this bleak waste of ice, glaciers, cold and toil." Fridtjof Nansen

Then it was over. On the 20th of January, 2001, at ten a.m., we were all back on good old terra firma in Bluff, New Zealand. We had been instructed to pack the night before, and to be ready to disembark early in the morning, but it didn't seem like we were really at the end of the trip. The last few hours, people gathered in the lounge, sat and read, stared into space. A feeling of bitter sweetness hung in the air. We told each other, and ourselves, that we would stay in touch, swapped addresses, both physical and email. Then about twenty-five of us got on a bus with our luggage and were driven to Invercargill. We were on our own, no more of someone telling us what time to do everything, where to be and what was going to happen next. The most startling thing was seeing new faces, which was also nice.

<u>Superlative</u> – Our captain said this journey had the most difficult ice conditions he had seen since he first came to Antarctica in 1992.

<u>Maybe not a Superlative</u> – The last movie shown on the cruise was *The Perfect Storm.*

<u>Superlative</u> – "I have been there, I have seen it, and I would go again. It is like a little heaven below." Sir Vivien Fuch's telegram to the British bases on his retirement from the British Antarctic Survey.

I was lucky. To visit Antarctica was a major treat. My goal of getting to the Dry Valleys, another deepest canyon, again just went to prove that the journey is in fact the destination. John Steinbeck wrote, "A journey is a person in itself; no two are alike. And all plans, safeguards, policies and coercion are fruitless. We find after years of struggle that we do not take a trip; a trip takes us." The people on this journey made for a large part of my enjoyment. The cost still stuck in my craw, but if I didn't have Quark to run the trip I would have paid between $150,000 and 300,000. Well, I could not have, but if I had the resources I could.

I knew Peru and its canyons would not be a pushover; it was time for a short pause in Hawaii with my brother, Mike, and sister-in-law, An, for a few days of sunset, balmy weather, kayaking, yoga, food, music, and family.

As it turned out my time in Hawaii with Mike and An would be the next-to-last time I would spend with An. She passed away a few months after I returned from the journey. During my Pacific Crest Trail hike it was she who sent my re-supply boxes along, often with an extra $10 or tub of honey. I will always recall the times with her in Hawaii, getting up early for a brisk walk, followed by some yoga on the beach, returning home for breakfast and coffee and a marathon crossword puzzle. The only rule An had was Be Home For Sunset. Not a bad rule. As Tom Hanks said, "Only a fool would squander the rich opportunities life affords us." An was not a squanderer.

Nvdo. MISMI
CONDOROMA
SIBAYO
VALLE DEL COLCA
CABANACONDE
CHIVAY
Nvdo. CHUCURA
Nvdo. AMPATO
VIZCACHANI
RESERVA NACIONAL DE SALINAS Y AGUADA BLANCA
Nvdo. CHACHANI
YURA
VOLCAN MISTI
RIO CHILI
PANAMERICANA
AREQUIPA
Nvdo. PICHU PICHU

Six

Peru
South America: Canon Del Colca & Canon del Cotahuasi

"Maybe we should stop searching for the meaning of life and enjoy the mystery instead"

Lilly Tomlin

I'd gotten soft, no doubt about it. Three weeks on a ship, followed by a week in Hawaii, then a few more days at my brother's Monrovia, California, house while waiting to go to Peru. I was rested, that was true, and while travel can be exhausting, I was in no shape for any serious hiking. The break also allowed time for my concerns, those old tests of the spirit that Colin Fletcher talks about to rise up again. They were familiar: language difficulties, questions of whether I would make it to the canyon and down, how would the transportation get worked out and what about the food? Would I remain lucky and not get sick? Would there be bottled water and how easy would it be to get? Could I stay within a reasonable budget? And, of course, there were bandits and wild animals. The guidebook mentioned pickpockets and muggers, as did the Lan Chile airline representative when I spoke to her. She asked where I was going to stay when I arrived. I said I would figure it out once I got there, but she would not have any of that. It was unsafe and not smart to arrive in Lima at midnight without a place to go, so she gave me some numbers to call. That seemed above and beyond the call of duty, but it smoothed my entrance into Peru, that is for sure.

Somehow I slipped through the eight million Lima residents, and was picked up, in person, by one of the owners of the Hotel Melodia, located on Ave. La Marine. I had a very nice room, woke up in the morning, and was transported back to the airport, where I flew off to Arequipa. Arequipa, in southern Peru, was my jumping-off spot; with a population of 700,000, it was easier for me to negotiate my way around than Lima. At the Arequipa Airport I again experienced my luggage beating me to the luggage pick-up area, and it was just inside the door. Leaving the airport, I noted that the bushes were trimmed into odd Disney-like figures that led into a palm tree-lined avenue, passing through what reminded me of a Tibetan landscape: brown, dusty scattered mud buildings on narrow, cobbled streets. Soon we passed into an area of Spanish architecture, two-story buildings with small wrought iron balconies overlooking the street, and Catholic churches with their square courtyards and promenading couples; yes, I was in South America.

Arequipa is almost 7,000 feet above sea level, and is surrounded by mountains and deserts. It is just off the Panamericana Highway, which goes from the coast up into the Andes highlands. This is not to be confused with the Pan American Highway, which runs to the tip of South America. Arequipa stakes claim to being the second largest city in Peru, but has to compete with Trujillo, which makes the same claim. The surrounding area has El Misti, an active volcano of 15,000 feet. Nearby are the taller peaks, Chachani and Pichu Pichu, all making for a beautiful sight on a clear day. I took a few strolls around the main plaza in town, the Plaza de Armas, and several times spotted these mountains, although, truth be told, I wasn't completely sure which was which. I was also not always sure where I was. The town was laid out in the fashion of smaller places, with the main square and church located in the center, and everything else spreading out from there. The streets weren't exactly checkerboard, but pretty close, and I had a map; nevertheless I did get lost now and then.

I found a nice place to stay, courtesy of the guidebook. The Hotel Miamaka was middle range, clean and quiet, and just a few blocks from the square. That is, it was quiet until the festival celebrating one of the virgins got started, about midnight to 5 a.m. I'd swear they were setting off the fireworks from on top of the Hotel Miamaka.

My job was then to figure out the logistics of the two canyons vying for the title of deepest South American canyon. The *Lonely Planet* said Colca Canyon claimed the title, but their book also said Cotahuasi (coat-uh-wha-see) claimed to be the deepest, and not just in South America but in the whole world! What to do? Why, visit them both.

As I walked around town looking for internet cafes and a guide or outfitter, I was struck by three things: hardly anyone was smoking cigarettes, speaking on a cell phone, or wearing baseball caps, forward or backwards. Once again, I turned to the guidebook for advice and found an outfitter. On the way to the outfitters, I waited in line at what I thought was the post office, but what turned out to be a bank. I was embarrassed after a twenty-minute wait in line, but the kind bankers took me by the hand and led me to the real post office.

I kept walking and came upon Colonial Tours. I met Luz, who understood my English. I explained my needs to her, and she told me that for $40.00 U.S. I could go to the Colca Canyon and get two nights and three days, plus guide, hotels, transportation, and a few meals to boot. I would have to pay the entrance fee for the hot springs, and there would be several other passengers. I said, "Let's do it." They would drop me off at a village called Cabanaconde, where I would walk to the river and be picked up the next day. This would allow me to walk to the bottom of Colca Canyon, I hoped, and back up the same day. Then I would come back to Arequipa and set off for Cotahuasi Canyon, thereby getting to see both canyons within my timeframe.

We also discussed the particulars of going to Cotahuasi, the rival canyon. Luz told me that it was a sixteen-hour bus ride, or I could rent a car, driver, and guide, which would be faster and safer. My worries included the knowledge that, sometimes, the buses slipped off the narrow dirt roads (upon returning home I read of an account in which just that happened, and at the exact place I'd been, and I wasn't up for the danger). The guidebook called them, "ram-shackle buses." Also, I am too tall for buses. They are okay for an hour, but not sixteen, and that was just an estimate. In one of the travel books I was reading, *Worst Journeys*, an author was going on about how readers only like to read about the trouble the writer gets into and how hard the travel was. It is my contention that sweat, blisters, sore muscles, and tears are okay, but not blood and gore. Particularly when it is my blood we're talking about. Since the buses were known to be ramshackle and risky, and I faced a time crunch, I chose the car and driver.

After settling up with Colonial Tours, or Agencia de Viajes Y Turismo, I took the obligatory walk through the heart of town, and saw La Catedral, built in the 1650s. It was destroyed by fire in 1844 and rebuilt only to be damaged by an earthquake in 1868, and rebuilt again. I also saw the Iglesia (church) de la San Agustin and the Iglesias of Compania with a pretty amazing façade. There was also the Church of San Francisco, also from the 16th century. I enjoyed the promenade as it gave me time to check out the locals, and for them to check me out, too. Again, my height seemed to draw attention, but I was used to it, and never took it personally. As I tramped around, other worries joined in: how would the roads be, how would the other drivers be? Heck, how would my driver be?

On the appointed morning, I met fourteen other tourists; we loaded up in an '80s Ford van and began our excursion towards Colca Canyon. Just outside Arequipa I spied the Hostel Elvis; a better omen I could not hope for. After one-and-a-half hours of driving, we were in the Andean Desert, as dry, rocky, and brown a place as I ever hoped to see. In the distance were 15,000- foot mountains, which gave me hope for the future of the drive. We continued to climb; after 50 miles of paved road we hit a dirt road that turned and twisted as we gained altitude. We saw Chilean Flamingos and Andean Gulls, along with alpaca and llamas. The houses were adobe, but the highlights were the incredible waist-high rock walls used for stock. One thing in abundance was rock, and it was put to good use.

We stopped at a small roadside rest stop, where it was suggested we buy coca tea and leaves. To make the point, a local woman traveling with us got out of the van and promptly collapsed. I thought she had stumbled, but when she didn't get right up, the other locals immediately plied her with coca leaves. The lesson was well presented, and the huge bruise on the cheek gave us a constant reminder. I bought some leaves, and kept them with me -- and used them, too -- until I got to the airport to return home. We were gaining more altitude, and were at about 15,000 feet. My stomach felt queasy and it was hard to breathe and walk at the same time. The sky was overcast, but an occasional glimpse of the distant mountains could be had if I looked long and hard enough. We stopped for lunch at the Los Sismos. On the menu was Alpaca steak with veggies. I passed, and went, instead, for a cheese omelet and coca tea. While lunching, we enjoyed the company of a baby alpaca that wandered in from the kitchen and checked through the trash for goodies, as well as nosing between our elbows to see if anything on the table was up for grabs. After lunch a dog came out of the kitchen to see if anything was left. It had orange eyebrows, which, I was told, gave the dog extra spirituality.

We continued to gain altitude as we headed for the village of Chivay, a village of about 4,000 people. The mountains reminded me of Tibet, but the real striking difference, aside from no yaks, was the stone walls that were everywhere. I couldn't imagine the work that must have gone into building them. Some were as big around as a football field, over waist high, and were reportedly made from river rocks, though I didn't see any nearby rivers. The terraced hills were also striking, some pre-Incan in their antiquity. We spent our first night in Chivay, where the locals were in traditional dress, at least most of the women. The village was about 400 years old. The Spanish, when they settled the area, forced the native people to move into villages for "administrative purposes," i.e., so they could keep track of them and work them harder. Chivay had the traditional town square with a pleasant church, folks strolling around, and a variety of shops lining the side streets: cafes, grocery, hotels and very small, hole-in-the-wall tourist shops. We were all dropped off at different hostels; mine was a compound and a five-bed dorm room, which I shared with just one other passenger: a young Brazilian named Gabrille. The building was adobe-walled, with a thatch roof and no heat, but lights. I experienced my first toilet with no seat on it (not first hole in the ground), and had to ask my roommate how to use it. He informed me that it was like any other toilet, just without a seat. After getting a lesson in bathroom etiquette, Gabrille and I were picked up again and transported to the Municpaldad Proviacial De Cayllorn Banos La Calera, a publicly owned thermal hot springs bath.

At the hot springs there were six different pools, some outdoors, some indoor, all differently shaped, and of varying age. I opted to try the more uptown one. It was surrounded on three sides by head-high lockers, with the fourth side open to the river, roofless, and facing the headwaters of the Colca River. It had a thermal waterfall that was just right, heat-wise. I chatted with my Brazilian roommate, who spoke English, as we tried not to watch the young couple canoodle across the pool.

After the bath we were transported back to our various abodes to prepare for dinner. Dinner was to be held in a restaurant that provided not only a traditional meal, but traditional music, as well. Several other tour outfits joined us, making for a pleasant night. One of the traditional aspects of Peruvian meals is to sit in very hard, and uncomfortable, tall, wooden chairs. I had tomato soup and spaghetti with tomato sauce. The highlight of the meal was a bowl of corn kernels, neither hard nor soft, but somehow toasted to a gentle texture that was very tasty. After dinner, the music began, courtesy of a five-piece group, which included pipes, guitar, ukulele, a drum, and an electric bass. A man and woman in at least five costume changes danced traditional dances, and then tried, successfully, to lure the visitors out on to the dance floor. If I hadn't been at 12,000 feet, I might have tried, but was content to watch the younger folks enjoy themselves, although now and then one of them had to take a break and get some oxygen replacement. I was back in the dorm by 10 p.m., already chomping at the bit for the following day's 6:30 a.m. departure, for the Cruz Del Condor and my drop off at Cabanaconde and my walk to Colca Canyon.

The next morning after the traditional breakfast of tea, bread, jam, and hard-backed chair, we loaded into the van and headed off to try and see condors. My fellow travelers were all excited, so I decided I was too. We passed more terraces, some dating back more than 10,000 years. These terraces are still studied today for the ingenuity of the irrigation system that was used. The

Colca River is not used for irrigation, as carrying water uphill was deemed to be counter-productive, so the various streams running down into it were connected and used, very ingeniously, apparently. The primary crops are maize, potatoes, and more recently, barley, and beans. We drove along looking for condors, but to little avail. The majority of the group was left at a popular viewing spot, and then Gabrille and I were taken to the end of the road for our hike to the bottom of the canyon.

We were dropped off at a hostel in Cabanaconde, where I left my unnecessary gear, and prepared for my walk to the bottom of the Colca Canyon. The guidebook said, "Cabanaconde is a good base for continuing on into the deepest parts of the Canon del Colca on foot. Ask for directions, or better, hire a local guide since there are several trails and it can be confusing." We were on the trail by 10:15 a.m. I lucked out, as Gabrille met a local who was going to a village past my destination for a festival, and they led me partly down the trail, and then left me in the dust to my own company. The first half-mile of trail was level and mostly along a ditch that was used for garbage, but at the rim the view was inspirational and then some! The Colca Canyon is a valley structure with very steep v-shaped sides rising up to 5,000-meter peaks. Across the river, the other side of the valley was green, terraced, with a huge, acres-wide, brownish colored patch. It broke up the green and made it that much more startling. A few villages were visible, and it wasn't long before the fog blew away and I could see the river way down in the canyon.

I know I started at 3,200 meters, about 10,500 American feet; the precipitous two-and-a-half- mile hike down to the river had a million switchbacks. I took a few pictures, and before I knew it, the fog was back covering up the river, and that became the day's routine, a glimpse and then fog. To say that the path was steep, rocky, and slow going, for me, would be accurate, but the locals seemed to think it was a freeway. There was a celebration at one of the villages, and I could hear the music and fireworks. Most people were heading there for a few days of celebration. The music was with me almost all the way down and up. It was steep; thank goodness switchbacks had been invented when this trail was built. The views remained magnificent, as I slowly plodded my way down and down past cacti, flowers, and chirping birds.

For the first time in my memory, I was actually breaking a sweat going *down* a mountain; it felt like I was really working. The altitude was definitely a factor in slowing me down; my thighs felt like they were made out of half-thawed ice cream. Usually, it is my knees and toes that bark and whine. After three hours I was at the oasis, my target, and right next to the river. I met four Spanish hippies who were luxuriating there, if sleeping in a thatch hut with a wooden floor and broken beds tilting every which way is luxuriating (the Lonely Planet said, "travelers should expect basic accommodations"). There was a local hostel manager keeping a fire going in the light drizzle, and I was served coca tea and sold a 1.5-liter bottle of water, which I drank down at once. The area had palm trees and a hot springs pool that was inviting; however, I wobbled on shaky legs to the river, collected my rock, wobbled back for more tea, and said adios. After fifteen minutes, I was heading back up the trail. It gets dark at about six p.m. there, and, while I had a flashlight, I wanted to be up before I had to use it. The Spaniards had told me they were waiting for horses to take them up, not a bad idea. If I had had any nerve or sense, I would have asked if I could ride up with them, but I thought they were talking about the next day.

I walked up slowly and methodically. Usually while hiking, I spend 90 percent of the time looking at my feet or where they were supposed to be going. On this hike, however, I seemed to be spending most of my time bent over, leaning with my left hand on my walking stick, right leg propped on a rock, backpack heaved way up on my back, trying to focus on the rock or dirt at my feet while panting so hard I could hardly see straight. I did occasionally get to peek at the vista views. It wasn't hot, mercifully, and even started to drizzle again to help cool me off. After one hour, I was at the spot where the trail divided; this filled me with false hope. I plodded and plodded on. Several locals passed me and offered encouragement saying, "Vamonos" and something that I assumed was, "It is going to rain and get dark, you better get a move on." A little old lady, in her upper 60s, with a huge sack of potatoes, passed me like I was standing still. I was. Every time someone passed me I was bent over double, going through my ritual inhalation, wheeze, exhalation and huff and puff, inhale, wheeze, exhale, and puff routine. If I wasn't bent over then I was sitting down, feet splayed, back against my pack, arms limp at my side, taking a break. I was sitting and making what must have seemed like some kind of ungodly whale noise. I felt like I had just climbed out of the ooze. But I continued to plod along, noting a few small memorials in passing, maybe to other gringos who had tried the same thing.

I kept telling myself, get up, get moving, keep breathing, you won't make any distance sitting here, keep moving. I would set a time, twenty minutes for a piece of candy or power bar or drink of water. Those were my immediate goals, and I kept putting one foot in front of the other, just barely. My normal stride is about three feet on the level, and maybe a bit less on an uphill stretch, about average for my height. On this little stretch of uphill, steep, rocky path, I was lucky to put one foot all the way in front of the other. Sometimes I wasn't even putting my foot half-way in front of the other. It was a struggle with the altitude; my comeuppance for trying to do in one day what ought to have been done in a few days. But I was heading up. And then it started to drizzle in earnest. On went the raincoat and hat. The clouds and the ever-darkening sky obscured the top, but on I went.

Six horses were headed down, and I noted it was about four p.m. Locals kept passing me going both ways, worried about me, but not for themselves. The "Vamonos!" encouragements got more urgent in tone. Onward I moved at my turtle's pace, and at about 5:45 p.m., topped out, to my surprise and relief. It was only about a half-mile to go, phew! Then it started to rain. At 6:15 p.m., I walked into the hostel, where the owner high-fived me. It was obvious he was very surprised to see me. I think he and the others there had taken bets on when I would reappear. I said my "Buneos tardes," went to my adobe room with the peeling walls and dirt floor, took off my wet clothes, and lay down for a short five-minute nap.

At 8:30 p.m., I awoke. I wandered into the little cantina attached to the hostel and my jaw dropped when I recognized the four Spaniards sitting, dry and warm with their feet up, jovially drinking beer! How'd they get up here so fast, I wondered? It took them three hours on horses to climb what I did in six hours on foot, and without the pain. Oh well, even though they looked hale and hearty, I knew that, after some rest, I would feel good about the exercise

I had expended to pocket this canyon. But while I was patting myself on the back for the heroic effort I had made, I was also shaking my finger at myself for my mistakes, which included not acclimatizing, not being in better shape, not allowing time to see the canyon, not having more food with me, not having a map, and not putting on rain pants when it started to pour. But as I sat and pondered, it hit me: this was truly a world-class canyon.

Everything was all new to me: green, steep valley walls, unlimited terraces across the way, and the sweet high clouds. I got to the river, got my rock, saw my canyon, felt it, touched it, and was touched by it. I fell asleep, knowing that I was supposed to be picked up the next morning at 7:30, part of the reason I didn't stay the night in the canyon. I knew I'd never get up the canyon in time to meet my ride if I spent the night at the bottom. As soon as I hit my rolled-up jacket/pillow, I was asleep.

In the morning I got up, had my tea, bread, and jam, packed, and who was sitting there? Young Gabrille, the Brazilian I had shared a room with two nights before and hiked part-way down the canyon with. He had just hiked up in two hours, and come farther than I did after partying all night at the village festival. I exclaimed, "How could you be so fast?" He responded, "I am young and beautiful." The morning sun was out and helped dry my still wet clothes and gave me a sunburn in forty minutes.

I waited for the ride back to Arequipa, and mused about a theory I was working on. I wanted a formula to help describe the beauty I had seen so it would have meaning to those who had not seen it. My equation went like this: pick an outdoor area that you really like -- mountains, ocean, river, valley, big sky, little glen, a national park, a small garden, a flower in a vase -- then close your eyes and focus on that spot or thing you really like, then multiply it by 10,000 in beauty and size and grandeur. That is what the Colca Canyon was to me, a magnum opus. How presumptuous was that? The very idea, to think my beauty equation could make a complete stranger understand how I felt. Who am I to say my view of the canyon is any more appreciative than your joy in your own rose garden, stamp collection, or whatever. Beauty, as we know, is in the eye of the beholder. I was brought back to ponder how to describe the extraordinary when it leaves me speechless. Might there be a formula to accomplish this? But they all felt flawed. Then I remembered the saying, "God is in the details." Maybe a way to describe how I felt is to say it is a living painting, on a huge canvas. Then again, all of Mother Nature's works are extraordinary. Let's just say this is one of her masterpieces, hanging in one of her most special galleries.

Maybe that is just the point of all this rambling. In fact the Colca Canyon was the best and grandest canyon I had seen on this quest, and I was somehow trying to justify it to myself, as well as apologize to the other canyons that they were not in the same league (back to worrying about bad vibing a canyon or messing with the good juju). And there I was, also sort of anthropomorphizing a canyon. How odd is that? And maybe that is just the point, the Colca was the best, hence my gushing about its beauty. I'd finally found a spot worthy of this canyon quest, and this was how I tried to define it.

Finally, the van back to Arequipa came and rescued me from more of this inane impossible Zen-type Koan on beauty. The ride back was a pleasure. My new cohorts were an Israeli, some Brits, Danes, and a few locals, too. Upon arrival in Arequipa, I did my usual chores: wrote some e-mails, took a shower, bought some more sunscreen, and walked the streets with my achy thighs. That night I made sure to get a good night's sleep, because the next day I was off to the Canon Del Cotahuasi, said to exceed 4000 meters in depth, and which according to some, was the deepest canyon in Peru, South America, if not the world!

The next day, Luz, the official guide, Liz her "trainee," and Juan, the driver, showed up at 11:10 a.m. sharp for our trip to Cotahuasi, which is located about 240 miles from Arequipa, mostly on dirt road. It was supposed to take at least twelve hours by pickup truck and sixteen by bus to get there. The guidebook notes that it is a traditional and rural area, which only recently has begun to be visited "by a handful of adventurous travelers" like myself.

Our transportation was a pretty new Toyota crew cab pickup with a short bed and roll bar in the back. We loaded our gear in the back and set off for our two-night three-day trip. We were soon on the Pan America Highway which I had read much about, passing through the outskirts of Arequipa, the landscaping gradually changing from tire shops, gas stations, and 7-11 shops, to trucks full of hay, grazing cows, and cornfields. Soon enough, we were cruising along the two-lane paved road through a totally arid, brown/white landscape with volcanic ash (from an eruption almost 1700 years ago). After two hours of climbing, we came to a rocky plateau, sparser than before. Just when I thought I'd never see green again, we wound our way down to a brown river, the valley green from irrigation. Then back up we went to the arid, hot, barren, and hazy landscape, stretching as far as the eye could see. We'd climb an hour or so, and then down we would flash to a green spot, and then back up we would climb to brown and dust.

After a few hours of the contrast, we came to the Toro Muerto Petroglyphs, an area liberally littered with petroglyphs. They were said to be pre-Incan, 1,400 to 1,500 years old. The story was that people who were traveling from the Machu Picchu area to trade with the coastal folks were elated when they crossed the mountains after an arduous, sandy, dirty, hot, sweaty, hike with little or no water, and spotted the river miles away. To show their pleasure, they left signs of their passing inscribed on the rocks: maps, thunderbirds, snakes, llamas, rivers, people, dancers, and much more. The area was barren and hot, but the sacredness of the site teased me. If it had been I that had made the journey, I'd be thinking of some way to give thanks to whomever or whatever got me there too, as well as let others know of my appreciation.

We headed up valley and it slowly got greener and greener, almost to a tropical lushness, the whole area scattered with palm trees, sugar cane, Hawaiian Big Island lush. I saw two tractors, which meant to me that it was a fairly prosperous area, given that these were the first tractors I had seen in any of the rural and remote areas I had visited to date. Our route took us up and out of this fertile valley back to the moonscape, with its iron reds, gold slashes of earth, and amazing sandstone formations. I was definitely not bored on this part of the drive. If I didn't like what I saw, all I had to do was wait five minutes and it would turn to something different. As we continued to climb, life began again, a few cacti eventually turning into a lot of cacti. We passed through several villages with narrow streets, the doors right on the road. We picked up an old man with two canes hitchhiking with three bags of firewood. He came up to my waist in height, but with his twenty-gallon hat, we were almost eye-to-eye.

At the village where we dropped the old hitchhiker off, we pulled into the bus stop. I was reminded of my happiness to not be riding the bus up and down those narrow, twisting roads. We decided to call it a night there in Chuquibamba (chew-key-bum-bah), still five hours from the canyon. Liz called ahead and learned of fog and snow, and it was getting dark. This area had lots of terraces with corn, sheep, maize, and a nice church square where people strolled in the plaza. I liked it. It was quiet, calm, and pretty with a few thousand residents. I missed the once-a-year bullfight, but the lurid signs were still up touting the four-day festival. How they got crowds of people there, and where they stayed, was a mystery to me. We stayed in a new hotel; my room was a twelve by twelve space with no window, and the bath down the hall had no hot water. The room smelled of insecticide, but I hoped it was just the new paint smell; as it turned out the bugs didn't get me that night. Walking around town looking for a place to eat, it was apparent that not many gringos got this far, about one a month maybe, according to Liz.

The following day was one of those if my eyes were teeth, they would have gotten cavities and rotted out of their sockets kind of days, it was that spectacular. We were up at five a.m. and on the road by six, sans breakfast. The locals get up earlier, but they work in their fields first, and then come to the village to eat at about nine. The road was gravel and dirt, and by 10:30 I had my first view of the Cotahuasi, a spacious valley, with a river meandering through, green terraces leading the eye down and down, the whole area scattered palm trees, and in the distance, the village. My first thought was of "Shangri-La," that James Hilton must have passed by this region before he wrote "*Lost Horizon*." We passed 15,000-foot snow covered mountains. Luz said we were in the Andes of Peru, the first Coropuna, said to be the highest mountain in Southern Peru at either 6,305 or 6,425 meters, take your pick. It took two hours to drive around it. Next up were more snowy mountains, Solimana, and then Firurce. The first mountain looked like huge scoops of vanilla ice cream with a giant extra helping in the middle, the second more like a giant rip saw in snowy relief. The last was a classic, prominent, snow-covered peak. In total, it was a six-and-a-half hour drive through paradise. There were waterfalls, lush, vibrant, green valleys, and twisty mountain roads. We saw one truck during the entire trip. It had broken down the night before, with its three men who had spent the night outside. We stopped and gave them a bag of candy and some extra avocados.

The road continued narrow and bumpy (note for when you design your next truck: do not put the "oh shit" handlebar next to the door where a person's head can hit it with every bounce). Just before the village of Cotahuasi, we came across a bulldozer clearing a landslide. The driver asked whether there were any slides where we had come from, at which Liz and Luz laughed. Later, they explained that, if there had been a landslide, we would never have gotten through.

The driving certainly made for an above average day. We drove past the village of Cotahuasi with the five-star hotel in town. It turned out that it had sewer pipe problems, so we opted for a more rustic one, with adobe walls, a tin roof, small courtyard, and bathroom around the corner with a pail used for the TP, and maybe hot water and electricity, depending on the village generator, but it was not yet time for bed. We continued on for about two hours beyond the village of Cotahuasi to a hot springs, reached by crossing the river on a narrow, old, wooden swinging bridge. This hot springs was a local gathering spot, and used as much for a communal bath as a place to relax. Luz and I went for a dip, and I watched the locals watch me; it was a very relaxing soak.

Later we walked back towards the village to get some exercise. It occurred to me that from a western point of view, this might look like paradise. The reality of actually living in paradise, though, might be quite different: get up early, work the fields by hand, travel long distances for necessities, and plow the fields with a pair of oxen and a wooden plow. I saw one tractor, a motorcycle, and a few cars for a village of 3,000 people. Most transportation was by foot, horse, or mule. No, viewing paradise and making a living there are two different things. The town of Cotahuasi is about 170 years old and of Spanish design. Being there was like going back in time: narrow roads, a few balconies, and a drainage ditch in the middle of the street. Where the houses stopped, the fields started.

The debate about which canyon is deepest will have to rage on. The Cotahuasi is supposed to be 5,335 meters at the highest point, and the river is at 1,500 meters, so the canyon is about 4,300 meters deep, a little over 14,000 feet in depth. The Colca Canyon makes the same claim, with a depth of more than 3,400 meters. The American Grand Canyon is 7,000 feet at the south rim and 8,000 at the north rim and the river is about one mile down on average, by way of comparison.

On the walk back I got my rock. Later we had a very nice dinner and I went to sleep with rain on the tin roof, tired but satisfied.

One of my reading materials, as noted before, was the book *Worst Journeys*. For those folks that believe travel ought to be done the cheapest, simplest, roughest way possible, and with certain danger, yes, I felt a twinge of guilt for another great day in Peru. I could have found my way on public transport to Cotahuasi, and found a "Kombi," local transport, to the river, and then back to a hostel. If I had done that, this is what I would have missed on this fine day: probably one of the best one-day trips of this journey, a truly glorious day, and the perfect wave syndrome day. As a passenger, it came to me that I didn't have to spend the majority of my time looking at my feet and watching for donkey dookey, or the other trailside hazards. As a driver, my attention would have to be focused on the road. No, I was happy to be a passenger and let my gaze roam free.

We rose at about six-thirty to a golden dawn. I had a breakfast of tasty omelet, about the best a vegetarian could do in these parts. We were on the road to the trailhead for Sepia Falls, which wasn't in the guidebook, and by nine-thirty, were on a trail in the Cotahuasi Canyon, which is about 100 miles long. The day before I had been almost to the headwaters, and today we would walk to the halfway point of the canyon, giving me some sense of satisfaction that I sort of earned this canyon. This part of the canyon, as a point of reference, had a lot of similarities to the Grand Canyon, like the clouds above the canyon horizon. We were probably about 6,000 to 8,000 feet below the walls, and the side drainages, although here the walls were greener.

A major difference between the Grand Canyon and Cotahuasi, though, was that Cotahuasi was a working canyon, not a tourist destination. The village at the bottom of the canyon, Tompepampa, had about 1,000 people living there. There were a few farm holdings along the trail to the waterfall, with a cow and a few goats, a garden, maize and yams. The people were pretty much self-sufficient, trading their goods up-canyon for flour and sugar. Even the children were in the fields helping the adults with the chores. The homes were thatched roof with adobe walls and rock walls for the stock. We were passed by a group of five men and ten mules taking supplies to the village, there being no road for cars or trucks. At one of the holdings, two oxen were pulling a wooden plow blade through the rock-strewn field.

By 11:30 we had reached the Sepia Falls, 500 feet deep, maybe 20 feet wide, a double rainbow in the mist murmuring a welcome to us. We lunched on avocado, cheese, oranges, bananas, and bread in the shade of an overhang not five feet from where the fall began its downward plunge. The water was coming so fast that it was difficult to focus on one surge before it was over the falls and gone; my eyes didn't have time to find the next surge before it, too, was cascading away. It was mesmerizing. After staring at the falls for ten minutes, I would look away and the entire earth seemed to be moving in harmony with the water. This was raw power, pure sex. Somewhere in my memory, when I was at a workshop in the mid '70s, my boss had a "psychological test" for the staff, one of those, "if you choose x, then you like y" type of exercises. There were a variety of different questions and choices, and, while I don't remember any of the other stuff, I do remember that if you answered "waterfalls" to one question, that meant that you apparently liked sex. Perhaps, this was what they were talking about.

Luz told a story about a Swedish kayaker who was trying to be the first to run this river. He came to the falls and the locals said, "This is very dangerous, don't do it." To my way of thinking, you'd have to be supremely confident in your skills, suicidal, or stupid to go over this fall; or perhaps all three. They found his body a few weeks later.

We returned the same way we had come, a pleasant stroll through the sun-splashed canyon, over the hanging bridge, leaping a few side creeks that moved rapidly down, found our driver Juan, and returned to Cotahuasi. There we gathered our swimsuits and returned back to the hot springs for another soothing soak. Afterwards heading back to our lodging, we stopped to look at some pre-Incan ruins, and our hitchhiker fed us the pears from the prickly pear cactus (Tuna in Spanish). It wasn't too bad. Then back for another nice dinner.

As awesome as the scenery was, having two friendly, knowledgeable, and humorous guides, who were beginning to feel like friends, was the icing on the cake. Between Liz and Luz, I must have heard more than 200 bits of information on the flora and fauna, correct pronunciations, traditional use of the plants, place names, geology, history, and countless stories.

On the ride home, I paid more attention as we passed through the village that had been my home for the last two days. The streets were narrow, with the doors of the houses opening almost onto the street. Most of the buildings were adobe with thatched roofs, the newer ones sporting corrugated iron, which was easier to put up. Some of the buildings looked quite old, with chipping adobe, their doors weathered and warped with huge, wrought iron hinges. Many had second floors with small balconies looking out over the street, but more for decoration than function, as they looked too small to even stand on. The roads were often cobbled or dirt. I saw tons of dogs, but not one cat. All the dogs were running free, but there was no dog doo. Donkey dookey and cow flop, yes, but no dog stuff. People on horseback, folks leading laden donkeys or pushing a wheelbarrow were the norm. The square had a nice old church with the traditional tall, white belfry. The stores were mostly selling the same things: soda pop, fruits and veggies, plastic doodads, and cowboy hats hanging from the ceilings. The police, I noticed did not seem to be wearing any guns, and in one small store, the police, proprietor, and hangers-on were playing guitars and singing. Eight hours later, they were still there making music.

Many of the buildings seemed to be built with an inner courtyard system. We would go into a room and pass through it, and suddenly find ourselves in a garden or small yard with rooms on all sides. We stayed at the Ludean Hostel. It was very rustic, as Liz said it would be. In this case, a rustic room meant a door that wouldn't close all the way due to age and weather, nor would it lock from the inside. I had to stoop to enter, as the door was only about five feet tall. My room, again windowless, had another door leading to I do not know where, a double bed with foam mattress (I could feel the wooden slats), and a chair. I slept in my sleeping bag, on top of my ensolite pad. The walls were adobe, peeling, and lit by a bare light bulb which only worked in the evening for a few hours.

The toilet around the corner had a strong smell of urine, a stall with no seat, and a bucket for the used toilet paper. There was a water spigot for hand washing, and the same for a shower. The little café sported three tables, had a glass counter display case, and two girly pictures advertising beer. The courtyard was hung with washing and other household items. It sounds kind of dreary, and maybe without the friendliness of the owner, it would have been. A high-school-aged woman was loaded with questions and great insights about my trip. Her little brother looked at me like I was from another planet, and for all intents and purposes I may as well have been, a tall, longhaired, bearded, aloha shirt-wearing gringo. Who could blame him? I only saw the men folk very early in the morning or in the evening after work; otherwise the hostel was run by women.

Walking down the street, folks either stared, gaped, or gave friendly nods or holas. One of the guides said I ought to run for mayor, but I am the sort who always says hello to everybody, whether I know them or not.

We left the village of Cotahuasi the next morning about 8:30 a.m. after a brief stop to visit the local bat expert, as in flying mammals. His first question was, "How can we improve tourism here, and what do you think of the city and valley?" My brain froze up; I was still looking for the bats, but I took a deep breath and asked him to repeat the question. As a point of fact, I have been interested in tourism for the past sixteen or so years. While living in Ketchikan, I'd worked as a part time kayak guide, was part-owner of a mountain bike tour business, and I was on the local Visitor Bureau board. In Sitka, I was starting my third summer as the owner/operator of a hike and bike, birding and photography business. So I have a bit more than a passing interest in the topic. The guide's interest was obvious, but what was the bat man's connection? Turns out he was also part of the local group trying to bring in more dollars.

I stumbled around a bit at first, but then caught my stride. I told him that, they had a world-class product. The question was, how to let people know about it, while at the same time protecting it from them, i.e. preventing them from loving it to death. The twelve-hour plus ride would solve part of that. The more we talked, the more I enjoyed the discussion. We concluded that he needed to target his audience; did he want bird watchers, mountain climbers, canyon freaks, shutterbugs, rafters, cultural snoops, or what? Then, he should find a willing partner to help promote the area. He could bring in travel writers from target areas and from big city newspapers, strengthen the infrastructure, roads, plumbing, hotels, etc. We also talked about how the locals felt about tourism. It was a wide-ranging discussion, though brief, and it got me to thinking about their tourism, and led me back to my own upcoming challenges.

By eight-thirty we were on the road again. We picked up three hitchhikers, it being the neighborly thing to do out in the middle of nowhere. By nine-thirty, we were stuck axle-deep in the mud. Juan, our driver, was avoiding a pregnant cow, and that was how we ended up spending the next three plus hours digging out of the muck, our only tool a small panga-like blade (like a small machete), which a passing young man reluctantly loaned us. We hand-dug a trench across the road to drain off as much of the calf-deep water as we could. Also we dug from under the right side of the truck to slowly build a rock road that would allow us to get a grip on the road and pull out. The hitchhikers helped without a second thought. Finally, the huge boulders heaved and tugged into place, all of us muddy up to our knees and elbows, and the truck jacked up for better leverage. We were standing back to admire our handiwork when a local kombi pulled up, and the driver jumped out and into our rig, fired it up, and drove it out of the mud, muck, and mire, much to our amazement. We washed off in the nearby creek, got in, and headed on up the road.

We climbed steadily for three or four hours before we hit the Andes plateau, just like on the way in. The beauty was still breathtaking, but this time we got the added bonus of rain, hail, and snow. On the way back, Liz and I got to talk more about local issues, such as drugs and alcohol, teen issues, employment, and politics. The more we talked, the more I realized that no matter where you are, the problems are similar. It took me back to what I had left back home, 28 years of the do-gooder business. I believe those were the first pangs of homesickness I'd felt since I'd left more than four months earlier.

We still needed some good juju to get back to Arequipa. We drove until eight-thirty at night, the last one-and-a-half hours of that in the dark; we needed all the good luck we could gather. Traffic was heavy and there were at least three surely drunk drivers making their way down the road, in some fashion or other. There were huge buses going both ways, trucks loaded with chickens, lambs, cows, and sheep being driven to slaughter. Juan continued to impress me with his driving skills.

Back in the hotel in Arequipa, I climbed into the shower and washed off four days of dirt and mud. The journey to Cotahuasi and environs was about as good as it gets. Like I tell the guides I work with, if the guides are good, they can take people through hell and make it interesting. Liz and Luz had the advantage of a truly exotic location, blissful hot springs, world-class scenery, they were interesting and fun company; it was the way it was supposed to be.

All in all, Peru was great. I skimmed it, got a brief glimpse of it, my time being short. I saw a lot, covered some miles, and had a great experience, but still, it was superficial in many ways. It took rushing through Peru to be reminded once again, of the lesson: slow down and smell the flowers. My obsession with the canyons had prevented me from experiencing more of the area, but it was the canyons that got me there in the first place. My only regret was that I wished I'd had more time.

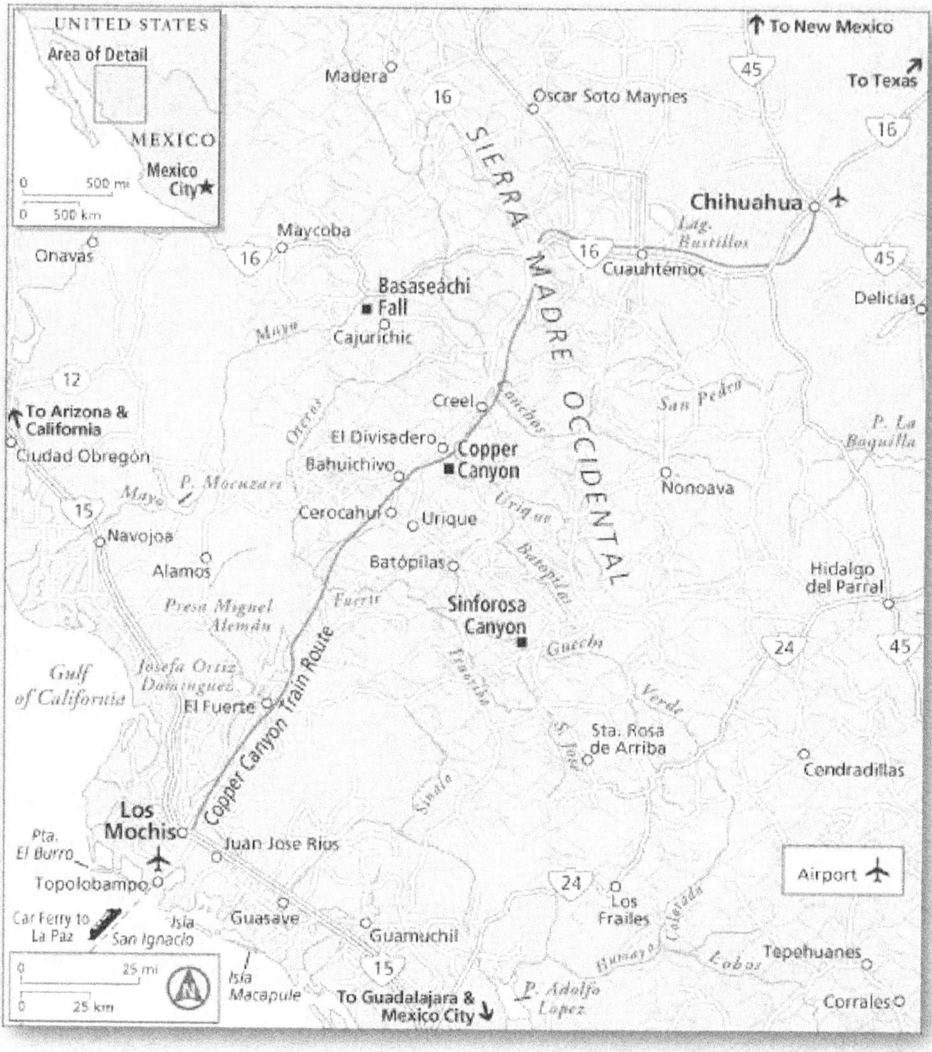
UNITED STATES
Area of Detail
MEXICO
Mexico City
0 500 mi
0 500 km
To New Mexico
To Texas
Madera
Oscar Soto Maynes
SIERRA MADRE OCCIDENTAL
Chihuahua
Lag. Bustillos
Cuauhtémoc
Delicias
Maycoba
Onavas
Basaseachi Fall
Cajurichic
Creel
El Divisadero
Copper Canyon
Bahuichivo
Cerocahui
Urique
Batópilas
Nonoava
San Pedro
P. La Boquilla
Hidalgo del Parral
Sinforosa Canyon
To Arizona & California
Ciudad Obregón
P. Mocuzari
Navojoa
Alamos
Presa Miguel Alemán
Gulf of California
Josefa Ortiz Domínguez
El Fuerte
Copper Canyon Train Route
Sta. Rosa de Arriba
Cendradillas
Los Mochis
Pta. El Burro
Juan Jose Rios
Topolobampo
Car Ferry to La Paz
Isla San Ignacio
Guasave
Guamuchil
Isla Macapule
To Guadalajara & Mexico City
P. Adolfo Lopez
Los Frailes
Tepehuanes
Corrales
Airport
0 25 mi
0 25 km

Seven

Mexico
Barranco Del Cobre

"Don't hurry, don't worry. You're only here on a short visit, so don't forget to stop and smell the flowers."

Walter Hagen

It seemed too easy getting to the next dance. My luck, magic, juju, or whatever it was, was holding out. I got an e-mail from Carl Franz, author of the quintessential Mexican guidebook, *The Peoples Guide to Mexico*, and he gave me great advice, saving me time and money. His advice was, "Don't go to Creel." Instead, he said, I should take a train from Los Mochis to Bahuichivo (bow-a-cheev-oh), about 60 miles short of Creel. One can hike or drive to the Urique Valley and River from there. Mr. Franz noted that it was very expensive to try and get to the canyon from Creel. My friend Jon in Sitka, who was still acting as a muse of sorts for the journey, tells me that it wasn't luck that got me to these places, but rather that people felt sorry for me. Be that as it may, I did feel fortunate in my travels, not just in Mexico, but for the entire trip.

My daughter Amelia flew in from Ashland, Oregon, where she was a student at Southern Oregon University. My brother and I picked her up in Burbank. The plan was for the three of us to fly from LAX to Los Mochis, train from there to Bahuichivo, stay at a ranchito, and get to the Urique River, the deepest part of the Copper Canyon river system.

I had looked through my guidebook and found several places to stay in Los Mochis, as we would need to overnight there before catching the early morning train to the canyon. Then I started calling the ranchitos to see where we could stay. A deal was struck for us to put up at the Paraiso del Oso (Paradise of the Bear) for four nights. The itinerary was set before we left the U.S. Amelia's main worry was that there would be no shops to buy gifts for her friends. Her e-mail to me, before the trip, noted, "I do expect to come back with a tan. Right? I will, right?"

One of my concerns --- I didn't really have my normal animal fears, as no one had gotten to me with snake or scorpion stories of Copper Canyon environs -- was the language barrier, but one of the reasons for Amelia to join my brother and I was to act as a translator; she was taking Spanish at school. In an e-mail, after the ticket was purchased, she opined, "I don't want your expectations to be so high, and for you to be disappointed. My Spanish is VERY so-so, but I will do my best and learn more while I am down there."

I was also a bit concerned with the currency aspect, and of course transportation and roads, but by that time I was pretty much blasé about all of it. I knew it would all fall together, but it would have to be quick; we had only six days to get to the canyon and back. I also felt a slight twinge of guilt, as again this trip would not be too rough by any hard core standard. We were paying $200 a night for the three of us for room and board. The room had no electricity or heat, but it did have a hot water shower, small wood stove, and oil lamps. The trip could be done more arduously and cheaply, but I didn't feel the need to run gauntlets and return with a missing limb or some tropical disease. The guidebook noted, to help salve my self- inflicted recriminations, "Ironically, while it's easier than ever to get to the region, it's trickier than ever to travel through it on your own." That we only had six days in Mexico soothed any serious concerns about the legitimacy of not doing this the hard way.

Another concern was train robbers. Amelia had heard stories of the trains being constantly robbed by masked men. "Hey," she'd e-mailed, "you do know that this train gets robbed by bandits every year, right?" The guidebook mentioned one such event, but noted the railroad now had its own armed guards.

I took fifteen minutes to pack my stuff, then sat around and watched Amelia and Mike spend more than two hours trying to get organized. I suppose five months of travel had taught me a thing or two about what to take and how to pack it. I watched in amusement as they struggled with all the stuff they wanted to take. How many pairs of shoes would one need for six days? How many hats? What about TP? Always carry spare TP - was my advice.

I must also note that while all the packing was going on, I was keeping an extra sharp eye on Mike. Back in 1994 when I'd been preparing for my through-hike of the Pacific Crest Trail, I spent the last few days at his place. He was going to hike the first three days with me, and his buddy and co-worker, Todd, was driving us to the trailhead. While I was fiddling with my gear, Mike casually asked if I would notice any extra weight. I told him I'd been working with my gear and pack for more than five months, and knew where everything was and what it weighed down to the ounce. I had even cut the handle off my toothbrush. We awoke the next morning, April Fool's Day, my favorite holiday, and drove to the California and Mexican border, where Todd dropped us to begin the hike. That night, fifteen miles later on, Mike went into my pack and pulled out four one-and-a-half pound weights. I was speechless and incredulous as well. So I kept an eye on him as we packed for Mexico.

The flight to Mexico was reminiscent of other flights, with brown landscape and mountains in the distance, but it was reassuring to have family with me. Despite my worries, we made it safe and sound to Los Mochis, past customs, and took a cab to our room at the San Anita Hotel. The room had two beds, but there were three of us. This was the start of a dilemma that would face us the rest of the short trip. Feeling sorry for her aged dad and uncle, Amelia usually took the floor with a mattress, but that wasn't the real evening drama. No, the drama was Amelia's mistaken idea that the older members of the party snored, were flatulent, and initiated other nighttime noises that made it hard for her to sleep. We were ordered to not fall asleep until she had done so. I provided earplugs, but they apparently didn't drown out the nocturnal noises. To her dismay (and our annoyance), we were awakened time and again to be told to go back to sleep, but only after she was asleep. Just to give you an idea of her level of distress, while in the ranchito, she woke herself up one night from a sound sleep by talking in her sleep, telling us to "be quiet." Truth was, Mike and I had been laying there not saying a word, trying to let her go to sleep first.

The next morning we were at the train station, right on time, to catch the Chihuahua al Pacifico (Chihuahua to the Pacific) railroad. It is renowned for making it all the way, almost 400 miles, through some of the most rugged country to test any engineer's skills. The trip included 39 bridges (one almost 1,000 feet tall), 86 tunnels (one more than a mile long), and we climbed nearly 8,000 feet along the journey. The Chihuahua al Pacifico goes from Los Mochis to Chihuahua, hence the name. The rail line was started in the late 19th century with the intent of finding the shortest route to Kansas City in order to facilitate trade. It was finally completed in the 1960s, missing the heyday of Kansas City. The train left right on time, give or take a few minutes. We headed off slowly through the dark. Our car was nice: seats with extra leg-room, and lots of storage space for our gear. There also happened to be riding in our car, a group of twenty-four Americans on tour. It had been quite some time since my country kin were that abundant, and it reminded me what it is like to be around a herd of Americans. As we rolled slowly through the industrial area of town, they mooed and snorted and bellowed about the inadequacies of the train and whatever else that didn't meet their standards. I don't mean to say that all American travelers are the stereotypical "ugly Americans." I certainly hoped that I wasn't. As the sun rose, we were starting to pass a few small houses, with women sweeping their dirt yards. There were cows, pigs, and goats, along with chickens, and kids going to school. We got friendly waves as we continued along the way. As it brightened up, it seemed that the countryside did, too. There were wildflowers mixed in with vibrant green and the brown earth.

Later we went forward to the café car, and I had hotcakes, which were okay, and bottled water, then back to the car for a snooze, waking off and on to check out the scenery as we slowly gained altitude. Mike had an altimeter on his watch, so we got hourly reports on our altitude progression. We passed kapok trees, big odd balls of cotton-looking stuff hanging from the trees, mixed in with cactus and yellow flowers and purple-tinged trees. The train journey really was quite pleasant. Passing over old-time train trestles, we had a view of some fairly deep gorges with greenish-blue colored water running through it, and our noontime shadow chasing us over the river.

"It's not down on any map, true places never are."

Herman Melville

We arrived in Bahuichivo about one p.m. This was really the first stop in the canyon country. I wouldn't call it a town, but rather more of a station or depot. Our driver, Angel, found us, along with a family of four from Kentucky, who were going our way to do some horseback riding, for which the ranchito was renowned. It was a pleasant half-hour drive over dirt road to the ranch. The Paraiso del Oso, named for the bear-like rock formation above it, boasted twenty-one rooms, clean but sparse, all facing a grassy courtyard. The buildings were white, with large dining, lounge, and bar areas for the guests. Doug "Diego" Rhodes, originally from Ohio, along with his wife, Anna Maria Chavez de Rhodes, a local, are the owners. They built the lodge about ten years ago; according to the various news articles tacked up around the dining area, they were well known for their horse-person-ship. Diego showed up – he'd just returned from a ten-day horseback-riding trip with a group of Germans and allowed as how he'd be drunk that night, but would get together with us in the morning, but not too early. My new worry now was whether we'd be able to pin this guy down so we could get to Urique Valley. That evening we enjoyed a pleasant dinner with the Kentucky folks. The next day Amelia went on a trail ride with our Kentucky friends and Diego, who Amelia had learned was a Pancho Villa fan. Although the horseback trip was a few hours behind schedule, none of us seemed to mind. The place had an air of friendly disorganization. It wasn't mean-spirited at all, but more of a just-exactly-what-is-the-hurry sort of spirit. When I reviewed my notes, I found that Carl Franz had sent a copy of a letter from some folks who had visited the Oso, and their comments were: "… it was a bit unorganized," but they, too, found it to be very friendly. People, both guests and hired hands, were coming and going; Diego, the owner, was caught between trying to say hello and good-bye, and overseeing the staff questions. I lurked nearby, ready to grab him when the time allowed, but I was already on Aloha time: to shift into Manana time was no effort. Mike went for a long hike and I took a short one. The ranchito is near the village of Cerocahui, about a mile away, at an elevation of 5,500 feet in the Sierra Madres. Pine trees, rocky outcrops, stone pillars, blue sky and wispy clouds were the order of the day. The ranchito got its name from a stone formation which, I swear, looked like Boo-Boo the bear from the Yogi Bear cartoon, as well as the bear-shaped bottle of honey we buy in the stores.

Amelia returned from her ride attesting to Diego's horse-person-ship, although he was riding a mule. We sat; father and daughter, watching the Germans parade back and forth getting ready to leave, some in high fashion and others in complete western garb. The time with Amelia was a treat, as it had been almost five months since I had seen her last, she being in her junior year of college, and me off to see some canyons. Neither of us is a candidate for a job on the fashion police force, me in jeans, aloha shirt, and Tevas, and she shoeless, in shorts and a tank top. This, however, has never stopped us from offering our opinions. So, Amelia and I leaned back and commenced to comment on the fashion sense of tourists in the Sierra Madres. If you have seen the movie *Treasure of the Sierra Madre,* and know the dusty outfits of those gold-seekers, just imagine the opposite. High society scarves, extra high-heeled boots, suede jackets in multi colors, and skintight pants were the haute couture for some. The others were in full-on cowboy or cowgirl motif, fine, hand-tooled cowboy boots, real western jeans with authentic leather chaps, ivory studded shirts, hand-tooled leather vests, and ten-gallon hats. I am not making this up. It was a strange parade, but who were we to rain on it?

We met our guide-to-be, Mica True, a gringo who spent summers in Colorado and winters in Mexico. He was a long distance trail runner and had befriended the natives, the Tarahumara, who are famous for their ability to run long distances, which included days-long races and the ability to run down deer or turkeys. Small world. Mica had met Richard Fisher, also a supporter of the Tarahumara Indians. Mica told a story of having run the Leadville (Colorado) 100 in less than twenty-four hours, and wanting to get the Tarahumara Indians to race. Apparently, they did race one year, and took many of the top place finishes, including first, which got one of the race sponsors, Reebok, in a dither. Reebok would not let the Indians return the following year. Mica's take on it was that the Tarahumara had run in Reeboks the first three miles, taking them off to run in their sandals, a slap in the face to Reebok.

Between Mica and Richard Fisher, I felt like a dilettante. I had some money, time, and good fortune on my side, and so was able to get to the canyons I am in love with. However, I admire them from a distance. The passion these two have makes mine pale in comparison. I didn't spend much time in the canyons, but I liked my goal, the challenge, and the sense of direction the quest gave me. Listening to real canyon aficionados, however, I could see I wasn't that high up on the pecking order of canyon dancers.

The Tarahumara Indians are the real stars of Chihuahua. They have been living and surviving in the Copper Canyon area for centuries. They are subsistence farmers and hunters. Their crops include corn, beans, apples, peaches, and other fruits. The hunting provides fish, deer and other game, and, not so appetizing to me, snakes and lizards. They also tend cattle, sheep, and pigs.

To get to Urique River, the deepest part of the Copper Canyon, I had several choices: I could walk, ride a vehicle, or go horseback. I knew I wasn't going to ride a horse, not for thirty miles without any butt training, no way. The idea of the walk was okay, but I had limited time, and the road was right there and so was the truck. So I took the easy way, with Mica as guide and Angel our driver. Mica talked a bunch and Angel didn't say a word, but he was another of the string of good drivers I was lucky to ride with.

On the way to the canyon we stopped in Cerocahui, a village that was around before and during the colonial period. It had about 600 people and boasted an old church that we visited. Diego gave us a tour of the 400-year-old church. The church was in a T shape if seen from the air, the long section narrow with pews that also looked about 400 years old, with three confessionals on each side. The center of the T was the altar, and the two short sides of the T were more pews. The back of the church had two stained glass windows, both painted, one quite incongruously, featuring a pagoda and a Chinese junk with a cross on it in the middle of a river. Nearer to us was a window depicting a dying priest attended by a person in a coolie-looking conical hat. We were then transferred from Diego to Mica and Angel for the ride to Urique.

Our road was about one-and-a-half lanes wide, dirt and rock, and filled with switchbacks and overhangs to oblivion. At the first glimpse of the canyon, I was again smitten. I liked it at first sight, and was reminded that I sure do like canyons. The views were breathtaking, huge stone monoliths, steep walls 5000 feet in depth, and green from recent rain. Far below we could see the aqua river as it meandered snake-like through the valley. The sky was azure with white swatches of cloud, and the sun gleamed off the buildings of Urique.

Along our way to the bottom, we stopped at a hole-in-the-wall place selling baskets. The shop, built in a natural indentation in the side of the cliff wall, was loaded down with handmade reed baskets. The front of the store was helter skelter boards cobbled together to form a wall. If you didn't know it was there, you'd think someone had left an old pile of wood leaning against the stone. Inside, a young woman was nursing her baby in one arm and weaving with the other. Amelia purchased a fair amount of baskets, and we continued down the switchbacks for two-and-a-half more hours before we arrived at the village of Urique. The tourist-friendly village has a population of about 1,500 people. In the old days it was a mining town, but now it is predominantly a farming community, with marijuana among the more financially successful crops. The four of us were the only gringos visible during our short stay. We ate at Mica's favorite place, and had a good lunch of cactus, beans, rice, and tortillas. The courtyard was thick with tropical plants, banana, mango, and grapefruit. After lunch we took a walk to an overlook of the river, where I stopped and got my rock from this deepest canyon in North America.

I realize some will take umbrage with this statement. There are those who say that Hells Canyon, between Oregon and Idaho, is the deepest in North America. But the simple fact is that Hells Canyon is officially a gorge. I had been to Hells Canyon back in 1980 with Amelia, when she was first born. It is 7,900 feet deep, some 1,800 feet deeper than Copper Canyon, but still a gorge. The Copper Canyon is 6,136 feet in depth and with its vast size and depth, it is the deepest canyon. So one is the deepest gorge in North America and the other the deepest canyon.

After gathering my stone, I gave thanks to the river god (or whatever deity or spirit was watching over me) for the good fortune that allowed me my canyon dance. I have never resolved the uncomfortableness of publicly being thankful. I am not a fall-on-my-knees, shout-for-joy-yelling-my-thanks-to-the-heavens kind of guy. My style is much more private, alone and quiet. Over the course of many years of outdoor travel, I have developed a routine, a chant or mantra, to offer up appreciation to the powers or spirits for the good fortune that saw me safely there and back home again. I am grateful for the privilege of visiting these places. I appreciate my great good luck in living in a country that allows me to own a house, sell it, and then have the freedom to take off and do such a whimsical thing without going through many trials and tribulations, or having to ask permission of some higher authority. I just saved my money and went.

The ride up was as pretty as it was going down. We again stopped at the basket shop, and Amelia was able to buy even more; thankfully they nested into each other, because otherwise I didn't know how we were going to get them all home. As father, I was constantly saying, "I am not going to help carry any of those." Amelia knew that was so much baloney and I did too.

We arrived back at the ranchito in time for dinner and to meet a new couple, a man and woman we had met on the train ride in. They were both educators and it was with both trepidation and satisfaction that I listened as the Mrs. gave Amelia the benefit of her thirty years of teaching wisdom. The satisfaction, of course, came when I agreed with her point of view, and the fear was mostly of Amelia not being able to stifle a yawn, but I needn't have worried; the differing points of view were handled with aplomb.

I was growing to enjoy the family-style dinners that the Ranchito del Oso provided. We never knew who our table companions would be. My only real complaint about the food was the coffee, which Mica called "no es café." But the real fun wasn't the food, it was the wide-ranging conversations, which often lasted until dark. We would linger, lamps lit, talking of all the things that travelers and strangers find to say.

One evening, over beers and the ranchito's specialty, margaritas, the fireplace casting its luminous glow, we got to talking about river trips. I told a story about a trip I'd taken with my friend Tim on the Porcupine River, which runs into the Yukon River at Fort Yukon, up in the interior of Alaska. Our plan was to be flown up, spend seven to ten days canoeing and camping, then drift and paddle back. It was the end of the season, in late September, just before freeze-up when we didn't have to worry much about mosquitoes, or sharing our wilderness with too many others. We were transported up river via a small floatplane. In those days you could strap your canoe on the pontoon, throw all your gear inside, and get all the equipment up there in one trip. We were dropped off and got our gear in order for the next day's start. I like canoe camping. I can bring everything: a folding chair, grill, big tent, cooler with favorite foods, and extra clothes. We even had a solar shower to keep us clean. We had a most pleasant camp and were up early the next morning to get a good start.

I will admit it: Tim is a much better canoeist than I am. He has paddled some extreme rivers, with big water and difficult navigation. I can follow directions, and am okay in the front of the boat. But we have different styles of going down a river. I like to take in the scenery. In fact, I like nothing better than to find a long, semi narrow piece of driftwood to put behind my back, put my feet up on the gunnels, and kind of gangster lean down the river, just digging the scene. That makes me really happy! Tim, on the other hand, if the river isn't challenging, will sit and read a book, and not just any book, mind you, but thick medical books (he is a nurse), books without one single picture! The kind of textbooks we were forced to read in college. Sometimes, he would even read government texts. After a few days, we changed places. I went to the back, and he to the front, so we could then both enjoy the river in our own fashions. This worked okay. I was supposed to keep an eye on the river and call for Tim's advice if needed.

A sweeper is a large fallen tree trunk with all the branches sticking out from the bank and the river. A real hazard, it can literally sweep you out of your boat. The number one rule, among many number one rules on the river, is don't go under a sweeper. I thought I could steer us around, but ... nope, into the drink we went. Another major rule is, don't let go of your paddle and for sure don't let go of the boat. Uh oh. It was, indeed, time to call the uh oh squad. We did manage to make it to shore intact, but the canoe and all the gear and the paddles and the ice chest and the tent and the food, well ... they drifted away. Mighty fast, too, for what was supposed to be a medium current river. We were out of the boat, in the water, and before I could blink, it was all gone. Now to be fair to myself, I was kind of shocked that we were in the water. I would like to say that I was also concerned about Tim's welfare, who didn't even see the sweeper coming, but that might not be true. We splashed around a bit and then made it to shore. Tim was not too happy about the whole affair.

Once on shore, after Tim's quite lengthy impeachment of my skills, denunciation of my parentage, and general all-around libelous, slanderous, and out-and-out bespirhment of my character and everything about me, we looked at the situation. We were, quite literally, up the creek without a paddle, or a canoe, or much of anything else, for that matter.

We sat down and took an inventory of what we had with us: two life jackets, our wet clothes -- which we began to dry around the fire -- and the items in our little survival kits (sewing kit, lots of fish line, a few pins and needles, matches, water purification tabs, a space blanket, and a couple of candy bars). We'd lost the maps and everything else, except, as Tim so carefully pointed out, "we" hadn't lost them.

The area we were in, the Yukon Flats, is called that for a reason. It is flat, with hundreds of sloughs, dozens of different braids in the river, and not one natural thing to give one an idea of where one is; no mountains, or hills, or anything of height to help us figure out where we were. We knew we had been on the river for three-and-a-half days, and we figured we had another three-and-a-half to go to reach Fort Yukon. Another feature of the area was that all the trees were the same height and not much good for anything but a forest fire, in season, which is where we had pitched up in, a recent fire area. So there was plenty of firewood, but nothing of much value, timber-wise, should we wish to, say, build a raft. It would be impossible to walk out, and the water was too cold to try to float out with just our PFD's, due to the potential of hypothermia. But these conclusions we came to later. Our first job was to get dry and warm. We took stock of our supplies: we had plenty of firewood and water to drink. We scraped together a makeshift lean-to and went to bed, without any "good nights" I might add.

The next morning dawned; we were warm, dry, and hungry. So we pulled out some fishing line, tied a hook, and then looked around for some bait. I was finally forced to give up a piece of my PowerBar for bait. Two things about the Porcupine River are relevant. First, it is fast and cold, and, second, and more importantly, it is silty. We couldn't see more than maybe a foot into the water. If fish could see or smell, our bait wasn't what they were after anyway. Any fish left that time of year were just heading upriver to spawn and are pretty nasty eating. We would not be having fish for dinner, lunch, or breakfast. It was to be a rationing of candy and Power-Bars for us. The day passed, quietly. I gathered firewood, cleaned up around camp, walked around the perimeter of our small island, if that was what it was, and mostly stayed away from the grouchy Tim. In the evening, we each had a bit of candy bar and went to sleep, although Tim swore my stomach growls kept him awake all night long.

The next days passed much like the first one. Tim did become more talkative. We got to talking about the trip arrangements. I was under the impression that Tim had told the outfitter to pick us up in Fort Yukon on x date, and Tim was under the impression of just the opposite. During this conversation, we recalled that the pilot had told us that we were the last group to go up and then (supposedly) come down the river. There would be no other boaters to give us a lift.

We had figured out we would not be able to make a raft or swim downriver. Even if we could go from island to island, which direction should we go? The compass was still on the boat. Yes we were warm and dry, but to my way of thinking, our situation was getting a bit desperate. Tim didn't agree, but he wasn't agreeing with anything I said. Our small stash of PowerBars and candy bars had long since been eaten. I knew you could survive for 30 days with no food, three days with no water, and maybe three minutes without air.

Well, we had plenty of water, that was true, but desperate straits were where we were. Tim just sat there, as usual, staring at the river, not saying anything. I had kind of lost track of days and time, but all of a sudden, Tim said, "We're saved!" Oh, no, I thought, he's gone off the deep end, harkening back to his missionary upbringing. But no.

Across the river, a flock of geese had landed. Tim said, "Give me your belt, and get the fishing line, and start tying different lengths with a slip knot on one end and the other end tied to your belt." My reaction was, "What???" I started to say something, but was cut off with a curt, "Get to work, now!" I did as I was told, thinking maybe he was going to make a sling shot and kill a goose, and we'd have roast goose for dinner, which sounded good to me. I got to work. I tied almost fifty varying lengths of fishing line to my belt with the mandated slip knot, and he did the same. He then put my belt around his chest, his around his waist, grabbed a huge stick from the fire, and jumped into the water! If this was some kind of jungle ritual he'd learned in boyhood, it was escaping me. I sat in horror; my only company had gone mad and jumped into the river. I was flabbergasted; was this really happening? I was too stunned to do anything. But this is what Tim was doing. He swam across the river, very skillfully and stealthily, I might add. Then just before he got to the geese, he slid under the water. He was coming up under the feet of the birds, and slipping the slip knot around their feet and tightening the nooses. Time after time after time. When he had finished, Tim jumped out of the water shrieking, swinging the piece of lumber like a club, and shouting for all he was worth. To say it startled me is one thing. To say it outright spooked, terrorized, and alarmed the birds is quite accurate. I don't think there is a word for what the birds must have thought. 100 waterfowl rose in unison, and there, hanging beneath them, suspended from various lengths of fishing line, was my friend Tim Johnson. It made me proud. It is a little known piece of bird lore, but when birds are startled, they automatically fly downriver, and in this case, in unison. This I saw with my own two eyes. Tim hanging from the birds, them honking and flapping and squawking, and flying away, away from me! What came to mind was, "Oh shit! Oh shit shit shit!!!" Tim flew, he said, with the birds' support, for about an hour, with the noise and bird doo falling on him. He said he started to get cold and was getting a bit concerned, but just then spotted the radar tower at Fort Yukon and knew it was all going to end right. The birds were heading in the right direction; he now only had to worry about how to land. No problem. As he neared the town, he started pulling birds down via the fishing line and clubbing them on the head; they then acted as ballast. He claims he landed on his feet in the middle of Fort Yukon. He traded the birds for a ride upriver, found the canoe safe and sound, with all our stuff, and he even came back for me. Well my story got a good laugh all around, and everyone went to bed with a smile on their face.

The next morning, while Mike and Amelia took another walk, I had time to reflect more on Copper Canyon. It was big and it was deep, and had the traditional shapes a good canyon needed. With its flat plateau or mesa-like top, but not totally flat, it had an unevenness to it that helped make it more rugged, in a sense, from that perspective. I was enamored with its plunging cliffs that fell straight down, only to run out into a gradually sloping landscape, only to, again after a bit, once again fall away towards the river which had eons ago begun this canyon.

I was intrigued that it was another "working" canyon where people lived and worked. It wasn't just for those who could afford a raft trip, a mule ride, or expend the energy to walk it for fun or adventure. People with a long history still made it their home, and it hadn't been loved to death, nor did it seem to be in danger of that, yet. Many of the locals are hoping to bring more and more visitors for economic reasons, but that may never happen. That people live and raise families there didn't take away from the beauty to me. I am familiar with the notion that for nature to have its singular beauty, many feel that no one, but perhaps himself or herself, ought to view it. I suppose whether a canyon is remote, isolated, or sparsely populated, can add to or subtract from its beauty, depending on the individual that is viewing the canyon. I was not offended that people were living in this canyon; there was plenty of remote space for the true hermit. But despite this, I was not overly awed. It was time to face the music, I was free of the need to not bad-vibe any of the canyons by comparing them to the Grand Canyon. From the beginning of my quest, the Grand Canyon had been in the back of my mind, but I had always managed to push it aside, so as not to jinx my travels to the next new canyon. It was kind of like my superstition to not make fun of the animals in the area for fear that they would then take their revenge on me in some untoward manner. This superstition had long been a part of my kit of tricks to foil any bad karma or vibrations that I might inadvertently set in motion.

I have no trouble understanding why ancient or tribal peoples worshipped rocks and stones or Mother Nature. So what if the Copper Canyon, or the Urique Valley, did not stand up to the Grand Canyon? It was true that the first view of the Grand Canyon and my heart was taken again. My first love was a woman from high school days. My first canyon love was the Grand Canyon, so in that sense I understood a part of the mental struggle I was going through. I was trying not to make comparisons and trying to judge each canyon on its own merit. I liked this Copper Canyon, but I knew I was also ready to go home.

Mike may have been ready to head back as well. Amelia and Mike had gone on a daylong hike. Somewhere during the hike, Amelia jumped down from a rock ledge and cried out in pain. Mike rushed to her in concern, only to learn that she was pulling his leg. Although they may have faced some real danger as they hiked in a field of bulls. The night watchman (who we called The Shadow), who had a .45 tucked into his pocket, as well as the goose in love with the barbecue, had also taken their toll on him.

We were up the next morning for a breakfast of cinnamon rolls and pancakes; they didn't make the top ten list, but they were good and hit the spot. Our goal for this last day was to hike up to the bear-shaped rock formation overlooking the ranchito. It still looked an awful lot like Boo-Boo, but would it from the other side? There was no trail up, so the three of us, Amelia, Mike, and I, bush-whacked our way up. We each chose our own path, sometimes on goat trails and other times just pulling our way up hand-over-hand, clutching the old cottonwood trees. We arrived at the top, and as I caught my breath, I noted that it felt good to get the old lungs working. Our view from the top was of shark and airplane-shaped clouds. We spent a few minutes just looking around at the vista and chatting. Then we wandered back, and slowly found our way to our homestead, going down a less difficult way. And no, the bear didn't look like a bear from the backside. The afternoon rolled on, Amelia sitting with a cat in her lap, writing. She was a trooper. I hadn't gotten the chance to chat with her as much as I would have liked, but it was okay just to spend time with her. I suppose that, like most parents, as we start to see our kids grow up, we begin to relish time to just be in some sort of proximity to them.

Later that day, on the train back to Los Mochis, I finally had a chance for a nice chat with Amelia. I asked her the usual questions: How was school? What was she thinking about for the future, both near and far? Who were her friends, what was she thinking about the bike business for the coming summer? She had been with the business as long as I, and as a guide -- an ace guide, at that - had some good insights. It was worthwhile to be able to bounce some thoughts off of her. It struck me, what a nice a person she was, gentle and caring, warm and polite with others, and with a love of animals. I suppose, like most kids around their parents, she was able to let her guard down around the folks and will certainly blow off some steam (though sometimes it seems like rocket fuel). She was, for sure, put off by the whiz pops and snoring, but aside from that she was an ideal travel companion. She was cautious, but I like that: so am I. Several times on the trip she'd caught a mistake I'd made in navigation.

Again, we managed to sit on the wrong side of the train for catching the best views of the countryside, but we could see the slot canyons and the river, the abundant colors of the flower trees -- white, yellow, pink and purple -- and the small surrounding communities, some with old railroad cars converted for housing, where families lived in overturned, graffiti-covered box cars, laundry lines strung between them. The vistas were still excellent and the train ride was worth the price of admission. I was still feeling guilty about not really working very hard for the Copper Canyon. It had grandeur, beauty, and probably the only reason it lacked that special connection for me was because we had driven. When I did hike, I didn't always get to see that much of the canyon. I was huffing and puffing, trying to catch my breath, my heart trying to pound its way out of my chest, paying more attention to my burning thighs, calves, and poor old barking dogs than I was to the canyon itself. Still, all those shortcomings on my part bring me closer emotionally and physically to the canyons that I did work for.

We made it safely to Los Mochis, where we were again ensconced in the San Anita Hotel. This time our room had two double beds, and also a small room with an exercise bike. Amelia immediately claimed that room for herself. We dragged a mattress off one of the beds, moved the bike, and she was a happy camper in her own room, sans the snores, etc.

We rose the next morning, caught a cab to the airport in time to get a pretty darn good breakfast of French Toast smothered in cinnamon sugar, fresh cantaloupe, and coffee (a decent cup, one of the few I had the entire five months of this adventure). The flight back to LA was uneventful, aside from me, the old world traveler, not catching that they were calling our flight number. I just passed it off that with family around I wasn't as careful as I would normally be.

We'd just come from a rural area, where the people farmed by hand, with no electricity, phones, mass transit, or street lights, and within eight hours were in a city of twelve million people; the world is truly getting smaller. I was again reminded that people really do make the journey, at least, in large part for me. The staff at the Oso had been smiling, helpful, and nice. While no one, other than Diego and Mica spoke English, they did not give us any funny looks when we asked for "non carne" (no meat), or told them that Amelia and I were vegiterano.

As I have noted several times, my height can have its drawbacks. Airplane and bus seats are cramped, to say the least. One of the nicest surprises I got, however, was when Aero Mexico offered me seats with extra leg room without my even asking, which I always have to do with other airlines. The Aero Mexico staff, both coming and going, looked me up and down and asked if I wanted extra leg room. That truly is of note for any airline traveler. The American companies, well, they try, but they do not try that hard.

One sad note, Mica True died March 27th 2012, while out on a run in southwest New Mexico.

Amelia's thank-you card:

"Dad, Thank-you for the Mexico trip. It was a much needed vacation from Ashland, & it was good to finally see you. Glad you're back all safe & everything. I'll work on getting the write up of Mexico to you, in any case, thanks again. I had a good time hiking & talking & reading and eating and train riding and driving and (not) sleeping and horseback riding. Talk to you soon. Love Amelia."

And in conclusion ...

It is almost sixteen years since I have returned. In the interim, I've read other travel stories, narratives, and adventure travel accounts, which was probably not a good idea, since I end up comparing their work to mine, and it is much like comparing canyons, with me as the Fish River and most of the other authors as the Grand Canyon. But I am compelled to try. Maybe that is what I most feel about this Canyon Dance, the satisfaction of the attempt, and the doing of it. There is much depth to the notion that the journey is the destination. I still have a raw spot from the itch of not getting to the canyon in Tibet, but ... one of these days.

After all that time my awe is renewed when I think of seeing the Potala Palace, the half-million penguins, and each of the canyons. Not a day goes by where something doesn't remind me of the trip and the good fortune I was amazingly graced with to go for this dream.

I was reminded that people are kind, for the most part, everywhere. Sure you've got to be alert, but in my experience, people are, mostly, good. There really is trail magic all over the world.

If I could offer my readers one piece of advice, it would be this: go for your dreams. What you really have to do is to want the trip, the dream. You have to want it, to desire it, maybe to need it. Maybe this trip could have been done for about half the price I spent, with much less gear, and with little or no planning. What it could not have been done without is the passion. So go for your dreams, enjoy, and have some fun. My favorite Chinese fortune cookie said, "When you think you are too old to do something – do it."

Author Biography

Jeff Budd has devoted his life to helping youth and adults treat substance abuse and addiction. Budd received a B.A. in Recreation Leadership from Bowling Green State University in Bowling Green, Ohio, and a master's in Juvenile Corrections from the University of Oregon in Eugene, Oregon.

After twenty-five years in his nonprofit career, Budd spent an additional ten years in the eco-tourism field in Alaska. Budd has hiked, biked, and kayaked some of the world's most challenging trails.

CPSIA information can be obtained
at www.ICGtesting.com
Printed in the USA
LVHW040531120423
744139LV00009B/496

9 781533 122216